What people are saying about

Pandora's Book

From the problem of free will to the ownership of nostrils, this philosophical questionnaire will disturb you into an exciting area of doubt and exploration. This book is the beginning of a wonderful adventure – an utter delight.
Robin Ince, comedian and writer

A fascinating invitation to philosophical thinking – provokes readers to explore the very deepest questions in the company of literary greats from Plato and Zhuangzi to Oscar Wilde and Lewis Carroll.
Katherine Hawley, Professor of Philosophy, University of St Andrews

Pandora's Book

401 Philosophical Questions to Help You Lose Your Mind (with answers)

Pandora's Book

401 Philosophical Questions to Help You Lose Your Mind (with answers)

David Birch

IFF
BOOKS

Winchester, UK
Washington, USA

JOHN HUNT PUBLISHING

First published by iff Books, 2021
iff Books is an imprint of John Hunt Publishing Ltd., No. 3 East Street, Alresford,
Hampshire SO24 9EE, UK
office@jhpbooks.com
www.johnhuntpublishing.com
www.iff-books.com

For distributor details and how to order please visit the 'Ordering' section on our website.

ISBN: 978 1 78904 571 0
978 1 78904 572 7 (ebook)
Library of Congress Control Number: 2020930847

A CIP catalogue record for this book is available from the British Library.

Design: Stuart Davies

UK: Printed and bound by CPI Group (UK) Ltd, Croydon, CR0 4YY
Printed in North America by CPI GPS partners

Contents

In memory of Félicitié Tomlinson

Acknowledgements

The curiosity of my students set this book in motion. Having written a dozen or so questions for my class at the London Academy of Excellence during the summer term of 2017, their demand for more prompted this proliferation. Subsequent conversations with students at Newham Sixth Form College and Kensington Park School were also invaluable, with especial thanks to Lucas Chancellor, Sude Elgun, Michalina Jarczyk and Janece Wong.

At the Philosophy Foundation I am grateful to Steve Hoggins for something or other, Andy West for his obliging input and Emma Worley for her support. I also wish to thank Lauren O'Rourke for her useful comments and Giulia Franzoni for her generous help with some Latin translation. My final thanks are to Sarah Birch, who has been so wonderful in so many ways.

Introduction

What is philosophy?

Philosophy starts when the world stops making sense. That is to say, it starts with loss. The loss of established belief, collective opinion, common understanding. This constitutes a crisis, though it is a crisis teeming with promise. Philosophy is an experiment into what loss can become once we have abandoned the search for salvation; into what thought is capable of once we have relinquished the need to be found. It is a quest for invention, a palpable longing for new ways of thinking about the world and our lives within it. It is homeless, boundless, untethered, an exile of forgotten origin.

Philosophy's quest for invention is impelled by a wish to overcome deep confusions. Ordinarily we are preoccupied with surface confusions. These are everyday worries that arise from the anomalous and unexpected. 'I have a hole in my trousers – how can that be?' is a surface confusion. Had the hole spontaneously appeared, it would violate our belief that everything has a cause. The question 'How can that be?' arises from a wish to reconcile this belief with the hole's presence. This is the nature of surface confusions. They aim to resolve conflicts that arise between our beliefs and our experiences. They wish to preserve the familiarity and order of the world.

Deep confusions occur when reconciliation is not an option, when the restoration of order is beyond hope. These are the remit of philosophy. Rather than addressing particular events, they address general concepts, such as time. 'I have a hole in my trousers – how can that be?' is not a philosophical question. 'Time passes – how can that be?' is. The latter question is not seeking to reconcile a particular event with prior beliefs: it is instead challenging the very viability of those beliefs. Deep confusions cannot be pacified with explanations because they arise when a general feature of our common understanding has stopped making sense.

With deep confusions the question 'How can that be?' is not an expression of curiosity but an exclamation of puzzlement, an outburst of disbelief. And within every deep confusion there is the desire for a new way of thinking. The time question, for instance, contains the nascent thought, 'Time *doesn't* pass – can it be?' And this touches on philosophy's need for invention: to answer this question, to explore this possibility, new concepts are required, for new concepts enable us to enter new territories of thought. Without them we are bound by the limits of received wisdom. Deep confusions, then, are portents of something new, a radical change.

Consider Lucy and Leila lying in bed together on a weeknight. It's 2am and Leila has awoken to find Lucy still reading:

Leila. It's late – go to sleep.
Lucy. Why?
Leila. You have work in the morning.
Lucy. Why should I go to work?
Leila. We need the money.
Lucy. Why?
Leila. To pay off the mortgage.
Lucy. Why do we need to pay off the mortgage?
Leila. To be secure.
Lucy. Why do you want to be secure?
Leila. I want to stop worrying all the time.
Lucy. What do you worry about?
Leila. The future.
Lucy. Why?
Leila. It's unknown.
Lucy. How can you be afraid of what you don't know?
Leila. I feel out of control.
Lucy. Why do you want to be in control?

Leila. I don't want to lose myself.
Lucy. What would be wrong with losing yourself?
Leila. I wouldn't be able to look after myself.
Lucy. Couldn't someone else look after you?
Leila. You can't rely on other people.
Lucy. Why?
Leila. We're all alone.
Lucy. Are we?
Leila. No one knows what I need.
Lucy. Why not?
Leila. Because no one knows who I am.
Lucy. Don't you know who you are?
Leila. Of course not! That's the terrifying thing.
Lucy. And this is why I need to go to work in the morning?
Leila. Exactly.

Lucy's questioning is not born of a desire to be a pain in the arse. She is genuinely puzzled by everything Leila says. The philosopher's disposition to think arises from a failure, and a desire, to understand. Lucy is trying to make sense of her apparent duties, but she can't. She no longer feels attuned to the world, but she is not content to muddle through. Having knocked her finger against the structure of ordinary explanations she has found a hollow timbre, a fundamental vacuity.

Lucy may well go to work the next day but she'll find herself preoccupied with Leila's answers. As is the tendency with philosophy, her initial question about why she should work generated further questions: Are we fundamentally isolated from each other? Should we fear the future? Can we know what we are? Should we strive to? Lucy is baffled. Yet, by thinking through these questions, she starts to fashion a trinity of concepts which articulate and extend her own thoughts on the world: *the intermingled self, the infinite present* and *the curious life*.

She returns home that night and tells Leila that she has

overcome the problems they discussed. 'You worry that you do not know who you are,' she starts, 'but this is because you are trying to find yourself through introspection. This is the wrong approach. You are an *intermingled self*. Since you cannot exist independently of other things, you are not an independent thing, and so you shouldn't search inside yourself for what you really are. This knowledge will only be found amid the objects and people around you. Since you are part of the world, the world is part of you.'

She goes on to expound the *infinite present*: 'You worry about the unknowable future, but the future cannot be known because it doesn't exist, so it makes no sense to say it is unknowable. We can only not-know what is, and the future is-not. All that exists is the present. And since something cannot be limited by non-existent things, the present cannot be limited by the future, or the past, so the present is effectively infinite.'

Finally, she describes her concept of the *curious life*: 'Everything you said last night was justified by fear. But fear is a poor justification for anything because it is fundamentally incurious. It hides rather than explores. It would rather we closed our eyes than kept them open. Fear is averse to knowledge. It doesn't want to know. It is ignorant. Yet ignorance is never a good justification for anything, so we should not base our decisions on fear. Rather we should live our lives motivated by curiosity, by an appetite to know.'

Lucy is doing philosophy. She started deeply confused with the question of why she should work, but Leila's answers only exacerbated her puzzlement, provoking further questions and deeper confusions. Yet, instead of burdening her, these questions unleashed a tremendous energy – philosophy is bewilderment made productive. Lucy's bewilderment fuelled the production of new concepts which offered a view of the world that she felt simultaneously attuned to and invigorated by. With these concepts available the world became clearer, but also radically different. Lucy replaced the vacuous with something, to her mind, sonorous and rich. How will she understand the duty to work now? How will she approach the future? That is impossible to say. But in the course of this philosophical episode she has, at the very least, invented for herself new possibilities of life.

Why does philosophy exist?

What lies at the foundation of these deep confusions? Why are we compelled to question? Why not make things easy for ourselves? Why not settle for simplicity? Why think at all?

I am inclined to see philosophy as arising from a basic aspect of our nature, a thought-drive we possess, the cognitive equivalent to the libido. This thought-drive, call it the *epinoia* (epi-no-ah), is an irreducible instinct within us to question, wonder, challenge, probe, explode, shake, shatter, rattle, prod, flip, whip, stretch… in a word, think. Whereas the libido seeks satisfaction, the *epinoia*, tireless and indefatigable, seeks the endless flight of thought. It never settles. It craves problems, seeks perplexities, and shows no interest in sound conclusions or tidy answers.

Our faculties of thought are ordinarily employed to address surface confusions: to make decisions, construct explanations, find answers. These faculties use thought to end thought, to put the mind at rest. But the object of the *epinoia* is the perpetual motion of thought, not its end. The *epinoia* reveals that there is more to thinking than the application of one's learning, more than the mere making of judgments. The *epinoia* takes us beyond the bounds of ordinary understanding; it addresses problems that exceed the remedial powers of our acquired wisdom. The deep confusions of the *epinoia* defeat our education and nullify the common repository of answers. Yet this is no source of anguish. For the *epinoia*, confusion is not an abject deficit of understanding but the very appetite of thought. The philosopher starts with a poverty of answers only to realise the exciting fecundity of questions. Answers are wanted only insofar as they ramify and breed further questions. Questions are an opportunity to unfetter thought. Every unanswerable question opens up a space in the world, making a void for something new, something different.

Following the *epinoia* into such voids is liable to be construed as the preserve of oddballs. Indeed, the 18th century Scottish philosopher David Hume worried that philosophy had turned him into a 'strange uncouth monster,' a creature unable to 'mingle and unite in society,' and he was right. The *epinoia* is the uncouth monster within you. It cannot be tamed or socialised, and since deference is a hindrance to thought, it fails to respect boundaries or acknowledge authority. The *epinoia* doesn't learn from experience. It is immune to norms. This is not rudeness or impudence but simply the raw stuff of nature. We can no more domesticate the *epinoia* than we can discipline the weather.

The role of the *epinoia* in philosophy shows why it is a misconception to regard the philosopher as wise. Though the word philosophy originally meant 'friend of wisdom', the *epinoia* proves how different friends can be. Pythagoras, the ancient Greek first thought to have labelled himself a philosopher, stressed that only the gods have wisdom; the philosopher is not herself wise. Whereas wisdom is still (a statue of thought) the *epinoia* is fluid (a river of thought). Unlike the wise person, the philosopher has nothing to bestow except provocation and potential. Her worth is determined not by the problems she solves but the new territories of thought she makes available.

In short, the philosopher is a *friend* of wisdom, not a *person* of wisdom. Friendship is not predicated on identity but occurs within a symbiosis of difference. The philosopher and the wise person may drink from the same wells of confusion, share the same questions, have similar preoccupations. The difference, however, is that the wise person tries to wrest his confusions from the forces of the *epinoia*. He seeks to silence his deep confusions, not amplify them or use their energy to fashion bizarre new concepts. Wisdom, in other words, is the ability to offer surface answers to deep confusions. It leaves everything as it is. As such, we are ultimately comforted and reassured by the presence of the wise person, far more so than his elusive and peculiar friend the philosopher. The philosopher wanders through strange spaces, occupying the regions between categories, a creature somewhere between the sage and the fool, somewhere between wisdom and lunacy.

Time touches the philosopher differently. She exists beyond the common dichotomies of beginnings and ends, innocence and experience. Peer through the curtains of an old people's home and you will find that the libido does not go gentle into that good night, and the same is true of the *epinoia*. There is no cosy fade to black, no notion of rest, it never settles down, and is, therefore, often a source of anxiety. So while some of us are wholly committed to the *epinoia*, it is understandable that others should endeavour to bury or repress theirs. In many of us it lies dormant, awaiting the slightest flutter of confusion to awaken. And for a few it is not buried but frustrated, active but aimless, like a libido without an object, desire in the absence of anything desirable. And that is where this book comes in.

What is this book?

This book is 401 attempts to help you lose your mind. The aim, to be clear, is not to challenge your sanity but to destabilise the structures of conventional wisdom that hold deep confusions at bay. If we picture the mind as an inert edifice of belief and opinion, the questions in this book hope to sweep it all away. To replace an object (statues of belief) with a process (rivers of thought). A kind of deliquescence.

To open the book is to invite chaos. Like Pandora's box, its questions seek to release a type of mayhem. They are not mere irritations to be scratched away. Your answer to a given question is only the start of the process, not the end. Once you have an answer, ask yourself why you think this. Search for your reasons, but not with the internal demand to justify your thoughts. Search with a fascination for where your thoughts may lead. And then consider why someone else might answer to the contrary. Be similarly curious about what it is you don't think.

Commit pencil to paper, mark your answers as you go. Try not to maintain a tidy distance. With many questions you may find that you cannot answer with a simple yes or no, and while such balance is commendable, do not shy away from your contradictions. Commit to yes and see where that takes you, then repeat with no. Permit yourself to be multitudinous, and grant each of your respective parts the unbridled freedom to think. Though a steady balance may in general keep us from falling, philosophy has no foundation, no solid ground to crash into, so why not fall?

More than a solitary exercise, I also encourage you to compare your answers with other people's. Discover the differences between you. These differences may occasion surprising conversations from which further thoughts may unfold. Such differences also serve to acquaint you with the idiosyncrasies of your own mind. Embracing one's irredeemable oddness is a prerequisite of *epinoic* thought.

In the second section, you will find that many questions are accompanied by so-called answers. These answers are in no way authoritative and warrant no deference. Their worth is in their catalytic powers, not their conclusiveness. Indeed, they do not always address their questions directly or expectedly. Sometimes they are taken from writers, such as D. H. Lawrence or Thomas De Quincey, not traditionally regarded as philosophers or commonly taught in university philosophy departments. The texts are selected on the basis of their potential effects, not their institutional status.

With the age, literary disposition and conceptual dexterity of these writers, some texts may be somewhat difficult to read. This presents you with a range of possible approaches. You can, for one, meticulously study an extract in a bid to discern its meaning. Or you can opt for indolence, regard obscurity as a blessing that liberates us from the burden of understanding, and read the extract in an oscitant state of dreamy abandon, leaving the words to work their magic, letting them slip away if they do nothing for you.

Approach this book with the spirit of Pandora. She sought to undo the endless tedium of perfection, inviting chaos and flux into our once too comfortable world. She, the patron saint of confusion and desire, sent the world off-kilter, and in so doing, provided the means for all that is interesting and vital in life.

'A lovely mischief to the soul of man.'
Hesiod, *Works and Days*

Questions

1. Do you know what you are? Yes / No.

2. Are you free? Yes / No.

3. Have you chosen the life that you lead? Yes / No.

4. Is there anything you cannot leave? Yes / No.

5. Are you certain you are alive? Yes / No.

6. Is it possible that your entire life has been a dream? Yes / No.

7. Are you a stranger to yourself? Yes / No.

8. Is it possible to know yourself completely? Yes / No.

9. Is it possible to be a slave without knowing it? Yes / No.

10. Is it possible that you are the only person in the world with thoughts and feelings? Yes / No.

11. Is your mind your property? Yes / No.

12. Do you own your nostrils? Yes / No.

13. Are you in control of yourself? Yes / No.

14. Is anyone else in control of you? Yes / No.

15. Are you in control of anyone other than yourself? Yes / No.

16. Imagine you are standing before two doors. Door 1 leads to an eternal world of peace, contentment, meaning and

order. Door 2 leads to a meaningless world of chaos, death, conflict and desire. Which one would you walk through?

17. Does anyone see the world in the same way that you do? Yes / No.

18. Does tomorrow exist? Yes / No. (The question is not *will* it exist, but *does* it exist.)

19. Does yesterday exist? Yes / No. (The question is not *did* it exist, but *does* it exist.)

20. Do your childhood fingers still exist? Yes / No.

21. Is existence a mystery? Yes / No.

22. Does the universe make sense? Yes / No.

23. Are you inside your body? Yes / No.

24. Are you wearing a face? Yes / No.

25. Are you conscious of your consciousness? Yes / No.

26. Does your mind have weight? Yes / No.

27. Is there anything you possess that could never be taken from you? Yes / No.

28. Are you one thing or many things? One thing / Many things.

29. Is the universe one thing or many things? One thing / Many things.

30. Is everything made of something else? Yes / No.

31. Are you well acquainted with your future corpse? Yes / No.

32. Are you an object? Yes / No.

33. Are you made of objects? Yes / No.

34. Is the River Thames an object? Yes / No.

35. 'Objects are things of use, so too are your hands, therefore your hands are objects.' Is this correct? Yes / No.

36. Is it possible that you have forgotten the most significant events of your life? Yes / No.

37. We speak of the past, present and future. Consider this moment now. Are you certain that it is the present? Yes / No.

38. Are you forever new? Yes / No.

39. Do you have an identity? Yes / No.

40. Where is your voice?

41. Does your voice exist while you are silent? Yes / No.

42. Are you a miracle? Yes / No.

43. Is your life a story? Yes / No.

44. Are we dying all the time? Yes / No.

45. Where does your history begin?

46. Did you have a nationality in the womb? Yes / No.

47. Was birth your first experience of rejection? Yes / No.

48. Are you a good advert for life? Yes / No.

49. Can you think without language? Yes / No.

50. Can you pray without words? Yes / No.

51. Is envy ever justified? Yes / No.

52. Is obsession ever admirable? Yes / No.

53. Can beauty ever be excessive? Yes / No.

54. Is it possible that your sexual orientation will change? Yes / No.

55. I am always listening to your thoughts though I have never heard you speak. Do I know the sound of your voice? Yes / No.

56. I am always reading your mind though I have never met you. Do I know your gender? Yes / No.

57. Every night I observe your dreams though in life you are a stranger to me. Do I know your desires? Yes / No.

58. When you lick your lips, are you licking the universe? Yes / No.

59. When you touch a beautiful object, are you touching its beauty? Yes / No.

60. When you eat a raspberry, are you eating its redness? Yes / No.

61. Can you do anything entirely original? Yes / No.

62. Are you an invention? Yes / No.

63. Do you have a purpose? Yes / No.

64. Is your body a machine? Yes / No.

65. Are you at home in the world? Yes / No.

66. Do you deserve to be loved? Yes / No.

67. Are you entitled to kindness? Yes / No.

68. Is there a true version of you? Yes / No.

69. Socrates said that it is impossible to love ugly things. Do you agree? Yes / No.

70. Is life an accident or a gift? Accident / Gift.

71. Are we born with the knowledge of death? Yes / No.

72. *Waves* ***have*** *motion.*
Waves ***are*** *motion.*
Which statement is correct?

73. *You **have** life.*
*You **are** life.*
Which statement is correct?

74. Is it possible to be closer to another person than you are to yourself? Yes / No.

75. Can you miss something you never had? Yes / No.

76. Can you imagine your own nonexistence? Yes / No.

77. Is there anyone in the world to whom you ought to be absolutely honest? Yes / No.

78. 'Debt is an illusion. Yes, we have laws that say borrowed money should be repaid etc. But outside of the law, no one really owes anyone anything.' Do you agree? Yes / No.

79. If all matter in the universe disappeared, would anything remain? Yes / No.

80. Can reality cease to exist? Yes / No.

81. Reality can be denied. Can it be escaped? Yes / No.

82. Are there degrees of existence? Yes / No.

83. Can the universe decay? Yes / No.

84. *Snow White exists as a fictional entity.*
Snow White does not exist.
Which statement is correct?

85. Does nothingness exist? Yes / No.

86. Does existence exist? Yes / No.

87. Are you worthy of life? Yes / No.

88. Do you know what it is like to be the ocean? Yes / No.

89. Do you know what it is like to be God? Yes / No.

90. Is everything you do motivated by desire? Yes / No.

91. Can desire ever be excessive? Yes / No.

92. Are we born with sexual desire? Yes / No.

93. Are there unnatural desires? Yes / No.

94. Is genocide natural? Yes / No.

95. Is there such a thing as human nature? Yes / No.

96. Is anyone more human than anyone else? Yes / No.

97. Are you incomplete? Yes / No.

98. Are most people boring? Yes / No.

99. Are humans fundamentally selfish? Yes / No.

100. Do we only fall in love because we want to be loved? Yes / No.

101. Is mortality a blessing? Yes / No.

102. Is mortality a disease? Yes / No.

103. Is the fear of death irrational? Yes / No.

104. Are you grateful that the universe exists? Yes / No.

105. Is democracy a wonderful thing? Yes / No.

106. Is capitalism a wonderful thing? Yes / No.

107. Would you rather a life of sobriety or passion? Sobriety / Passion.

108. Which would you most like to excel in: strength, intelligence, kindness or beauty?

109. Is it always wrong to blame other people for our failures? Yes / No.

110. Are you always waiting? Yes / No.

111. Are you impossible to understand? Yes / No.

112. Can I experience your experience? Yes / No.

113. Can you know yourself without knowing what other people think of you? Yes / No.

114. Can emotions lie? Yes / No.

115. Can music lie? Yes / No.

116. Is it possible to distinguish between what we genuinely believe and what we have been made to believe? Yes / No.

117. Is it possible to live without beliefs? Yes / No.

118. Do butterflies have beliefs? Yes / No.

119. Are thoughts physical? Yes / No.

120. When you shake your head are you shaking your thoughts too? Yes / No.

121. Since waking up today, have you had a series of different thoughts or a single continuously changing thought? Series / Single.

122. Thoughts, they say, are in the head. Try to imagine instead that they are on the surface of your eyes or within the cavity of your mouth. Can you? Yes / No.

123. Is the pain of a stubbed toe in your toe or your mind? Toe / Mind.

124. *When you wince I see your pain.*
When you wince I see the effect of your pain.
Which statement is correct?

125. Do you experience sleep? Yes / No.

126. Are you performing an action when you dream? Yes / No.

127. Was Juliet in love with Romeo even whilst she slept? Yes / No.

128. Do sleeping bats have upside down dreams? Yes / No.

129. Can drugs enhance our perception of reality? Yes / No.

130. Can music enhance our perception of reality? Yes / No.

131. Can you be certain that you will never murder the people you love? Yes / No.

132. Can you be certain that the people you love will never murder you? Yes / No.

133. Is sacrificing your own life to save another the greatest act of love? Yes / No.

134. 'One has renounced the great life when one renounces war,' wrote the philosopher Friedrich Nietzsche. Do you agree? Yes / No.

135. Is it easier to imagine true love or true hate? True love / True hate.

136. Is addiction a form of loyalty? Yes / No.

137. Is self-control a kind of tyranny? Yes / No.

138. What do you most want: wealth, fame, power or love?

139. Do you want a revolution? Yes / No.

140. Should we love everyone? Yes / No.

141. Is confusion a talent? Yes / No.

142. Is boredom an ability? Yes / No.

143. Is blind faith admirable or foolish? Admirable / Foolish.

144. Is the willingness to die for one's country absurd? Yes / No.

145. 'There is great joy in darkness,' wrote the Persian poet Sana'i. Do you agree? Yes / No.

146. If you knew that you were destined to repeat your life endlessly, would you live it differently? Yes / No.

147. Do you believe in salvation? Yes / No.

148. Should we only hope for what is possible? Yes / No.

149. Does perfection exist? Yes / No.

150. Does purity exist? Yes / No.

151. Can one fail at life? Yes / No.

152. Can one master life? Yes / No.

153. Is dependence a weakness? Yes / No.

154. Is weakness ever more desirable than strength? Yes / No.

155. Do you use the world more than it uses you? Yes / No.

156. Do you want more than the world can provide? Yes / No.

157. Is aging a process of acquisition or loss? Acquisition / Loss.

158. What is the greater possession, innocence or experience? Innocence / Experience.

159. If there were a god, would you worship Him? Yes / No.

160. Is anyone in a position to tell you how you should live your

life? Yes / No.

161. Has education been designed to make us more intelligent or more compliant? Intelligent / Compliant.

162. Can intelligence ever be excessive? Yes / No.

163. Is stupidity a right? Yes / No.

164. Is effort necessary for a good life? Yes / No.

165. Do some people understand life better than others? Yes / No.

166. Among the living, are some people more alive than others? Yes / No.

167. Are some people's lives worth more than others? Yes / No.

168. Can bad people have good lives? Yes / No.

169. Would a life without other people be worth living? Yes / No.

170. What would be worse, a world of total or zero obedience? Total / Zero.

171. Should we follow laws we don't agree with? Yes / No.

172. Is a prisoner who wants to be in prison free? Yes / No.

173. Should there be a statute of limitation on murder? Yes / No.

174. Should murderers who are truly sorry be given a lesser

punishment than those who aren't? Yes / No.

175. Should a murderer of children be punished more severely than a murderer of adults? Yes / No.

176. If existence is necessary for victimhood, does it follow that murder is a victimless crime? Yes / No.

177. Is incarceration more inhumane than corporal punishment? Yes / No.

178. We are sometimes punished for mistreating others. Should we ever be punished for mistreating ourselves? Yes / No.

179. Should we ever apologise for another person's actions? Yes / No.

180. Is it wrong to steal that which no one will miss? Yes / No.

181. In certain circumstances do you approve of revenge? Yes / No.

182. Irrespective of one's actions, is it wrong to have racist thoughts? Yes / No.

183. Is good graffiti vandalism? Yes / No.

184. Is colonialism intrinsically wrong? Yes / No.

185. Is humanity flawed? Yes / No.

186. Is humanity becoming more intelligent over time? Yes / No.

187. Are humans fundamentally barbaric? Yes / No.

188. Are you more dignified than a pig? Yes / No.

189. Are you more civilised than a rat? Yes / No.

190. Can one be too civilised? Yes / No.

191. Is it possible to have dignified sex? Yes / No.

192. Is lust a form of admiration? Yes / No.

193. Is it adulterous to be tickled by someone other than your partner? Yes / No.

194. Is it possible to commit adultery with an inanimate object? Yes / No.

195. Is seduction consensual? Yes / No.

196. Should all consensual acts be legal? Yes / No.

197. He has a hole called a mouth. You have one too. When you and he kiss, how many holes are there? One / Two / None.

198. While he speaks and you listen, are his words entering your body? Yes / No.

199. While you speak and he listens, is your voice inside him? Yes / No.

200. Is your silence as unique and personal to you as your voice is? Yes / No.

201. Is saying what you mean the same as meaning what you say? Yes / No.

202. An American and a German are sitting together beneath the night sky. 'I love the moon,' thinks the American. 'Ich liebe den Mond,' thinks the German. Are they thinking the same thing? Yes / No.

203. Though the word 'pineapple' doesn't appear to contain a pineapple, does the word 'hello' contain a hello? Yes / No.

204. Thinking that 'orange' refers to apples, I say, 'I love oranges.' Have I declared my love for oranges or apples? Oranges / Apples.

205. She unwittingly makes a comment regarded as homophobic. 'It can't have been homophobic,' she protests, 'since I didn't mean it like that.' Is she right? Yes / No.

206. You can imagine words without meaning. Can you imagine meanings without words? Yes / No.

207. In the year 3000 Homo sapiens are extinct. All that remains of the species is a lone copy of *Oliver Twist*. Though the printed words are intact, do their meanings still exist? Yes / No.

208. Now that Rasputin is dead, does the name 'Rasputin' still refer to something? Yes / No.

209. Can language exist without grammar? Yes / No.

210. Do thoughts have grammar? Yes / No.

211. Is the rhythm of your speech the rhythm of your thoughts? Yes / No.

212. Is complete fluency in one's native tongue possible? Yes / No.

213. Can the description of an object be more realistic than your experience of it? Yes / No.

214. Can the painting of a landscape be more realistic than your experience of it? Yes / No.

215. Consider the opening lines of Lewis Carroll's poem 'Jabberwocky':

'Twas brillig, and the slithy toves
Did gyre and gimble in the wabe:
All mimsy were the borogoves,
And the mome raths outgrabe.

Are they true? Yes / No / Possibly.

216. *'Rain' is a word.*
'Rain' is the representation of a word.
Which statement is correct?

217. 'Slavery is wrong.' Is this a fact? Yes / No.

218. You pass a stranger hanging from a cliff. Is it your responsibility to help her? Yes / No.

219. You pass a stranger starving and malnourished. Is it your responsibility to feed her? Yes / No.

220. According to Catholicism there are seven deadly sins: wrath, sloth, gluttony, avarice, lust, envy and pride. Which of these is the worst?

221. If there were a pill that eliminated one's capacity to feel shame, would you take it? Yes / No.

222. If there were a pill that eliminated one's capacity to feel disgust, would you take it? Yes / No.

223. 'To your faults be true,' wrote the poet W. H. Auden. Is this good advice? Yes / No.

224. 'No one is truly insane. Some people are just harder to understand.' Do you agree? Yes / No.

225. Can you be certain that you are not insane? Yes / No.

226. Can you look at a word without reading it? Yes / No.

227. Can you look at an object without categorising it? Yes / No.

228. In Leonardo's *Mona Lisa* there is a woman, there is a river, there are mountains. Is there air? Yes / No.

229. He looks at the vacant chair where his dead friend once sat. She looks at the same chair, though she knows nothing of his friend. Do they see the same thing? Yes / No.

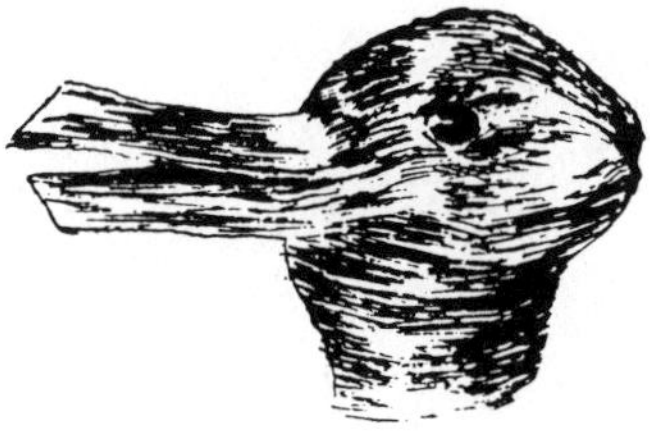

230. She thinks that the drawing is of a duck. He thinks it's of a rabbit. Do they see the same thing? Yes / No.

231. We can see with light but can we see light itself? Yes / No.

232. Is darkness invisible? Yes / No.

233. Is darkness an absence or a presence? Absence / Presence.

234. Is desire an absence or a presence? Absence / Presence.

235. Can an absence be present? Yes / No.

236. 'Beneath every surface is another surface. Probe and peer as you wish, the depths can never be seen. We are only ever looking at surfaces.' Is this correct? Yes / No.

237. If a congenitally blind person were suddenly able to see, using sight alone would she be able to identify empty spaces? Yes / No.

238. Are there infinite colours? Yes / No.

239. 'If an eye loses its sight,' wrote Aristotle, 'it is no longer an eye.' Do you agree? Yes / No.

240. When you look at the stars are you in contact with them? Yes / No.

241. You study a photograph of Martin Luther King in which he is staring down the lens of the camera. Are you looking into the living eyes of a dead man? Yes / No.

242. You hear a parakeet overhead while sipping lemonade.
These are two experiences.
These are two parts of the same experience.
Which statement is correct?

243. The uterus has a use. Does it have a purpose? Yes / No.

244. Are his warts *on* his body or *part* of his body? On / Part.

245. *I am digesting a meal.*
My organs are digesting a meal.
Which statement is correct?

246. Are meat eaters murderers? Yes / No.

247. Is eating the body of a dead animal as intimate as having sex with it? Yes / No.

248. Is the life of a human worth more than the life of a goat? Yes / No.

249. Do you have more in common with Michelangelo's *David* or an earthworm? *David* / earthworm.

250. If every particle within a statue is in motion, is the statue itself in motion? Yes / No.

251. Is anything in the world entirely still? Yes / No.

252. Can you hold a thought entirely still? Yes / No.

253. 'I have no time to age since I am always growing older.' Does this make sense? Yes / No.

254. Is the space between us a something or a nothing? Something / Nothing.

255. Does the centre of a circle have a centre? Yes / No.

256. She sings a low note followed by a high. Do you hear the first note, then the second, and *judge* that there is a change in pitch, or do you *hear* a change in pitch? Judge / Hear.

257. 'Everything you can see is an entity, and you can see change, therefore change is an entity.' Is this correct? Yes / No.

258. When you move into and occupy a certain portion of space, does that portion of space continue to exist? Yes / No.

259. Imagine the space inside a French train carriage. As the train travels from Paris to London, is that portion of space being carried to England? Yes / No.

260. If everything in existence – from rulers to fig leaves to comets – instantaneously became a thousand times larger, would anything have changed? Yes / No.

261. ●, ■, ▲ and — are the only objects in existence. They are positioned as follows -

● ▲
■ —

Imagine they are rearranged like so -

— ■
▼ ●

Has anything changed? Yes / No.

262. She stands at the border between England and Scotland with one foot inside each country. Is she in two places at once? Yes / No.

263. Do the borders between adjacent countries have width? Yes / No.

264. Is space composed of parts? Yes / No.

265. Is time composed of parts? Yes / No.

266. Is the time at which you started reading this question still part of the present? Yes / No.

267. Does the present have duration? Yes / No.

268. Does time exist in a vacuum? Yes / No.

269. Is the year 2020 older than the year 1920? Yes / No.

270. Do clocks measure time or shape it? Measure / Shape.

271. Do seconds pass on Jupiter? Yes / No.

272. Are you literally moving through time? Yes / No.

273. Does the present contain the past? Yes / No.

274. Does the past contain the future? Yes / No.

275. Is the past immutable? Yes / No.

276. 'Since the past no longer exists, and you cannot have what does not exist, it follows that you have no past.' Is this correct? Yes / No.

277. 'Since the future does not yet exist, and you cannot have what does not exist, it follows that you have no future.' Is

this correct? Yes / No.

278. 'Whatever I perceive must be present and to remember an event is to perceive the past, so when I remember an event, the past must be present.' Is this correct? Yes / No.

279. With the passing of time, do moments perish or become new? Perish / Become new.

280. With every choice you make are you annihilating possible futures? Yes / No.

281. Can you feel the passage of time on the surface of your skin? Yes / No.

282. Is yesterday more real than tomorrow? Yes / No.

283. If you have memories of being 5 years old, does this mean that you have retained the mind of a 5-year-old? Yes / No.

284. Do memories age with you? Yes / No.

285. Is the memory of pain painful? Yes / No.

286. Is the memory of warmth warm? Yes / No.

287. Can pleasure ever be excessive? Yes / No.

288. Is monogamy a kind of greed? Yes / No.

289. Is terrorism ever justified? Yes / No.

290. Is anger inherently ugly? Yes / No.

291. Is sex inherently intimate? Yes / No.

292. Is perseverance a kind of paralysis? Yes / No.

293. Is humility a character flaw? Yes / No.

294. Is selflessness a virtue or an affliction? Virtue / Affliction.

295. She is incapable of feeling guilt. Is this a sickness or a blessing? Sickness / Blessing.

296. Is gambling the apotheosis of hope? Yes / No.

297. Is hope only for the impotent? Yes / No.

298. Is gratitude ever a duty? Yes / No.

299. Is humanity a kind of family? Yes/ No.

300. Is family a social invention? Yes / No.

301. Can society ever be too diverse? Yes / No.

302. Is the world infinitely interesting? Yes / No.

303. Do you believe that you have a head? Yes / No.

304. Do you hold any beliefs that are beyond doubt? Yes / No.

305. I hold a belief that is of tremendous help to me, but I find evidence to suggest that it is false. Would it be more rational to ignore the evidence or abandon the belief? Ignore / Abandon.

306. Imagine you saw a file of angels pass through your body and disappear. Would it be possible to prove whether the experience had been real or illusory? Yes / No.

307. Generally speaking, should we trust appearances? Yes / No.

308. Could acquiring greater knowledge of a certain thing ever lessen our understanding of it? Yes / No.

309. Is disappointment always the fault of the disappointed? Yes / No.

310. Is moaning ever poetic? Yes / No.

311. 'We are never free of moods,' wrote the philosopher Martin Heidegger. Do you agree? Yes / No.

312. Does the calm person see the world more clearly than the angry person? Yes / No.

313. Are some of us more adept at recognising beauty than others? Yes / No.

314. Can animals perceive beauty? Yes / No.

315. Could an evil act ever be worthy of admiration? Yes / No.

316. Is evil a brand of stupidity? Yes / No.

317. Is it always wrong to take pleasure in another person's pain? Yes / No.

318. Can beauty be terrifying? Yes / No.

319. Can good art be ugly? Yes / No.

320. Can art be immoral? Yes / No.

321. Does art have a function? Yes / No.

322. Is there progress in art? Yes / No.

323. Is pornography art? Yes / No.

324. Is perfume art? Yes / No.

325. Can art make you a better person? Yes / No.

326. Is poetry flammable? Yes / No.

327. Do birds literally sing? Yes / No.

328. Has Shakespeare outlived his life? Yes / No.

329. Is the author the foremost authority on the meaning of her work? Yes / No.

330. Does anything ever happen without a cause? Yes / No.

331. Can you conceive of an act that has no effect? Yes / No.

332. Is there anything that is not itself? Yes / No.

333. Is the new only a reconfiguration of the old? Yes / No.

334. Are you confined to a single body? Yes / No.

335. Are you inescapably human? Yes / No.

336. Is it possible to leave yourself behind? Yes / No.

337. Do all things resemble each other in at least one aspect? Yes / No.

338. Can the exact same event occur more than once? Yes / No.

339. How long can this moment last?

340. Are moments divisible? Are there half-moments, say? Yes / No..

341. Are events divisible? Are there half-events, say? Yes / No.

342. When you take a step forward are you performing one action – a single step – or multiple actions – four quarter-steps, say? One / Multiple.

343. An egg hatches. This is an event. An hour passes. Is this an event? Yes / No.

344. When you watch a pot of water boil at 100 degrees Celsius, are you watching a fact? Yes / No.

345. Is there anyone whom you wouldn't change in any way? Yes / No.

346. Are you more certain of your political or your sexual orientation? Political / Sexual.

347. Are you hidden or revealed by your clothes? Hidden / Revealed.

348. The pleasures of eating and the pleasures of sex: a difference

in degree or a difference in kind? Degree / Kind.

349. He believes that God exists. She believes that He does not. Is one of them wrong? Yes / No.

350. He believes that God exists. She believes that He does not. Is there a significant difference between them? Yes / No.

351. Could an omnipotent being create a tennis ball that was not a tennis ball? Yes / No.

352. Does it matter how the universe began? Yes / No.

353. 'If the universe is infinitely large, it makes no sense to say we are inside it.' Is this correct? Yes / No.

354. Were you created or produced by your parents? Created / Produced.

355. Can we give back to our parents more than we have received from them? Yes / No.

356. 'They fuck you up, your mum and dad,' wrote the poet Philip Larkin. Do you agree? Yes / No.

357. Do artists create or produce their work? Create / Produce.

358. 'To produce a work of genius one needs to be a genius, but no one is a genius until they have produced a work of genius, therefore there are no works of genius.' Is this correct? Yes / No.

359. There is a list that details every fact about you. There is another list that details every fact about the full-stop at the

end of this sentence. Is your list longer? Yes / No.

360. Do babies deserve our respect? Yes / No.

361. Do babies know that they exist? Yes / No.

362. Does an octopus know what it is? Yes / No.

363. Does the ocean have a skin? Yes / No.

364. Do trees have flesh? Yes / No.

365. Is gravity a form of oppression? Yes / No.

366. With a single word how would you describe the world?

367. In the absence of the law, would we still have rights? Yes / No.

368. In the absence of the law, would we still have property? Yes / No.

369. In the absence of God is nothing blasphemous? Yes / No.

370. Should MPs in the House of Commons be permitted to call each other cunts? Yes / No.

371. Could you trust a politician who had an awful taste in music? Yes / No.

372. Are citizens in democratic countries responsible for atrocities committed by their leaders? Yes / No.

373. Does your employer own your labour? Yes / No.

374. Is a high-school massacre the act of a crazed individual or a crazed society? Individual / Society.

375. What is the greater misfortune, to be an adult or a child? Adult / Child.

376. What is the greater misfortune, to be a woman or a man? Woman / Man.

377. Painting A depicts the crucifixion of a single person. Painting B depicts the crucifixion of five people. Does painting B depict more suffering than painting A? Yes / No.

378. Cancer exists. Does it make sense to say that it *shouldn't?* Yes / No.

379. Despite the impositions of pain and misfortune, is being alive intrinsically pleasurable? Yes / No.

380. Is it possible to have too little pain in one's life? Yes / No.

381. 'Life, friends, is boring,' wrote the poet John Berryman. Is this an adequate justification for suicide? Yes / No.

382. If all the beauty in the world were to disappear, would life be worth living? Yes / No.

383. Is an unintelligent life worth living? Yes / No.

384. Can you let 10 waking seconds pass without making a single decision? Yes / No.

385. Is following your desire a form of compliance? Yes / No.

386. Is following your conscience a type of obedience? Yes / No.

387. When you wriggle your toes is your body obeying you? Yes / No.

388. Is it possible to wholly disobey yourself? Yes / No.

389. Is it possible to invent new emotions? Yes / No.

390. With two hands we can simultaneously perform different tasks. With two mouths, could we simultaneously hold different conversations? Yes / No.

391. Try to imagine your body dissolving into thin air, starting with your toes, and then slowly rising, till all that remains are your disembodied thoughts. Can you? Yes / No.

392. 'Your voice is a large part of who you are, and your voice is made of air, so you are largely made of air.' Is this correct? Yes / No.

393. 'Given that you were once an embryo, and embryos do not have minds, it follows that you are distinct from your mind.' Is this correct? Yes / No.

394. 'Since your body will continue to exist after you have stopped existing, it follows that you are distinct from your body.' Is this correct? Yes / No.

395. If she disappeared into thin air and never returned, would it be accurate to describe her as dead? Yes / No.

396. If she suddenly froze and never moved again, changeless and without aging, would she still exist? Yes / No.

397. Herodotus wrote of an Indian tribe that ate its dead. Is this practice any stranger than cremation or burial? Yes / No.

398. When someone close to us dies, does their love for us die with them? Yes / No.

399. Do the dead have a right to privacy? Yes / No.

400. Do smaller creatures have smaller deaths? Yes / No.

401. Is anything eternal? Yes / No.

Answers

1. Do you know what you are?

In the summer of 1734 the 23-year-old **David Hume** (1711-1776) left Britain for France in search of solitude and cheap living. His aim was to jettison philosophical preconceptions and write an account of human nature based solely on the raw data of experience. Three years later he returned with *A Treatise of Human Nature.*

In the following extract Hume considers whether experience alone is enough to convince us of the existence of a self. Though we experience particular sensations and feelings, do we experience an enduring self that has these sensations and feelings? Hume thought not, and concluded that we are 'nothing but a bundle or collection of different perceptions, which succeed each other with an inconceivable rapidity, and are in a perpetual flux and movement'.

'There are some philosophers, who imagine we are every moment intimately conscious of what we call our SELF; that we feel its existence and its continuance in existence; and are certain, beyond the evidence of a demonstration, both of its perfect identity and simplicity…

For my part, when I enter most intimately into what I call *myself*, I always stumble on some particular perception or other, of heat or cold, light or shade, love or hatred, pain or pleasure. I never can catch *myself* at any time without a perception, and never can observe any thing but the perception. When my perceptions are removed for any time, as by sound sleep; so long am I insensible of *myself*, and may truly be said not to exist. And were all my perceptions removed by death, and could I neither think, nor feel, nor see, nor love, nor hate after the dissolution of my body, I should be entirely annihilated, nor do I conceive what is farther requisite to make me a perfect non-entity. If any one, upon serious and unprejudiced reflection thinks he has a different notion of *himself*, I must confess I can reason no longer with him. All I can allow him is, that he may be in the right as well as I, and that we are essentially different in this particular. He may, perhaps, perceive something simple and continued, which he calls *himself*; though I am certain there is no such principle in me.

But setting aside some metaphysicians of this kind, I may venture to affirm of the rest of mankind, that they are nothing but a bundle or collection of different perceptions, which succeed each other with an inconceivable rapidity, and are in a perpetual flux and movement. Our eyes cannot turn in their sockets without varying our perceptions. Our thought is still more variable than our sight; and all our other senses and faculties contribute to this change; nor is there any single power of the soul, which remains unalterably the same, perhaps for one moment. The mind is a kind of theatre, where several perceptions successively make their appearance; pass, re-pass, glide away, and mingle in an infinite variety of postures and situations.'

For Hume, see *Q*. 90.

6. Is it possible that your entire life has been a dream?

Zhuangzi (*c.* 396-286 BCE) was once invited by the king of Chu (an ancient Chinese state) to become the region's prime minister. Greatly offended by the honour, he declined, claiming that such high office would demean him. To live beholden to duty or the veneration of others is a curtailment of one's freedom. We should have no truck with toil or ambition. Life ought to be passed in a plume of insouciance.

It was possibly this ideal of a floating flitting life which gave Zhuangzi the propensity to dream of butterflies.

'Those who dream of the banquet may wake to lamentation

and sorrow; those who dream of lamentation and sorrow may wake to join the hunt. While they dream, they do not know that they dream. Some will even interpret the dream while they are dreaming; but only when they awake do they know it was a dream. By and by comes the Great Awakening, and then we shall find out that this life is really a great dream. Fools think they are awake now, and flatter themselves they know if they are really princes or peasants...

Once upon a time, I, Zhuangzi, dreamt I was a butterfly, fluttering hither and thither, a veritable butterfly, enjoying itself to the full of its bent, and not knowing it was Zhuangzi. Suddenly I awoke, and came to myself, the veritable Zhuangzi. Now I do not know whether it was then I dreamt I was a butterfly, or whether I am now a butterfly dreaming I am a man.'

For Zhuangzi, see *Q*. 152.

7. Are you a stranger to yourself?

According to the Second Book of Samuel in the Old Testament, David, king of Israel, fell in love with Bathsheba, a married woman, slept with her, and then arranged for her husband, Uriah the Hittite, to be killed in battle. Neither the adultery nor the murder troubled his conscience.

In *Fifteen Sermons Preached at the Rolls Chapel* the Anglican bishop **Joseph Butler** (1692-1752) expressed his astonishment that so virtuous and pious a figure as David could have behaved so wickedly. He believed this was indicative of a serious and pervasive moral problem: self-deceit. Our partiality towards ourselves means that we are unable to see our own conduct clearly. We unwittingly apply different standards to our own behaviour.

'There is not any thing, relating to men and characters, more surprising and unaccountable, than this partiality to themselves, which is observable in many as there is nothing of more melancholy reflection, respecting morality, virtue, and religion. Hence it is that many men seem perfect strangers to their own characters. They think, and reason, and judge quite differently upon any matter relating to themselves, from what they do in cases of others where they are not interested. Hence it is one hears people exposing follies, which they themselves are eminent for; and talking with great severity against particular vices, which, if all the world be not mistaken, they themselves are notoriously guilty of. This self-ignorance and self-partiality may be in all different degrees. It is a lower degree of it, which David himself refers to in these words, "Who can tell how oft he offendeth? O cleanse thou me from my secret faults." This is the ground of that advice of Elihu to Job: "Surely it is meet to be said unto God,– That which I see not teach thou me; if I have done iniquity, I will do no more." And Solomon saw this thing in a very strong light when he said, "He that trusteth his own heart is a fool." This likewise was the reason why that precept, *Know thyself*, was so frequently inculcated by the philosophers of old. For if it was not for that partial and fond regard to ourselves, it would certainly be no great difficulty to know our own character, what passes within the bent and bias of our mind; much less would there be any difficulty in judging rightly of our own actions. But from this partiality it frequently comes to pass, that the observation of many men's being themselves last of all acquainted with what falls out in their own families, may be applied to a nearer home, to what passes within their own breasts.

There is plainly, in the generality of mankind, an absence of doubt or distrust, in a very great measure, as to their moral character and behaviour; and likewise a disposition to take for granted, that all is right and well with them in these respects. The former is owing to their not reflecting, not exercising their judgment upon themselves; the latter, to self-love. I am not speaking of that extravagance, which is sometimes to be met with; instances of persons declaring in words at length, that they never were in the wrong, nor had ever any diffidence of the justness of their conduct, in their whole lives: no, these people are too far gone to have any thing said to them. The thing before us is indeed of this kind, but in a lower degree, and confined to the moral character; somewhat of which we almost all of us have, without reflecting upon it. Now, consider how long, and how grossly, a person of the best understanding might be imposed upon by one of whom he had not any suspicion, and in whom he placed an entire confidence; especially if there were friendship and real kindness in the case: surely this holds even stronger with respect to that self we are all so fond of. Hence arises in men a disregard of reproof and instruction, rules of conduct and moral discipline, which occasionally come in their way: a disregard, I say, of these, not in every respect, but in this single one, namely, as what may be of service to them in particular towards mending their own hearts and tempers, and making them better men. It never in earnest comes into their thoughts, whether such admonitions may not relate, and be of service to themselves; and this quite distinct from a positive persuasion to the contrary, a persuasion from reflection that they are innocent and blameless in those respects.'

10. Is it possible that you are the only person in the world with thoughts and feelings?

In the extract below, from *An Examination of Sir William Hamilton's Philosophy*, the English philosopher **John Stuart Mill** (1806-1873) endeavours to solve the following problem: 'By what evidence do I know, or by what considerations am I led to believe, that there exist other sentient creatures; that the walking and speaking figures which I see and hear, have sensations and thoughts, or in other words, possess Minds?'

His answer is a striking inversion of the psychoanalyst Donald Winnicott's thoughts on child development. Winnicott claims that we first develop a sense of self, of our own feelings, through the responsive face of the mother. The mother's face is a mirror in which we see ourselves and through which we discover our minds. That is, for Winnicott we find our sentience through our observations of other people.

For Mill, on the contrary, we find the sentience of other people through observations of ourselves. Winnicott regards other people as constitutive of self-awareness. Mill takes our self-awareness to be original: the awareness of others is derivative. Winnicott believes we work from the outside in. Mill, from the inside out.

'I conclude that other human beings have feelings like me, because, first, they have bodies like me, which I know, in my own case, to be the antecedent condition of feelings; and because, secondly, they exhibit the acts, and other outward signs, which in my own case I know by experience to be caused by feelings. I am conscious in myself of a series of facts connected by an uniform sequence, of which the beginning is modifications of my body, the middle is feelings, the end is outward demeanour. In the case of other human beings I have the evidence of my senses for the first and last links of the series, but not for the intermediate link. I find, however, that the sequence between the first and last is as regular and constant in those other cases as it is in mine. In my own case I know that the first link produces the last through the intermediate link, and could not produce it without. Experience, therefore, obliges me to conclude that there must be an intermediate link; which must either be the same in others as in myself, or a different one: I must either believe them to be alive, or to be automatons: and by believing them to be alive, that is, by supposing the link to be of the same nature as in the case of which I have experience, and which is in all other respects similar, I bring other human beings, as phenomena, under the same generalizations which I know by experience to be the true theory of my own existence. And in doing so I conform to the legitimate rules of experimental enquiry. The process is exactly parallel to that by which Newton proved that the force which keeps the planets in their orbits is identical with that by which an apple falls to the ground. It was not incumbent on Newton to prove the impossibility of its being any other force; he was thought to have made out his point when he had simply shown, that no other force need be supposed. We know the existence of other beings by generalization from the knowledge of our own: the generalization merely postulates that what experience shows to be a mark of the existence of something within the sphere of our consciousness, may be concluded to be a mark of the same thing beyond that sphere.'

For Mill, see *Q*. 178.

13. *Are you in control of yourself?*

Thomas Henry Huxley (1825-1895) held that 'a man shall not say he knows or believes that which he has no scientific grounds for professing to know or believe'. He coined a now familiar term to enshrine this principle: agnosticism.

Huxley's agnosticism steered him towards a variety of unorthodox conclusions, one of which was epiphenomenalism. This is the view that the mind has no control over the body. The body is a machine which mechanically reacts to stimuli. Our choices and decisions are the consequences rather than the causes of these reactions. We are marionettes living under the illusion of autonomy. To believe otherwise, he thought, is to ignore the available evidence.

Huxley's evidence partly consisted of experiments

carried out on frogs. These frogs had portions of the brain responsible for conscious perception removed, and yet, despite lacking consciousness, continued to exhibit normal forms of behaviour. For instance, as discussed here in his 1874 lecture 'On the Hypothesis that Animals Are Automata, and Its History', a frog missing two-thirds of its brain was still able to swim when thrown in water. Consciousness, in short, is not in the driving seat.

'Suppose that only the anterior division of the brain – so much of it as lies in front of the "optic lobes" – is removed. If that operation is performed quickly and skilfully, the frog may be kept in a state of full bodily vigour for months, or it may be for years; but it will sit unmoved. It sees nothing: it hears nothing. It will starve sooner than feed itself, although food put into its mouth is swallowed. On irritation, it jumps or walks; if thrown into the water it swims. If it be put on the hand, it sits there, crouched, perfectly quiet, and would sit there for ever. If the hand be inclined very gently and slowly, so that the frog would naturally tend to slip off, the creature's fore paws are shifted on to the edge of the hand, until he can just prevent himself from falling. If the turning of the hand be slowly continued, he mounts up with great care and deliberation, putting first one leg forward and then another, until he balances himself with perfect precision upon the edge; and if the turning of the hand is continued, he goes through the needful set of muscular operations, until he comes to be seated in security, upon the back of the hand. The doing of all this requires a delicacy of coordination, and a precision of adjustment of the muscular apparatus of the body, which are only comparable to those of a rope-dancer. To the ordinary influences of light, the frog, deprived of its cerebral hemispheres, appears to be blind. Nevertheless, if the animal be put upon a table, with a book at some little distance between it and the light, and the skin of the hinder part of its body is then irritated, it will jump forward, avoiding the book by passing to the right or left of it. Therefore, although the frog appears to have no sensation of light, visible objects act through its brain upon the motor mechanism of its body…

When we speak of the actions of the lower animals being guided by instinct and not by reason, what we really mean is that, though they feel as we do, yet their actions are the results of their physical organisation. We believe, in short, that they are machines, one part of which (the nervous system) not only sets the rest in motion, and co-ordinates its movements in relation with changes in surrounding bodies, but is provided with special apparatus, the function of which is the calling into existence of those states of consciousness which are termed sensations, emotions, and ideas…

It may be assumed, then, that molecular changes in the brain are the causes of all the states of consciousness of brutes. Is there any evidence that these states of consciousness may, conversely, cause those molecular changes which give rise to muscular motion? I see no such evidence. The frog walks, hops, swims, and goes through his gymnastic performances quite as well without consciousness, and consequently without volition, as with it; and, if a frog, in his natural state, possesses anything corresponding with what we call volition, there is no reason to think that it is anything but a concomitant of the molecular changes in the brain which form part of the series involved in the production of motion.

The consciousness of brutes would appear to be related to the mechanism of their body simply as a collateral product of its working, and to be as completely without any power of modifying that working as the steam-whistle which accompanies the work of a locomotive engine is without influence upon its machinery. Their volition, if they have any, is an emotion indicative of physical changes, not a cause of such changes…

It is quite true that, to the best of my judgment, the argumentation which applies to brutes holds equally good of men; and, therefore, that all states of consciousness in us, as in them, are immediately caused by molecular changes of the brain-substance. It seems to me that in men, as in brutes, there is no proof that any state of consciousness is the cause of change in the motion of the matter of the organism. If these positions are well based, it follows that our mental conditions are simply the symbols in consciousness of the changes which take place automatically in the organism; and that, to take an extreme illustration, the feeling we call volition is not the cause of a voluntary act, but the symbol of that state of the brain which is the immediate cause of that act. We are conscious automata, endowed with free will in the only intelligible sense of that much-abused term – inasmuch as in many respects we are able to do as we like – but none the less parts of the great series of causes and effects which, in unbroken continuity, composes that which is, and has been, and shall be – the sum of existence.'

18. Does tomorrow exist?

St Augustine's (354-430) *Confessions* recounts the moment when at the age of 32 he finally committed to an abstinent life of Christian devotion. The conversion occurred in a Milanese garden where he heard a child from a nearby house repeatedly sing 'Take it and read'. Believing this to be a sign, he opened the Bible at random and was wonderstruck, transfigured, by a verse from Romans: 'Not in revelling and drunkenness, not in lust and wantonness, not in quarrels and rivalries. Rather, arm yourselves with the Lord Jesus Christ; spend no more thought on nature and nature's appetites.'

The experience of conversion is intertwined with notions of time. It constitutes a moment of the present in which the past is renounced and a new future is committed to. Having undergone his conversion, questions of time were close to Augustine's heart.

'Who will tell me that there are not three times (as we learned when boys, and as we have taught boys), the past, present, and future, but only present, because those two are not? Or are they also; but when from future it becometh present, cometh it forth from some secret place, and when from the present it becometh past, doth it retire into anything secret? For where have they, who have foretold future things, seen these things, if as yet they are not? For that which is not cannot be seen. And they who relate things past could not relate them as true, did they not perceive them in their mind. Which things, if they were not, they could in no wise be discerned. There are therefore things both future and past.

Permit me, Lord, to seek further. O my hope, let not my purpose be confounded. For if there are times past and future, I desire to know where they are. But if as yet I do not succeed, I still know, wherever they are, that they are not there as future or past, but as present. For if there also they be future, they are not as yet there; if even there they be past, they are no longer there. Wheresoever, therefore, they are, whatsoever they are, they are only so as present. Although past things are related as true, they are drawn out from the memory,— not the things themselves, which have passed, but the words conceived from the images of the things which they have formed in the mind as footprints in their passage through the senses. My childhood, indeed, which no longer is, is in time past, which now is not; but when I call to mind its image, and speak of it, I behold it in the present, because it is as yet in my memory. Whether there be a like cause of foretelling future things, that of things which as yet are not the images may be perceived as already existing, I confess, my God, I know not...

In whatever manner, therefore, this secret preconception of

future things may be, nothing can be seen, save what is. But what now is is not future, but present. When, therefore, they say that things future are seen, it is not themselves, which as yet are not (that is, which are future); but their causes or their signs perhaps are seen, the which already are. Therefore, to those already beholding them, they are not future, but present, from which future things conceived in the mind are foretold. Which conceptions again now are, and they who foretell those things behold these conceptions present before them. Let now so multitudinous a variety of things afford me some example. I behold daybreak; I foretell that the sun is about to rise. That which I behold is present; what I foretell is future,— not that the sun is future, which already is; but his rising, which is not yet. Yet even its rising I could not predict unless I had an image of it in my mind, as now I have while I speak. But that dawn which I see in the sky is not the rising of the sun, although it may go before it, nor that imagination in my mind; which two are seen as present, that the other which is future may be foretold. Future things, therefore, are not as yet; and if they are not as yet, they are not. And if they are not, they cannot be seen at all; but they can be foretold from things present which now are, and are seen.'

For Augustine, see *Qs.* 80 and 191.

19. Does yesterday exist?

Henri Bergson (1859-1941) is the only philosopher to have been awarded the Nobel Prize for Literature for a predominantly metaphysical body of work. Such was his popularity during the belle époque that the Catholic Church found it necessary to proscribe his writings for seeking 'to shatter grand fundamental principles and truths'.

Central to Bergson's philosophy was the idea that we have an intellectual predisposition to erroneously conflate space and time, that is to say, we conceive of events and moments as sitting side-by-side each other in time just as objects sit side-by-side each other in space. This, he claimed, is wrong. Time is not like this. It does not consist of discrete parts but is a continuous indivisible flow.

From 'The Perception of Change' –

'We are inclined to conceive of the past as nonexistent, and philosophers encourage this natural tendency in us. For them, and for us, only the present exists: if the past does survive, it is only with the help and charity of the present, that is to say, only via the intervention of memory, a faculty whose function is to select and preserve certain portions of the past by storing them away in a kind of box. — This, I assure you, is an illusion, which, though useful and necessary to life, is nevertheless extremely dangerous to theorising. Here we find in a nutshell most of the illusions capable of vitiating philosophical thought.

Let us think about this solely-existing "present". What exactly is it? If it is the current instant – I mean, a mathematical instant that is to time what the mathematical point is to the line – it is clear that such an instant is a pure abstraction, a fantasy; it cannot have real existence. You could no more make time out of such instants than you could make a line out of mathematical points. Suppose it does exist: how could there be an instant prior to it? The two instants could not be separated by an interval of time since, by hypothesis, time is reduced to a juxtaposition of instants. Therefore, they would be separated by nothing, and consequently they would be one: when mathematical points touch, they coalesce. But let us put these subtleties aside. Common sense tells us that when we speak of the present we are thinking of an interval of time, a certain duration. What duration? It's impossible to define exactly. It is inconstant. My present at this moment is the sentence I am speaking. But this is because I want to limit my field of attention to this sentence. This attention can be made longer or shorter, like the interval between the two points of a compass. For the moment, the points are just wide enough to reach from the beginning to the end of my sentence; but, if I felt like moving them further away, my present would embrace both my last sentence and the one before it: I'd simply have to adopt different punctuation. We can go further: a field of attention which could be extended indefinitely would contain in its view, along with the preceding sentence, all the previous sentences of the lecture, and the events which preceded the lecture, and as large a portion of what we call the past as we wanted. The distinction we make between our present and our past is therefore, if not arbitrary, at least relative to how much of one's life is embraced by one's field of attention. The "present" occupies just as much space as this effort. As soon as our attention releases any part of that which it holds within its view, immediately that portion of the present become *ipso facto* part of our past. In short, our present falls back into the past when we cease to attribute current interest to it. This is true of both individuals and nations: an event belongs to the past and becomes history when it is no longer of direct interest to the politics of the day and can be neglected without there being any practical consequence. So long as an action is felt, it belongs to the life of the nation and remains present to it.

As such, nothing prevents us from extending back as far as possible the line of separation between our present and our past. An attention to life, sufficiently powerful and sufficiently free of practical concerns, would thus embrace in an undivided present the entire past history of the cognisant person — not as a simultaneity, but as something which is at the same time continually present and continually moving.'

For Bergson, see *Qs*. 126, 213, 265 and 389.

20. Do your childhood fingers still exist?

'All of us, I presume, more or less, are led beyond the region of ordinary facts. Some in one way and some in others, we seem to touch and have communion with what is beyond the visible world. In various manners we find something higher, which both supports and humbles, both chastens and transports us,' wrote the English philosopher **F. H. Bradley** (1846-1924) in *Appearance and Reality,* describing the appetite for transcendence, for that which lies beyond the sensory and apparent; an appetite he assuredly possessed.

In the following passage Bradley disputes the seemingly obvious reality of *things.* Your fingers, as they are now, and considered as *things,* do not really exist. Thingness necessitates identity, and identity necessitates continuity over time, so to claim that such digital things exist we'd need to specify by virtue of what they are the same fingers that existed yesterday, or a month ago, even decades ago. The rub, however, is that there is no definitive criterion of sameness.

'For a thing to exist it must possess identity; and identity seems a possession with a character at best doubtful. If it is merely ideal, the things itself can hardly be real. First, then, let us inquire if a thing can exist without identity. To ask this question is at once to answer it; unless, indeed, a thing is to exist, and is to hold its diversity combined in an unity, somehow quite outside of time. And this seems untenable. A thing, if it is to be called such, must occupy some duration beyond the present moment, and hence succession is essential. The thing, to be at all, must be the same after a change, and the change must, to some extent, be predicated of the thing. If you suppose a case so simple as the movement of an atom, that is enough for our purpose. For, if this "thing" does not move, there is no motion. But, if it moves, then succession is predicated of it, and the thing is a bond of identity in differences. And, further, this identity is ideal, since it consists in the content, or in the "what we are able to say of the thing". For raise the doubt at the end of our atom's process, if the atom is the same. The question raised cannot be answered without an appeal to its character. It is different in one respect – namely, the change of place; but in another respect – that of its own character – it remains the same. And this respect is obviously identical content…

A thing is a thing, in short, by being what it was. And it does not appear how this relation of sameness can be real. It is a relation connecting the past with the present, and this connection is evidently vital to the thing. But, if so, the thing has become, in more senses than one, the relation of passages in its own history. And if we assert that the thing is this inclusive relation, which transcends any given time, surely we have allowed that the thing, though not wholly an idea, is an idea essentially. And it is an idea which at no actual time is ever real.

And this problem is no mere abstract invented subtlety, but shows itself in practice. It is often impossible to reply when we are asked if an object is really the same. If a manufactured article has been worked upon and partly remade, such a question may have no sense until it has been specified. You must go on to mention the point or the particular respect of which you are thinking. For questions of identity turn always upon sameness in character, and the reason why here you cannot reply generally, is that you do not know this general character which is taken to make the thing's essence. It is not always material substance, for we might call an organism identical, though its particles were all different. It is not always shape, or size, or colour, or, again, always the purpose which the thing fulfils. The general nature, in fact, of a thing's identity seems to lie, first, in the avoidance of any absolute break in its existence, and, beyond that, to consist in some qualitative sameness which differs with different things. And with some things – because literally we do not know in what character their sameness lies – we are helpless when asked if identity has been preserved. If any one wants an instance of the value of our ordinary notions, he may find it, perhaps, in Sir John Cutler's silk stockings. These were darned with worsted until no particle of the silk was left in them, and no one could agree whether they were the same old stockings or were new ones. In brief, the identity of a thing lies in the view which you take of it. That view seems often a mere chance idea, and, where it seems necessary, it still remains an idea. Or, if you prefer it, it is a character, which exists outside of and beyond any fact which you can take. But it is not easy to see how, if so, any thing can be real. And things have, so far, turned out to be merely appearances.'

23. Are you inside your body?

Miguel de Unamuno (1864-1936) was a Spanish writer whose individualism – 'The individual is the end of the universe' – was a repeated source of conflict between himself and state forces. After his vocal opposition to General Miguel Primo de Rivera's dictatorship, he was exiled to Fuerteventura in the Canary Islands in 1924. Though pardoned several months later, he had no wish to return and moved to Paris till Primo de Rivera's resignation in 1930. Six years later, however, after denouncing the Falangists, he was placed under house arrest by General Francisco Franco and died shortly after.

The following extract is from his essay 'Solitude'.

'It is only solitude that dissolves that thick cloak of shame that isolates us from one another; only in solitude do we find ourselves; and in finding ourselves, we find in ourselves all our brothers in solitude. Solitude unites us, believe me, just as much as society separates us. And if we do not know how to love one another, it is because we do not know how to be alone...

We men are impenetrable. Spirits, like solid bodies, can only communicate with one another by the contact of surfaces, not by penetrating one another, still less by fusing together.

You have heard me say a thousand times that most spirits seem to me like crustaceans, with the bone outside and the flesh inside. And when in some books that I have forgotten I read what a painful and terrible thing it would be if the human spirit were to be incarnated in a crab and had to make use of the crab's senses, organs, and members, I said to myself: "This is what actually happens; we are all unfortunate crabs, shut up in hard shells."

And the poet is he whose flesh emerges from the shell, whose soul oozes forth. And when, in our hours of anguish or joy, our soul oozes forth, we are all of us poets.

And that is why I believe that it is necessary to agitate the masses, to shake men and winnow them as in a sieve, to throw against one another, in order to see if in this way their shells will not break and their spirits flow forth, whether they will not mingle and unite with one another, and whether the real collective spirit, the soul of humanity, may not thus be welded together.

But the sad thing is, if we are to go by past experience, that all these mutual rubbings and clashings, far from breaking the shells, harden, thicken, and enlarge them. They are like corns that grow larger and stronger with rubbing. Although perhaps it is that the clashes are not violent enough. And in any case it must be clashing, not rubbing. I do not like to rub against people but to clash against them; I do not like to approach people obliquely and glance off them at a tangent, but to meet them frontally, and if possible split them in two. It is the best service I can do them. And there is no better preparation for this task than solitude.

It is very sad that we have to communicate with one another by touching, at most by rubbing, through the medium of the hard shells that isolate us from one another. And I am convinced that this hard shell becomes weaker and more delicate in solitude until it changes into the most tenuous membrane which permits the action of osmosis and exosmosis. And this is why I believe that it is solitude that makes men really sociable and human.'

25. Are you conscious of your consciousness?

Dugald Stewart (1753-1828) was so captivating a lecturer that he could ensorcell his students merely by clearing his throat. 'There was eloquence in his very spitting,' one remarked. His sputum, of course, belonged to a broader rapture: 'To me his lectures were like the opening of the heavens: I felt that I had a soul.'

Stewart himself had been a student of Thomas Reid's before going on to hold the chair of moral philosophy at the University of Edinburgh for 25 years. Upon his death, friends and colleagues erected a monument in his honour, a neoclassical structure that still sits on Calton Hill overlooking the city.

From *Elements of the Philosophy of the Human Mind* –

'According to the common doctrine of our best philosophers, it is by the evidence of *consciousness* we are assured that we ourselves exist. The proposition, however, when thus stated, is not accurately true; for our own existence (as I have elsewhere observed) is not a direct or immediate object of consciousness, in the strict and logical meaning of that term. We are conscious of sensation, thought, desire, volition: but we are not conscious of the existence of mind itself; nor would it be possible for us to arrive at the knowledge of it (supposing us to be created in the full possession of all the intellectual *capacities* which belong to human nature), if no impression were ever to be made on our external senses. The moment that, in consequence of such an impression, a sensation is excited, we learn two facts at once;—

the existence of the sensation, and our own existence as sentient beings;—in other words, the very first exercise of consciousness necessarily implies a belief, not only of the present existence of what is felt, but of the present existence of *that* which feels and thinks; or (to employ plainer language) the present existence of that being which I denote by the words *I* and *myself*. Of these facts, however, it is the former alone of which we can properly be said to be conscious, agreeably to the rigorous interpretation of the expression. A conviction of the latter, although it seems to be so inseparable from the exercise of consciousness, that it can scarcely be considered as posterior to it in the order of *time*, is yet (if I may be allowed to make use of a scholastic distinction) posterior to it in the order of *nature*; not only as it supposes consciousness to be already awakened by some sensation, or some other mental affection; but as it is evidently rather a judgment accompanying the exercise of that power, than one of its immediate intimations concerning its appropriate class of internal phenomena. It appears to me, therefore, more correct to call the belief of our own existence a concomitant or accessory of the exercise of consciousness, than to say, that our existence is a fact falling under the immediate cognizance of consciousness, like the existence of the various agreeable or painful sensations which external objects excite in our minds.'

For Stewart's esteemed teacher, see *Qs*. 124 and 267.

26. Does your mind have weight?

For substance dualists – those who believe that mind and body are distinct entities – the mere presence of a living breathing body does not entail the presence of a conscious feeling mind. **René Descartes** (1596-1650), for instance, a dualist, would stick his fingers into the beating hearts of living dogs and, reputedly, throw cats out of windows confident in the belief that they, as mindless beings, didn't feel a thing.

In the passage below from *Discourse on Method,* Descartes argues for the distinction between mind and body on the grounds that he can doubt the existence of his body (it may be an illusion) whereas he cannot doubt the existence of himself as a thinking thing (since doubting is thinking). He concludes that the mind is immaterial and non-spatial.

'In the next place, I attentively examined what I was, and as I observed that I could pretend that I had no body, and that there was no world nor any place in which I might be; but that I could not therefore pretend that I was not; and that, on the contrary, from the very circumstance that I thought to doubt of the truth of other things, it most clearly and certainly followed that I was; while, on the other hand, if I had only ceased to think, although all the other objects which I had ever imagined had been in reality existent, I would have had no reason to believe that I existed; I thence concluded that I was a substance whose whole essence or nature consists only in thinking, and which, that it may exist, has need of no place, nor is dependent on any material thing; so that "I," that is to say, the mind by which I am what I am, is wholly distinct from the body, and is even more easily known than the latter, and is such, that although the latter were not, it would still continue to be all that it is.'

For Descartes, see *Q.* 351.

29. Is the universe one thing or many things?

Little is known of the ancient Greek philosopher **Melissus** (*fl.* 441 BCE). He was a native of the island of Samos. He was an admiral. He once succeeded in repelling Pericles's Athenian fleet, though he was ultimately defeated. He wrote a treatise entitled *On Nature, or On What Is,* which is lost.

Despite this paucity we are acquainted with aspects of his thinking. We know that he regarded assertions made about the gods as fruitless since knowledge of them is impossible. And thanks to verbatim fragments of his treatise preserved by the 6th century philosopher Simplicius, we also know that he was a monist. Whereas pluralists believe that there are many things, monists believe there is only one. Melissus argued that the universe is a single, homogenous, everlasting, spatially infinite and changeless thing.

'What was was ever, and ever shall be. For, if it had come into being, it needs must have been nothing before it came into being. Now, if it were nothing, in no wise could anything have arisen out of nothing.

Since, then, it has not come into being, and since it is, was ever, and ever shall be, it has no beginning or end, but is without limit. For, if it had come into being, it would have had a beginning (for it would have begun to come into being at some time or other) and an end (for it would have ceased to come into being at some time or other); but, if it neither began nor ended, and ever was and ever shall be, it has no beginning or end; for it is not possible for anything to be ever without all being.

Further, just as it ever is, so it must ever be infinite in magnitude.

Nothing which has a beginning or end is either eternal or infinite.

If it is infinite, it must be one; for if it were two, it could not be infinite; for then they would be bounded by one another.

So then it is eternal and infinite and one and all alike. And it cannot perish nor become greater, nor does it suffer pain or grief. For, if any of these things happened to it, it would no longer be one. For if it is altered, then the real must needs not be all alike, but what was before must pass away, and what was not must come into being. Now, if it changed by so much as a single hair in ten thousand years, it would all perish in the whole of time.

Further, it is not possible either that its order should be changed; for the order which it had before does not perish, nor does that which was not come into being. But, since nothing is either added to it or passes away or is altered, how can any real thing have had its order changed? For if anything became different, that would amount to a change in its order...

Nor is anything empty: For what is empty is nothing. What is nothing cannot be.

Nor does it move; for it has nowhere to betake itself to, but is full. For if there were aught empty, it would betake itself to the empty. But, since there is naught empty, it has nowhere to betake itself to.

And it cannot be dense and rare; for it is not possible for what is rare to be as full as what is dense, but what is rare is at once emptier than what is dense.

This is the way in which we must distinguish between what is full and what is not full. If a thing has room for anything else, and takes it in, it is not full; but if it has no room for anything and does not take it in, it is full.

Now, it must needs be full if there is naught empty, and if it is full, it does not move.

This argument, then, is the greatest proof that it is one alone; but the following are proofs of it also. If there were a many, these would have to be of the same kind as I say that the one is. For if there is earth and water, and air and iron, and gold and fire, and if one thing is living and another dead, and if things are black and white and all that men say they really are,—if that is so, and if we see and hear aright, each one of these must be such as we first decided, and they cannot be changed or altered, but each must be just as it is. But, as it is, we say that we see and hear and understand aright, and yet we believe that what is warm becomes cold, and what is cold warm; that what is hard turns soft, and what is soft hard; that what is living dies, and that things are born from what lives not; and that all those things are changed, and that what they were and what they are now are in no way alike. We think that iron, which is hard, is rubbed away by contact with the finger; and so with gold and stone and everything which we fancy to be strong, and that earth and stone are made out of water; so that it turns out that we neither see nor know realities. Now these things do not agree with one another. We said that there were many things that were eternal and had forms and strength of their own, and yet we fancy that they all suffer alteration, and that they change from what we see each time. It is clear, then, that we did not see aright after all, nor are we right in believing that all these things are many. They would not change if they were real, but each thing would be just what we believed it to be; for nothing is stronger than true reality. But if it has changed, what was has passed away, and what was not is come into being. So then, if there were many things, they would have to be just of the same nature as the one.'

32. *Are you an object?*

Immanuel Kant (1724-1804) had a ferocious love of lemons. This, at least, was implied by his characterisation of the depravity of sex: 'Sexual love makes of the loved person an Object of appetite; as soon as that appetite has been stilled, the person is cast aside as one casts away a lemon which has been sucked dry.'

Did libidinal frustration incite his ravenous desiccations? Perhaps, since he was also disparaging about masturbation, more so in fact. Whereas sex makes us subhuman, masturbation makes us sub-animal. 'It is the most abominable conduct of which a man can be guilty,' he wrote, admitting that he felt nauseous just thinking about it.

The immorality of sex resides in its objectifying nature. As outlined in the extract below from *Fundamental Principles of the Metaphysics of Morals,* humans are rational beings who should not be used as mere objects. Here he takes exception to suicide, but for Kant suicide and masturbation were morally comparable.

'Now I say: a human being and generally any rational being exists as an end in himself, not merely as a means to be arbitrarily used by this or that will, but in all his actions, whether they concern himself or other rational beings, must be always regarded at the same time as an end. All objects of the inclinations have only a conditional worth, for if the inclinations and the wants founded on them did not exist, then their object would be without value. But the inclinations, themselves being sources of want, are so far from having an absolute worth for which they should be desired that on the contrary it must be the universal wish of every rational being to be wholly free from them. Thus the worth of any object which is to be acquired by our action is always conditional. Beings whose existence depends not on our will but on nature's, have nevertheless, if they are irrational beings, only a relative value as means, and are therefore called things; rational beings, on the contrary, are called persons, because their very nature points them out as ends in themselves, that is as something which must not be used merely as means, and so far therefore restricts freedom of action (and is an object of respect). These, therefore, are not merely subjective ends whose existence has a worth for us as an effect of our action, but objective ends, that is, things whose existence is an end in itself; an end moreover for which no other can be substituted, which they should subserve merely as means, for otherwise nothing whatever would possess absolute worth; but if all worth were conditioned and therefore contingent, then there would be no supreme practical principle of reason whatever...

He who contemplates suicide should ask himself whether his action can be consistent with the idea of humanity as an end in itself. If he destroys himself in order to escape from painful circumstances, he uses a person merely as a mean to maintain a tolerable condition up to the end of life. But a man is not a thing, that is to say, something which can be used merely as means, but must in all his actions be always considered as an end in himself. I cannot, therefore, dispose in any way of a man in my own person so as to mutilate him, to damage or kill him.'

For Kant, see *Q.* 246.

39. Do you have an identity?

With the death of his 19-year-old wife in 1831, **Ralph Waldo Emerson's** (1803-1882) life was permanently changed. The loss was profound. He visited her tomb daily, once opening the coffin, and continued to write her letters and poems. And though he had been working as a Unitarian minister at Second Church in Boston, a year or so after her death he resigned, citing his disbelief in the value of communion. 'I dare attempt to lay out my own road,' he wrote in his journal shortly after, and within a few months he had sold his belongings and left for Europe.

Emerson returned to the US to become a peripatetic lecturer. Though he sometimes worked as a guest minister, he never reconciled with the church: 'The true Christianity, – a faith like Christ's in the infinitude of man, – is lost.'

From his essay 'Circles' –

'The life of man is a self-evolving circle, which, from a ring imperceptibly small, rushes on all sides outwards to new and larger circles, and that without end. The extent to which this generation of circles, wheel without wheel, will go, depends on the force or truth of the individual soul. For it is the inert effort of each thought, having formed itself into a circular wave of circumstance,—as for instance an empire, rules of an art, a local usage, a religious rite,—to heap itself on that ridge and to solidify and hem in the life. But if the soul is quick and strong it bursts over that boundary on all sides and expands another orbit on the great deep, which also runs up into a high wave, with attempt again to stop and to bind. But the heart refuses to be imprisoned; in its first and narrowest pulses, it already tends outward with a vast force and to immense and innumerable expansions...

In nature every moment is new; the past is always swallowed and forgotten; the coming only is sacred. Nothing is secure but life, transition, the energizing spirit. No love can be bound by oath or covenant to secure it against a higher love. No truth so sublime but it may be trivial to-morrow in the light of new thoughts. People wish to be settled: only as far as they are unsettled is there any hope for them.

Life is a series of surprises. We do not guess to-day the mood, the pleasure, the power of to-morrow, when we are building up our being. Of lower states,—of acts of routine and sense, we can tell somewhat, but the masterpieces of God, the total growths and universal movements of the soul, he hideth; they are incalculable. I can know that truth is divine and helpful; but how it shall help me I can have no guess, for so to be is the sole inlet of so to know. The new position of the advancing man has all the powers of the old, yet has them all new. It carries in its bosom all the energies of the past, yet is itself an exhalation of the morning. I cast away in this new moment all my once hoarded knowledge, as vacant and vain. Now for the first time seem I to know any thing rightly. The simplest words,—we do not know what they mean except when we love and aspire...

The one thing which we seek with insatiable desire is to forget ourselves, to be surprised out of our propriety, to lose our sempiternal memory, and to do something without knowing how or why; in short, to draw a new circle. Nothing great was ever achieved without enthusiasm. The way of life is wonderful: it is by abandonment. The great moments of history are the facilities of performance through the strength of ideas, as the works of genius and religion. "A man," said Oliver Cromwell, "never rises so high as when he knows not whither he is going." Dreams and drunkenness, the use of opium and alcohol are the semblance and counterfeit of this oracular genius, and hence their dangerous attraction for men. For the like reason, they ask the aid of wild passions, as in gaming and war, to ape in some manner these flames and generosities of the heart.'

For Emerson, see Q. 160.

42. *Are you a miracle?*

> Born in West Sussex and drowned at sea, **Percy Bysshe Shelley's** (1792-1822) short life was punctuated by expulsion, expatriation and elopement. He was a writer, chiefly a poet, who advocated atheism and egalitarianism. In T. S. Eliot's estimation 'the ideas of Shelley seem to me always to be the ideas of adolescence', but we shan't let that discourage us. This passage is from his essay 'On Life'.

'Life and the world, or whatever we call that which we are and feel, is an astonishing thing. The mist of familiarity obscures from us the wonder of our being. We are struck with admiration at some of its transient modifications, but it is itself the great miracle. What are changes of empires, the wreck of dynasties, with the opinions which support them; what is the birth and the extinction of religious and of political systems, to life? What are the revolutions of the globe which we inhabit, and the operations of the elements of which it is composed, compared with life? What is the universe of stars, and suns, of which this inhabited earth is one, and their motions, and their destiny, compared with life? Life, the great miracle, we admire not because it is so miraculous. It is well that we are thus shielded by the familiarity of what is at once so certain and so unfathomable, from an astonishment which would otherwise absorb and overawe the functions of that which is its object.

If any artist, I do not say had executed, but had merely conceived in his mind the system of the sun, and the stars, and planets, they not existing, and had painted to us in words, or upon canvas, the spectacle now afforded by the nightly cope of heaven, and illustrated it by the wisdom of astronomy, great would be our admiration. Or had he imagined the scenery of this earth, the mountains, the seas, and the rivers; the grass, and the flowers, and the variety of the forms and masses of the leaves of the woods, and the colours which attend the setting and the rising sun, and the hues of the atmosphere, turbid or serene, these things not before existing, truly we should have been astonished, and it would not have been a vain boast to have said of such a man, "Non merita nome di creatore, se non Iddio ed il Poeta" [no one merits the name of creator except God and the Poet]. But how these things are looked on with little wonder, and to be conscious of them with intense delight is esteemed to be the distinguishing mark of a refined and extraordinary person. The multitude of men care not for them. It is thus with Life – that which includes all.'

44. Are we dying all the time?

Friedrich Nietzsche (1844-1900) was a nomadic German whose ill-health excused him from two afflictions: the German climate and gainful employment. Living in voluntary exile he used his freedom to write polemical books that virtually no one read on the bloodthirsty anaemia of conventional morality. Valuing strength, power and vitality, he was sickened by those weak souls who exercise piety, judgment and condemnation in order to suppress the healthy forces of life. Among the weak souls are 'the preachers of death', whom Nietzsche described in *Thus Spoke Zarathustra*.

'There are those with consumption of the soul: hardly are they born when they begin to die and long for doctrines of weariness and renunciation.

They would like to be dead, and we should welcome their wish! Let us beware of waking the dead and disturbing these living coffins!

They meet an invalid, or a geriatric, or a corpse and immediately they say: "Life is refuted!"

But only they are refuted, and their eyes, which see only this one face of existence.

Enveloped in heavy melancholy and hungry for those little accidents that bring death, thus do they wait with clenched teeth...

And you, too, for whom life is frantic work and unrest – are you not very tired of life? Are you not very ripe for the sermon of death?

All of you to whom frantic work is dear, and whatever is fast, new, and strange – you find it hard to bear yourselves, your industry is escape and the will to forget yourselves.'

For Nietzsche, see *Qs*. 146 and 295.

45. Where does your history begin?

Robert Darwin betrayed a distinct lack of foresight when he told his teenage son, 'You care for nothing but shooting, dogs and rat-catching, and you will be a disgrace to yourself and all your family'.

Among his son **Charles Darwin's** (1809-1882) eventual accomplishments was *The Descent of Man*. This is its closing passage.

'The main conclusion arrived at in this work, namely, that man is descended from some lowly organised form, will, I regret to think, be highly distasteful to many. But there can hardly be a doubt that we are descended from barbarians. The astonishment which I felt on first seeing a party of Fuegians on a wild and broken shore will never be forgotten by me, for the reflection at once rushed into my mind—such were our ancestors. These men were absolutely naked and bedaubed with paint, their long hair was tangled, their mouths frothed with excitement, and their expression was wild, startled, and distrustful. They possessed hardly any arts, and like wild animals lived on what they could catch; they had no government, and were merciless to every one not of their own small tribe. He who has seen a savage in his native land will not feel much shame, if forced to acknowledge that the blood of some more humble creature flows in his veins. For my own part I would as soon be descended from that heroic little monkey, who braved his dreaded enemy in order to save the life of his keeper, or from that old baboon, who descending from the mountains, carried away in triumph his young comrade from a crowd of astonished dogs—as from a savage who delights to torture his enemies, offers up bloody sacrifices, practices infanticide without remorse, treats his wives like slaves, knows no decency, and is haunted by the grossest superstitions.

Man may be excused for feeling some pride at having risen, though not through his own exertions, to the very summit of the organic scale; and the fact of his having thus risen, instead of having been aboriginally placed there, may give him hope for a still higher destiny in the distant future. But we are not here concerned with hopes or fears, only with the truth as far as our reason permits us to discover it; and I have given the evidence to the best of my ability. We must, however, acknowledge, as it seems to me, that man with all his noble qualities, with sympathy which feels for the most debased, with benevolence which extends not only to other men but to the humblest living creature, with his god-like intellect which has penetrated into the movements and constitution of the solar system—with all these exalted powers—Man still bears in his bodily frame the indelible stamp of his lowly origin.'

For Darwin, see Q. 249.

47. Was birth your first experience of rejection?

Otto Rank (1884-1939) was an Austrian psychoanalyst who had long been a disciple of Sigmund Freud, but with the publication of his book *The Trauma of Birth* he found himself ostracised from the psychoanalytic community.

Freud believed that the child's erotic desire for the parent of the opposite sex and the concomitant rivalry with the parent of the same sex was the foundational crisis in our mental development. This he called the Oedipus complex. Rank, however, claimed that the foundational crisis occurs earlier, with birth itself, the 'primal separation'. According to Rank, life's anxieties have their genesis in the trauma of birth and the desperate longing to return to the womb.

'In attempting to reconstruct for the first time from analytic experiences the to all appearances purely physical birth trauma with its prodigious psychical consequences for the whole development of mankind, we are led to recognize in the birth trauma the ultimate biological basis of the psychical...

If we look at the psychical development of the child from this point of view, it may be said that the human being needs many years—namely, his whole childhood—in which to overcome this first intensive trauma in an approximately normal way. Every child has anxiety, and from the standpoint of the average healthy adult, one can, with a certain amount of justification, designate the childhood of individuals as their normal neurosis. Only this may continue into adult life in the case of certain individuals, the neurotics, who therefore remain infantile or are called infantile.

Instead of numerous examples with the same simple mechanism, let us investigate the typical case of infantile anxiety which occurs when the child is left alone *in a dark room* (usually the bedroom at bed-time). This situation reminds the child, who still is close to the experience of the primal trauma, of the womb situation—with the important difference that the child is now consciously separated from the mother, whose womb is only "symbolically" replaced by the dark room or warm bed. The anxiety disappears, according to Freud's brilliant observation, as soon as the child again becomes conscious of the existence (the nearness) of the loved person (contact, voice, etc.).

From this example we can understand the anxiety mechanism, which is repeated almost unaltered in cases of phobia (claustrophobia, fear of railways, tunnels, travelling, etc.), as the unconscious reproduction of the anxiety at birth…

[J]ust as the anxiety at birth forms the basis of every anxiety or fear, so *every pleasure has as its final aim the re-establishment of the intrauterine primal pleasure.* The child's normal functions, the assimilation of nourishment (sucking) and the expulsion of the product assimilated, both of which functions analysis recognizes as libidinal, betray the tendency to continue as long as possible the unlimited freedom of the pre-natal state…

More clearly still do the "childish faults," resulting from a too persistent clinging to these sources of pleasure, show the origin and tendency of this libido-gratification. I mean such "faults" as sucking on the one hand, and wetting and dirtying themselves on the other, when these go beyond a certain length of time or to a certain degree of intensity (for instance, in the exquisite "neurotic" symptom of enuresis nocturna). In the consciously uncontrollable and apparently automatic ejection of urine and discharge of faeces ("as proof of love" for the mother) the child behaves as if it were still in the womb...

Ferenczi has ingeniously shown [that] the man, penetrating into the vaginal opening, undoubtedly signifies a partial return to the womb, which by identification with the penis known as a symbol for a child becomes not only a complete but also an infantile return. But in the case of the woman, the attitude is quite similar, as analytic material has shown. By means of the clitoris libido, experienced so intensely in masturbation, the woman is able—often only too able—to identify herself with the penis or the man and so indirectly to approach the return into the womb. The tendency to apparent masculinity revealed in it rests on the unconscious identification with the father and finally aims at becoming, at least a participator in the inestimable advantage which the man has over the woman, and which consists in his being able partially to go back into the mother, by means of the penis, itself representing the child. For the woman there results a still more far-reaching and normal gratification of this primal wish manifesting itself as mother love in the identification with the fruit of the body...

Sexual love, then, which reaches its climax in the mating of two beings, proves to be the most sublime attempt partially to re-establish the primal situation between mother and child, which only finds its complete realisation in a new embryo.'

57. Every night I observe your dreams though in life you are a stranger to me. Do I know your desires?

In June 1900 **Sigmund Freud** (1856-1939) sent a letter to his friend Wilhelm Fliess from a holiday home near Vienna in which he mused: 'Do you suppose that some day a marble tablet will be placed on the house inscribed with these words:

In This House, on July 24th, 1895
the secret of Dreams was Revealed
to Dr Sigm. Freud'

July 24th, 1895 was the date that Freud had reached the conclusion that dreams are essentially wish-fulfilments, often of unconscious desires. Though such a plaque does now exist, it is perhaps unfair to Plato who had offered a similar insight almost 2500 years earlier in the *Republic*. Plato suggested that we are all born with 'violent and lawless' desires which emerge during the abeyance of the rational mind. When we sleep the 'bestial savage' mind awakens and commits, through dreams, shameless acts of incest, bestiality and murder.

The novelty of Freud's approach, however, as outlined in *The Interpretation of Dreams*, was to claim that our wishes, due to their troubling nature, are often buried beneath the surface of dreams, and so to exhume the wishes we must interpret the dream.

'[O]ur doctrine is not based upon the estimates of the obvious dream-content, but relates to the thought-content, which, in the course of interpretation, is found to lie behind the dream. Let us compare and contrast the *manifest* and the *latent dream-content*. It is true that there are dreams the manifest content of which is of the most painful nature. But has anyone ever tried to interpret these dreams—to discover their latent thought-content? If not, the objections to our doctrine are no longer valid; for there is always the possibility that even our painful and terrifying dreams may, upon interpretation, prove to be wish-fulfilments...

[A dream of a] gloomy character was offered me by a female patient in contradiction of my theory of the wish-dream. This patient, a young girl, began as follows: "You remember that my sister has now only one boy, Charles. She lost the elder one, Otto, while I was still living with her. Otto was my favourite; it was I who really brought him up. I like the other little fellow, too, but, of course, not nearly as much as his dead brother. Now I dreamt last night that I *saw Charles lying dead before me. He was lying in his little coffin, his hands folded; there were candles all about; and, in short, it was just as it was at the time of little Otto's death, which gave me such a shock*. Now tell me, what does this mean? You know me—am I really so bad as to wish that my sister should lose the only child she has left? Or does the dream mean that I wish that Charles had died rather than Otto, whom I liked so much better?"

I assured her that this latter interpretation was impossible. After some reflection, I was able to give her the interpretation of the dream, which she subsequently confirmed. I was able to do so because the whole previous history of the dreamer was known to me.

Having become an orphan at an early age, the girl had been brought up in the home of a much older sister, and had met, among the friends and visitors who frequented the house, a man who made a lasting impression upon her affections. It looked for a time as though these barely explicit relations would end in marriage, but this happy culmination was frustrated by the sister, whose motives were never completely explained. After the rupture the man whom my patient loved avoided the house; she herself attained her independence some time after the death of little Otto, to whom, meanwhile, her affections had turned. But she did not succeed in freeing herself from the dependence due to her affection for her sister's friend. Her pride bade her avoid him, but she found it impossible to transfer her love to the other suitors who successively presented themselves.

Whenever the man she loved, who was a member of the literary profession, announced a lecture anywhere, she was certain to be found among the audience; and she seized every other opportunity of seeing him unobserved. I remembered that on the previous day she had told me that the Professor was going to a certain concert, and that she too was going, in order to enjoy the sight of him. This was on the day before the dream; and the concert was to be given on the day on which she told me the dream. I could now easily see the correct interpretation, and I asked her whether she could think of any particular event which had occurred after Otto's death. She replied immediately: "Of course; the Professor returned then, after a long absence, and I saw him once more beside little Otto's coffin." It was just as I had expected. I interpreted the dream as follows: "If now the other boy were to die, the same thing would happen again. You would spend the day with your sister; the Professor would certainly come to offer his condolences, and you would see him once more under the same circumstances as before. The dream signifies nothing more than this wish of yours to see him again—a wish against which you are fighting inwardly. I know that you have the ticket for to-day's concert in your bag. Your dream is a dream of impatience; it has anticipated by several hours the meeting which is to take place to-day."

In order to disguise her wish she had obviously selected a situation in which wishes of the sort are commonly suppressed—a situation so sorrowful that love is not even thought of. And yet it is entirely possible that even in the actual situation beside the coffin of the elder, more dearly loved boy, she had not been able to suppress her tender affection for the visitor whom she had missed for so long...

The disagreeable sensation which such dreams arouse is of course precisely identical with the antipathy which would, and usually does, restrain us from treating or discussing such subjects—an antipathy which must be overcome by all of us if we find ourselves obliged to attack the problem of such dreams. But this disagreeable feeling which recurs in our dreams does not preclude the existence of a wish; everyone has wishes which he would not like to confess to others, which he does not care to admit even to himself. On the other hand, we feel justified in connecting the unpleasant character of all these dreams with the fact of dream-distortion, and in concluding that these dreams are distorted, and that their wish-fulfilment is disguised beyond recognition, precisely because there is a strong revulsion against—a will to repress—the subject-matter of the dream, or the wish created by it. Dream-distortion, then, proves in reality to be an act of the censorship. We shall have included everything which the analysis of disagreeable dreams has brought to light if we reword our formula thus: *The dream is the (disguised) fulfilment of a (suppressed, repressed) wish.*'

For Freud, see *Q*. 187.

60. When you eat a raspberry, are you eating its redness?

Pity **John Locke** (1632-1704). He had to wait over five decades before he found the time to concentrate on philosophy. Danger was his eventual blessing.

In 1683 the Rye House Plot to assassinate Charles II and his brother the Duke of York was uncovered. Not only were arrests made and executions ordained, but Oxford theatrically burnt a number of books (Thomas Hobbes's *Leviathan* included) which espoused 'damnable doctrines', such as the right to resist tyrants. The political climate was not favourable to Locke. He, the holder of a studentship at Christ Church, had been working on a manuscript which contained such doctrines. He was, moreover, given his connections, concerned about becoming implicated in the plot. To avoid the turbulence he stole away to Holland for five years.

Exile afforded Locke the freedom to work on philosophy and it was during this period that he wrote *An Essay Concerning Human Understanding*, a monumental work which he prefaced with these words: 'This, reader, is the entertainment of those who let loose their own thoughts, and follow them in writing;

which thou ought not to envy them, since they afford thee an opportunity of the like diversion, if thou wilt make use of thy own thoughts in reading.'

'Flame is denominated hot and light; snow, white and cold; and manna, white and sweet, from the ideas they produce in us, which qualities are commonly thought to be the same in those bodies that those ideas are in us, the one the perfect resemblance of the other, as they are in a mirror; and it would by most men be judged very extravagant, if one should say otherwise. And yet he that will consider that the same fire that at one distance produces in us the sensation of warmth, does at a nearer approach produce in us the far different sensation of pain, ought to bethink himself what reason he has to say, that this idea of warmth which was produced in him by the fire, is actually in the fire, and his idea of pain which the same fire produced in him the same way is not in the fire. Why is whiteness and coldness in snow and pain not, when it produces the one and the other idea in us, and can do neither but by the bulk, figure, number, and motion of its solid parts?

The particular bulk, number, figure, and motion of the parts of fire or snow are really in them, whether any one's senses perceive them or no; and therefore they may be called real qualities, because they really exist in those bodies. But light, heat, whiteness, or coldness, are no more really in them than sickness or pain is in manna. Take away the sensation of them; let not the eyes see light or colours, nor the ears hear sounds; let the palate not taste, nor the nose smell; and all colours, tastes, odours, and sounds, as they are such particular ideas, vanish and cease, and are reduced to their causes, i.e., bulk, figure, and motion of parts...

Let us consider the red and white colours in porphyry; hinder light but from striking on it, and its colours vanish; it no longer produces any such ideas in us. Upon the return of light, it produces these appearances on us again. Can anyone think any real alterations are made in the porphyry by the presence or absence of light, and that those ideas of whiteness and redness are really in porphyry in the light, when it is plain it has no colour in the dark? It has indeed such a configuration of particles, both night and day, as are apt, by the rays of light rebounding from some parts of that hard stone, to produce in us the idea of redness, and from others the idea of whiteness. But whiteness or redness are not in it at any time, but such a texture that hath the power to produce such a sensation in us.'

For Locke, see *Qs*. 71 and 368.

61. Can you do anything entirely original?

> 'Court mediocrity, avoid originality, and sacrifice to fashion,' wrote John Caspar Lavater in his book of aphorisms, only for **William Blake** (1757-1827) to add 'and go to hell' in the margins of his copy. Blake's habitual inability to read without writing was an illustration of his belief in the need to soar with one's own wings.
>
> Below are further marginalia from his copy of the artist Joshua Reynolds' lecture series *Discourses*.

'When a Man talks of Acquiring Invention & of learning how to produce Original Conception he must expect to be called a Fool by Men of Understanding; but such a Hired Knave cares not for the Few. His Eye is on the Many. or rather on the Money. The man who says that the genius is not born, but taught—is a knave.

How ridiculous it would be to see the Sheep Endeavouring to walk like the Dog. or the Ox striving to trot like the Horse just as Ridiculous it is to see One Man Striving to Imitate Another Man varies from Man more than Animal from Animal of Different Species

Reynolds Thinks that Man Learns all that he Knows I say on the Contrary that Man Brings All that he has or Can have Into the World with him. Man is Born Like a garden ready planted & sown This world is too poor to produce one Seed

I always thought that the Human Mind was the most Prolific of All Things & Inexhaustible

He who Can be bound down is No Genius Genius cannot be Bound it may be Rendered Indignant & Outrageous'

65. Are you at home in the world?

> **St Cyprian** (200-258), bishop of Carthage, despaired at the violence and greed he saw in the world around him. The prospect and contemplation of a world beyond this one offered him great solace, and in 258 he was granted the opportunity to join it. This was the year that the Roman emperor Valerian issued an edict mandating the execution of all bishops.
>
> Either as an act of pre-emptive forgiveness, a passive aggressive gesture of disgust, or possibly a tip, before he died Cyprian handed his executioner 25 gold pieces.
>
> The following extract is taken from his sermon *De mortalitate*.

'We must consider, dear friends, and constantly reflect that we have renounced the world and are meanwhile sojourning here as foreigners. Let us embrace the day which allocates us to our own home, which rescues us from the snares of this world and restores us to paradise and the kingdom of heaven. Which of us, when in a foreign country, would not hurry back to our native land? Which of us, hurrying to return to our friends, would not eagerly desire a favourable wind, that we might sooner embrace those dear to us? We reckon paradise as our native land. We have begun already to think of the patriarchs as our parents. Why do we not hurry and run to see our native land and greet our parents? There a crowd of dear ones are waiting for us: parents, brothers and sisters, and children. A great crowd are longing for us, still anxious for our safety while already secure in their own immortality. What a great joy it will be to see each other and embrace! What pleasure is found in the kingdom of heaven, without any fear of dying, and with an eternity of life! What total and everlasting happiness!'

For early Christian theologians, see *Qs*. 350 and 356.

70. Is life an accident or a gift?

In the depths of Hades, among the miserable dead, were the Danaids, the 49 sisters who in their terrestrial lives had beheaded their 49 husbands on the night of their collective wedding. The ensuing punishment was the torture of futility. They were condemned to spend eternity trying to fill a leaky vessel with water.

The German philosopher **Arthur Schopenhauer** (1788-1860) regarded their hell as a portrait of our lives: a vain longing for satisfaction, a humourless farce, the sorry endeavour to be filled up. Relief, when it comes, is only a fleeting interlude amid the endless throes of deprivation and boredom.

From his essay 'On the Vanity of Existence' –

'The vanity of existence finds expression in the whole way in which things exist: in the infinite nature of time and space, as opposed to the finite nature of the individual in both; in the fleeting present as the only mode of actual existence; in the contingency and relativity of all things; in continual becoming without ever being; in constant wishing and never being satisfied; in the long battle which forms the history of life, where every effort is checked by difficulties, and stopped until they are overcome. Time is that in which all things pass away; it is merely the form under which the will to live – the thing-in-itself and therefore imperishable – has revealed to it that its efforts are in vain; it is that agent by which at every moment all things in our hands become as nothing, and lose any real value they possess...

Human life must be some kind of mistake. The truth of this will be sufficiently obvious if we only remember that man is a compound of needs and necessities hard to satisfy; and that even when they are satisfied all he obtains is a state of painlessness, where nothing remains to him but abandonment to boredom. This is direct proof that existence has no real value in itself; for what is boredom but the feeling of the emptiness of life? If life – the craving for which is the very essence of our being – were possessed of any positive intrinsic value, there would be no such thing as boredom at all: mere existence would satisfy us in itself, and we should want for nothing. But as it is, we take no delight in existence except when we are struggling for something; and then distance and difficulties to be overcome make our goal look as though it would satisfy us – an illusion which vanishes when we reach it; or else when we are occupied with some purely intellectual interest – where in reality we have stepped forth from life to look upon it from the outside, much after the manner of spectators at a play. And even sensual pleasure itself means nothing but a struggle and aspiration, ceasing the moment its aim is attained. Whenever we are not occupied in one of these ways, but cast upon existence itself, its vain and worthless nature is brought home to us; and this is what we mean by boredom. The hankering after what is strange and uncommon – an innate and ineradicable tendency of human nature – shows how glad we are at any interruption of that natural course of affairs which is so very tedious.'

For Schopenhauer, see Q. 130.

71. Are we born with the knowledge of death?

In *An Essay Concerning Human Understanding* **John Locke** (1632-1704) argued that we do not arrive in the world equipped with an innate understanding of it. Innate knowledge requires innate ideas, but all ideas derive from experience. Prior to experience our minds are akin to blank sheets of paper or empty cabinets.

Locke did not explicitly address the idea of death. By suggesting, however, that there are prenatal experiences, that newborns do perhaps have 'some faint ideas of hunger, and thirst, and warmth, and some pains, which they may have felt in the womb', he left enough fuel for speculation.

Is hunger a minor annihilation? Is thirst? Are these precursors of our final annihilation? Could the experience of these privations, these manifestations of dependence and thus mortality, furnish the mind with the idea of death? Is the idea of death anything other than the awareness of dependent existence?

'If we will attentively consider new-born children, we shall have little reason to think that they bring many ideas into the world with them. For, bating perhaps some faint ideas of hunger, and thirst, and warmth, and some pains, which they may have felt in the womb, there is not the least appearance of any settled ideas at all in them; especially of *ideas answering the terms which make up those universal propositions that are esteemed innate principles.* One may perceive how, by degrees, afterwards, ideas come into their minds; and that they get no more, nor other, than what experience, and the observation of things that come in their way, furnish them with; which might be enough to satisfy us that they are not original characters stamped on the mind…

Let us then suppose the mind to be, as we say, white paper, void of all characters, without any ideas:—How comes it to be furnished? Whence comes it by that vast store which the busy and boundless fancy of man has painted on it with an almost endless variety? Whence has it all the *materials* of reason and knowledge? To this I answer, in one word, from EXPERIENCE. In that all our knowledge is founded; and from that it ultimately derives itself. Our observation employed either, about external sensible objects, or about the internal operations of our minds perceived and reflected on by ourselves, is that which supplies our understandings with all the *materials* of thinking. These two are the fountains of knowledge, from whence all the ideas we have, or can naturally have, do spring…

He that attentively considers the state of a child, at his first coming into the world, will have little reason to think him stored with plenty of ideas, that are to be the matter of his future knowledge. It is *by degrees* he comes to be furnished with them. And though the ideas of obvious and familiar qualities imprint themselves before the memory begins to keep a register of time or order, yet it is often so late before some unusual qualities come in the way, that there are few men that cannot recollect the beginning of their acquaintance with them. And if it were worth while, no doubt a child might be so ordered as to have but a very few, even of the ordinary ideas, till he were grown up to a man. But all that are born into the world, being surrounded with bodies that perpetually and diversely affect them, variety of ideas, whether care be taken of it or not, are imprinted on the minds of children. Light and colours are busy at hand everywhere, when the eye is but open; sounds and some tangible qualities fail not to solicit their proper senses, and force an entrance to the mind;—but yet, I think, it will be granted easily, that if a child were kept in a place where he never saw any other but black and white till he were a man, he would have no more ideas of scarlet or green, than he that from his childhood never tasted an oyster, or a pine-apple, has of those particular relishes.'

For Locke, see *Qs*. 60 and 368.

76. Can you imagine your own nonexistence?

There are at least two ways by which we might try to imagine our nonexistence: as the nothingness of non-being or as the world without us. The Irish philosopher **George Berkeley** (1685-1753) thought that the latter approach was impossible: to watch the world in my absence presupposes my presence. Berkeley used this impossibility to argue for the mind-dependence of everything. If we cannot imagine the world without us, then the world cannot exist without us (or, at the very least, its mind-independence is unintelligible).

Berkeley's view that the world is mind-dependent is known as idealism. Idealists believe that the world does not exist independently of our perceptions of it. When the moon is not being perceived, it ceases to be. Sound queer? Not according to Berkeley. He thought there was nothing strange in this theory: 'Some truths are so near and obvious to the mind that a man need only open his eyes to see them. Such I take this important one to be: all the choir of heaven and furniture of the earth, in a word all those bodies which compose the mighty frame of the world, have not any subsistence without a mind, that their being is to be perceived or known...'

From *Treatise Concerning the Principles of Human Knowledge*–

'I am content to put the whole upon this issue – if you can but conceive it possible for one extended moveable substance, or, in general, for any one idea, or anything like an idea, to exist otherwise than in a mind perceiving it, I shall readily give up the cause. And, as for all that *compages* of external bodies you contend for, I shall grant you its existence, though you cannot either give me any reason why you believe it exists, or assign any use to it when it is supposed to exist. I say, the bare possibility of your opinion's being true shall pass for an argument that it is so.

But, say you, surely there is nothing easier than for me to imagine trees, for instance, in a park, or books existing in a closet, and nobody by to perceive them. I answer, you may so, there is no difficulty in it; but what is all this, I beseech you, more than framing in your mind certain ideas which you call *books* and *trees*, and at the same time omitting to frame the idea of any one that may perceive them? But do not you yourself perceive or think of them all the while? This therefore is nothing to the purpose: it only shews you have the power of imagining or forming ideas in your mind; but it does not shew that you can conceive it possible the objects of your thought may exist without the mind. To make out this, it is necessary that you conceive them existing unconceived or unthought of, which is a manifest repugnancy. When we do our utmost to conceive the existence of external bodies, we are all the while only contemplating our own ideas. But the mind, taking no notice of itself, is deluded to think it can and does conceive bodies existing unthought of or without the mind, though at the same time they are apprehended by or exist in itself. A little attention will discover to any one the truth and evidence of what is here said, and make it unnecessary to insist on any other proofs against the existence of [mind independent] *material substance*.'

80. Can reality cease to exist?

If we regard the absence of being as an absence of reality, then **St Augustine** (354-430) would not only claim that reality can cease to exist, but that its vacancies are all around us.

For nearly a decade Augustine was an adherent of Manichaeism, a religious movement founded by the prophet Mani from Mesopotamia in the 3rd century CE, which held that good and evil are two cosmic forces in perpetual conflict with each other. But once he had abandoned Manichaeism for the view that all things were created by God, a perfect and purely good being, the existence of evil became harder to fathom.

Augustine's solution was to deny the existence of evil. Evil is not a presence in the world but a deficiency, a lack, the absence of being. Since we were not created out of the substance of God but *ex nihilo*, from nothing, we are liable to regress to that non-state of emptiness, the emptiness we call evil. To try to discover the cause of evil 'is as if one sought to see darkness, or hear silence'.

The following extract is from 'On the Morals of the Manichaeans'.

'You Manichaeans often, if not in every case, ask those whom you try to bring over to your heresy, Whence is evil? Suppose I had now met you for the first time, I would ask you, if you please, to follow my example in putting aside for a little the explanation you suppose yourselves to have got of these subjects, and to commence this great inquiry with me as if for the first time. You ask me, Whence is evil? I ask you in return, What is evil? Which is the more reasonable question? Are those right who ask whence a thing is, when they do not know what it is; or he who thinks it necessary to inquire first what it is, in order to avoid the gross absurdity of searching for the origin of a thing unknown? Your answer is quite correct, when you say that evil is that which is contrary to nature; for no one is so mentally blind as not to see that, in every kind, evil is that which is contrary to the nature of the kind. But the establishment of this doctrine is the overthrow of your heresy. For evil is no nature, if it is contrary to nature. Now, according to you, evil is a certain nature and substance. Moreover, whatever is contrary to nature must oppose nature and seek its destruction. For nature means nothing else than that which anything is conceived of as being in its own kind. Hence is the new word which we now use derived from the word for being, — essence namely, or, as we usually say, substance, — while before these words were in use, the word nature was used instead. Here, then, if you will consider the matter without stubbornness, we see that evil is that which falls away from essence and tends to non-existence.

Accordingly, when the Catholic Church declares that God is the author of all natures and substances, those who understand this understand at the same time that God is not the author of evil. For how can He who is the cause of the being of all things be at the same time the cause of their not being, — that is, of their falling off from essence and tending to non-existence? For this is what reason plainly declares to be the definition of evil. Now, how can that race of evil of yours, which you make the supreme evil, be against nature, that is, against substance, when it, according to you, is itself a nature and substance? For if it acts against itself, it destroys its own existence; and when that is completely done, it will come at last to be the supreme evil. But this cannot be done, because you will have it not only to be, but to be everlasting. That cannot then be the chief evil which is spoken of as a substance.'

For Augustine, see *Qs*. 18 and 191.

85. Does nothingness exist?

A topic of contention among ancient Greek philosophers was whether emptiness, the void, exists. Melissus (see *Q*. 29) argued against its possibility, writing, 'Nor is anything empty: For what is empty is nothing. What is nothing cannot be'. From the impossibility of the void he deduced the impossibility of motion. The atomists, however, inverted this reasoning: the existence of motion (as well as contraction, enlargement and containment) necessitates the existence of the void.

The atomists held that the world is comprised of being and non-being: every entity, every event, is a momentary flourish in the eternal dance of atoms in the void. Such was the view of the 5th century BCE philosophers **Leucippus** and **Democritus**, whose works do not survive, but whose ideas can be pieced together from other writers; in the following case, Aristotle in *Physics* and *Metaphysics*.

'Leucippus and his associate Democritus hold that the elements are the full and the void, affirming that the former is what-is and the latter what-is-not. The full and solid is what-is; the void and attenuated is what-is-not. Hence they say that what-is has no more existence than what-is-not, because void exists just as much as solidity...

Their arguments are, first, that there could not be such a thing as local movement at all (whether of transference or of growth) without [a] void for it to move into, since the full could not allow anything to move into it. Because, if the full could receive anything into itself so that two bodies coincided, then any number of bodies might coincide; for no reason can be given why not three and so forth, if two. And, if that were so, the smallest body could receive the greatest into itself; for many smalls make a great, so that if many equals can coincide, so can many unequals...

Such then is one of the alleged proofs of the existence of the void. Another is that certain substances seem to contract and to thicken. This is exemplified in the alleged fact that casks can receive their full complement of wine and the wine-skins as well, which is attributed to the bodily substances drawing up into the vacant interspaces and so becoming denser.

And further it is generally supposed that growth is made possible only by the void, food being a bodily substance and its coincidence with the fed being therefore impossible. In support of this, what is said about ashes — that they will absorb as much water as the vessel they are in would hold if it were empty — is appealed to.'

88. Do you know what it is like to be the ocean?

The psychoanalyst Sándor Ferenczi believed that we are possessed of an unconscious longing to return to the sea, the site of our primeval origin. He called this the 'thalassal regressive trend'. Like Rank (see *Q.* 47) he saw sex as the erotic wish to return to the womb, but he went further in claiming that the womb, our aquatic nest, is only a symbol and substitute for the sea.

Herman Melville (1819-1891) spent several years working as a seaman and though he sometimes characterised the sea's uniform mass as a sublime alterity, in *Moby-Dick* he also described moments of mystical union with the water. But this was no 'thalassal regression'. The sea does not take us to the beginning of things. Rather, it takes us to the realisation that there are no beginnings.

'Let me make a breast of it here, and frankly admit that I kept but sorry guard. With the problem of the universe revolving in me, how could I—being left completely to myself at such a thought-engendering altitude,—how could I but lightly hold my obligations to observe all whale-ships' standing orders, "Keep your weather eye open, and sing out every time."

And let me in this place movingly admonish you, ye ship-owners of Nantucket! Beware of enlisting in your vigilant fisheries any lad with lean brow and hollow eye; given to unseasonable meditativeness; and who offers to ship with the Phædon instead of Bowditch in his head. Beware of such an one, I say; your whales must be seen before they can be killed; and this sunken-eyed young Platonist will tow you ten wakes round the world, and never make you one pint of sperm the richer. Nor are these monitions at all unneeded. For nowadays, the whale-fishery furnishes an asylum for many romantic, melancholy, and absent-minded young men, disgusted with the carking cares of earth, and seeking sentiment in tar and blubber. Childe Harold not unfrequently perches himself upon the mast-head of some luckless disappointed whale-ship, and in moody phrase ejaculates:—

"Roll on, thou deep and dark blue ocean, roll!
Ten thousand blubber-hunters sweep over thee in vain."

Very often do the captains of such ships take those absent-minded young philosophers to task, upbraiding them with not feeling sufficient 'interest' in the voyage; half-hinting that they are so hopelessly lost to all honourable ambition, as that in their secret souls they would rather not see whales than otherwise. But all in vain; those young Platonists have a notion that their vision is imperfect; they are short-sighted; what use, then, to strain the visual nerve? They have left their opera-glasses at home.

"Why, thou monkey," said a harpooneer to one of these lads, "we've been cruising now hard upon three years, and thou hast not raised a whale yet. Whales are scarce as hen's teeth whenever thou art up here." Perhaps they were; or perhaps there might have been shoals of them in the far horizon; but lulled into such an opium-like listlessness of vacant, unconscious reverie is this absent-minded youth by the blending cadence of waves with thoughts, that at last he loses his identity; takes the mystic ocean at his feet for the visible image of that deep, blue, bottomless soul, pervading mankind and nature; and every strange, half-seen, gliding, beautiful thing that eludes him; every dimly-discovered, uprising fin of some undiscernible form, seems to him the embodiment of those elusive thoughts that only people the soul by continually flitting through it. In this enchanted mood, thy spirit ebbs away to whence it came; becomes diffused through time and space; like Cranmer's sprinkled Pantheistic ashes, forming at last a part of every shore the round globe over.

There is no life in thee, now, except that rocking life imparted by a gently rolling ship; by her, borrowed from the sea; by the sea, from the inscrutable tides of God. But while this sleep, this dream is on ye, move your foot or hand an inch; slip your hold at all; and your identity comes back in horror. Over Descartian vortices you hover. And perhaps, at mid-day, in the fairest weather, with one half-throttled shriek you drop through that transparent air into the summer sea, no more to rise for ever. Heed it well, ye Pantheists!'

For Melville, see *Q*. 311.

89. Do you know what it is like to be God?

The German philosopher **Ludwig Feuerbach** (1804-1872) argued that God was the projection of our own human nature on to the idea of a non-human being. His qualities mirror our own collective human qualities. His wisdom is our wisdom, his benevolence our benevolence. And our belief that God possesses these qualities to an infinite degree reflects our sense of our own infinite potential as a species; the gap we recognise between the greatness of God and the insignificance of ourselves correlates to the gap between the greatness of the human species and the insignificance of the individual. God's transcendence and immortality is actually the immortality and transcendence of the human spirit. By failing to realise these connections, by failing to see that we made Him in our own image, we thereby fail to know ourselves.

The following excerpt is from George Eliot's translation of *The Essence of Christianity*.

'God is the highest being; therefore, to feel God is the highest feeling. But is not the highest feeling also the highest feeling of self? So long as I have not had the feeling of the highest, so long I have not exhausted my capacity of feeling, so long I do not yet fully know the nature of feeling. What, then, is an object to me in my feeling of the highest being? Nothing else than the highest nature of my power of feeling. So much as a man can feel, so much is (his) God. But the highest degree of the power of feeling is also the highest degree of the feeling of self. In the feeling of the low I feel myself lowered, in the feeling of the high I feel myself exalted. The feeling of self and feeling are inseparable, otherwise feeling would not belong to myself. Thus God, as an object of feeling, or what is the same thing, the feeling of God, is nothing else than man's highest feeling of self. But God is the freest, or rather the absolutely only free being; thus God is man's highest feeling of freedom. How couldst thou be conscious of the highest being as freedom, or freedom as the highest being, if thou didst not feel thyself free? But when dost thou feel thyself free? When thou feelest God. To feel God is to feel oneself free. For example, thou feelest desire, passion, the conditions of time and place, as limits. What thou feelest as a limit thou strugglest against, thou breakest loose from, thou deniest. The consciousness of a limit, as such, is already an anathema, a sentence of condemnation pronounced on this limit, for it is an oppressive, disagreeable, negative consciousness. Only the feeling of the good, of the positive, is itself good and positive – is joy. Joy alone is feeling in its element, its paradise, because it is unrestricted activity. The sense of pain in an organ is nothing else than the sense of a disturbed, obstructed, thwarted activity; in a word, the sense of something abnormal, anomalous. Hence thou strivest to escape from the sense of limitation into unlimited feeling. By means of the will, or the imagination, thou negativest limits, and thus obtainest the feeling of freedom. This feeling of freedom is God. God is exalted above desire and passion, above the limits of space and time. But this exaltation is thy own exaltation above that which appears to thee as a limit. Does not this exaltation of the divine being exalt thee? How could it do so, if it were external to thee? No; God is an exalted being only for him who himself has exalted thoughts and feelings. Hence the exaltation of the divine being varies according to that which different men or nations perceive as a limitation to the feeling of self, and which they consequently negative or eliminate from their ideal.'

90. Is everything you do motivated by desire?

Immanuel Kant believed that for an act to be truly good it must be motivated by duty alone; feeling and emotion should hold no sway. Yet if this were so, it would follow from the ideas of **David Hume** (1711-1776) that there are no good acts. This is because Hume believed that an act could not be purely rational. No act is ever impelled by the forces of reason; the passions are what drive us. Indeed, so impotent is reason that it cannot even enter into conflict with feeling. A tug of war between the two would be a contest no more engaging than a race between lions and sloths.

Tangentially, it is interesting to note that Hume further argued that since only judgments and opinions can be assessed by reason, and since the passions express no judgments or opinions – they are mere feelings which say nothing about the world – it follows that they cannot in themselves be unreasonable: 'It is not contrary to reason to prefer the destruction of the whole world to the scratching of my finger.'

From *A Treatise of Human Nature* –

'Nothing is more usual in philosophy, and even in common life, than to talk of the combat of passion and reason, to give the preference to reason, and assert that men are only so far virtuous as they conform themselves to its dictates. Every rational creature, it is said, is obliged to regulate his actions by reason; and if any other motive or principle challenge the direction of his conduct, he ought to oppose it, till it be entirely subdued, or at least brought to a conformity with that superior principle. On this method of thinking the greatest part of moral philosophy, antient and modern, seems to be founded; nor is there an ampler field, as well for metaphysical arguments, as popular declamations, than this supposed pre-eminence of reason above passion. The eternity, invariableness, and divine origin of the former have been displayed to the best advantage: The blindness, unconstancy, and deceitfulness of the latter have been as strongly insisted on. In order to shew the fallacy of all this philosophy, I shall endeavour to prove first, that reason alone can never be a motive to any action of the will; and secondly, that it can never oppose passion in the direction of the will.

The understanding exerts itself after two different ways, as it judges from demonstration or probability; as it regards the abstract relations of our ideas, or those relations of objects, of which experience only gives us information. I believe it scarce will be asserted, that the first species of reasoning alone is ever the cause of any action. As its proper province is the world of ideas, and as the will always places us in that of realities, demonstration and volition seem, upon that account, to be totally removed, from each other. Mathematics, indeed, are useful in all mechanical operations, and arithmetic in almost every art and profession: But it is not of themselves they have any influence: Mechanics are the art of regulating the motions of bodies to some designed end or purpose; and the reason why we employ arithmetic in fixing the proportions of numbers, is only that we may discover the proportions of their influence and operation.

A merchant is desirous of knowing the sum total of his accounts with any person: Why? but that he may learn what sum will have the same effects in paying his debt, and going to market, as all the particular articles taken together. Abstract or demonstrative reasoning, therefore, never influences any of our actions, but only as it directs our judgment concerning causes and effects; which leads us to the second operation of the understanding.

It is obvious, that when we have the prospect of pain or pleasure from any object, we feel a consequent emotion of aversion or propensity, and are carryed to avoid or embrace what will give us this uneasines or satisfaction. It is also obvious, that this emotion rests not here, but making us cast our view on every side, comprehends whatever objects are connected with its original one by the relation of cause and effect. Here then reasoning takes place to discover this relation; and according as our reasoning varies, our actions receive a subsequent variation. But it is evident in this case that the impulse arises not from reason, but is only directed by it. It is from the prospect of pain or pleasure that the aversion or propensity arises towards any object: And these emotions extend themselves to the causes and effects of that object, as they are pointed out to us by reason and experience. It can never in the least concern us to know, that such objects are causes, and such others effects, if both the causes and effects be indifferent to us. Where the objects themselves do not affect us, their connexion can never give them any influence; and it is plain, that as reason is nothing but the discovery of this connexion, it cannot be by its means that the objects are able to affect us.

Since reason alone can never produce any action, or give rise to volition, I infer, that the same faculty is as incapable of preventing volition, or of disputing the preference with any passion or emotion. This consequence is necessary. It is impossible reason could have the latter effect of preventing volition, but by giving an impulse in a contrary direction to our passion; and that impulse, had it operated alone, would have been able to produce volition. Nothing can oppose or retard the impulse of passion, but a contrary impulse; and if this contrary impulse ever arises from reason, that latter faculty must have an original influence on the will, and must be able to cause, as well as hinder any act of volition. But if reason has no original influence, it is impossible it can withstand any principle, which has such an efficacy, or ever keep the mind in suspence a moment. Thus it appears, that the principle, which opposes our passion, cannot be the same with reason, and is only called so in an improper sense. We speak not strictly and philosophically when we talk of the combat of passion and of reason. Reason is, and ought only to be the slave of the passions, and can never pretend to any other office than to serve and obey them.'

For Hume see *Q*. 1.

91. Can desire ever be excessive?

It is unlikely that the Roman writer **Lucretius** (*fl.* 1st c BCE) was driven mad by a love potion and committed suicide. Yet this is the only account we have of his life. No matter, for his masterpiece *De rerum natura* – 'On the Nature of Things' – survives; a philosophical text unusually composed in verse so that the 'dulcet strains of poesy' might render its ideas more palatable.

What does lend the fanciful tale an odour of truth, however, is the fact that Lucretius regarded love as a kind of madness. Though the sexual appetites of lovers can undergo periods of quiescence, there is no final satisfaction. They each expend their energies feverishly trying to disappear into the other's body, but this is an impossibility, the desire is insatiable, and so, perhaps, excessive, for it precludes ataraxy, a state Lucretius regarded as the greatest good.

The following passage is from John Dryden's 1685 translation.

'When love its utmost vigour does employ,
Even then 'tis but a restless wandering joy:
Nor knows the lover in that wild excess,
With hands or eyes, what first he would possess:
But strains at all, and, fastening where he strains,
Too closely presses with his frantic pains;
With biting kisses hurts the twining fair,
Which shows his joys imperfect, insincere:
For, stung with inward rage, he flings around,
And strives to avenge the smart on that which gave the wound.
But love those eager bitings does restrain,
And mingling pleasure mollifies the pain.
For ardent hope still flatters anxious grief,
And sends him to his foe to seek relief:
Which yet the nature of the thing denies;
For love, and love alone of all our joys,
By full possession does but fan the fire;
The more we still enjoy, the more we still desire.
Nature for meat and drink provides a space,
And, when received, they fill their certain place:
Hence thirst and hunger may be satisfied;
But this repletion is to love denied:
Form, feature, colour, whatsoe'er delight
Provokes the lover's endless appetite,
These fill no space, nor can we thence remove
With lips, or hands, or all our instruments of love:
In our deluded grasp we nothing find,
But thin aerial shapes, that fleet before the mind.
As he, who in a dream with drought is cursed,
And finds no real drink to quench his thirst;

Runs to imagined lakes his heat to steep,
And vainly swills and labours in his sleep;
So love with phantoms cheats our longing eyes,
Which hourly seeing never satisfies:
Our hands pull nothing from the parts they strain,
But wander o'er the lovely limbs in vain:
Nor when the youthful pair more closely join,
When hands in hands they lock, and thighs in thighs they
twine,
Just in the raging foam of full desire,
When both press on, both murmur, both expire,
They grip, they squeeze, their humid tongues they dart,
As each would force their way to t'other's heart:
In vain; they only cruise about the coast;
For bodies cannot pierce, nor be in bodies lost;
As sure they strive to be, when both engage
In that tumultuous momentary rage;
So tangled in the nets of love they lie,
Till man dissolves in that excess of joy.
Then, when the gathered bag has burst its way,
And ebbing tides the slackened nerves betray,
A pause ensues; and nature nods awhile,
Till with recruited rage new spirits boil;
And then the same vain violence returns;
With flames renewed the erected furnace burns.
Again they in each other would be lost,
But still by adamantine bars are crossed.
All ways they try, successless all they prove,
To cure the secret sore of lingering love.'

For Lucretius, see *Q*. 243.

93. Are there unnatural desires?

The **Marquis de Sade** (1740-1814) – progenitor of the term 'sadism' – was a French aristocrat whose unconventional and abusive appetites resulted in lengthy periods of incarceration. The cycle started in 1763 when he was arrested for, in his father's words, 'horrifying impiety'. Having masturbated over a crucifix in the presence of a sex worker, he then forced her to trample on the holy symbol before trying to give her an enema to make her defecate on it. In 1768, he was arrested again, this time for luring a beggar back to his house, binding her in rope and whipping her till he climaxed. In 1772, having fled to Italy, he was found guilty *in absentia* and executed in effigy for sodomy and poisoning several sex workers with the putative aphrodisiac cantharidin. The revolving door of freedom and detention continued turning till his death in Charenton asylum.

Amid France's revolutionary fervour, de Sade used his 1795 book *Philosophy in the Boudoir* to make a series of utopian proposals for a libertine society. This society would abide by an axiomatic embrace of nature, of our natural proclivities, of the appetites we actually have rather than those we believe we ought to have. De Sade implies that the idea of an unnatural desire is effectively a contradiction: the only unnatural desire is the desire to thwart desire.

'Now that we have returned from the horde of religious errors that held us captive, and now that the number of prejudices we have annihilated has brought us closer to nature, we listen only to its voice, well assured that the only crime is to resist the inclinations it inspires in us, rather than embrace them. Believing that lust is a result of such inclinations, these passions should not be legislated against or extinguished, but rather granted the freedom to be satisfied in peace…

Our laws must be favourable to the lascivious nature of women. It is absurd to identify their honour and virtue with the unnatural force they exert resisting those inclinations which nature has bestowed upon them in far greater abundance than in men. This injustice of our morals is all the more striking when men endeavour to weaken them through seduction, yet at the same time punish them when they yield to their advances. It seems to me that all the nonsense of our morals is ingrained in this unjust outrage, and that this short discussion should make us feel the desperate need to purify our morals.

I say, therefore, that women, who have been given lustful tendencies far wilder than men, should be permitted to indulge them, entirely free from the bonds of virginity, from the false judgments of modesty, and be absolutely restored to the state of nature. I want the law to permit them as many men as they wish. I want them to be granted the delights of all the sexes, and of all parts of their bodies…

There will therefore be houses intended for the libertinage of women, which, like men's, will be under government protection; here women will be supplied with as many people of either sex as they desire, and the more they visit these houses the higher they will be esteemed. There is nothing so barbarous and so ridiculous as to have attached the honour and virtue of women to their resistance to the desires which nature has given them, and which continually inflame those hypocritical enough to censure them. From the most tender age, a girl, freed from her paternal bonds, no longer having to preserve her chastity for marriage (completely abolished by the noble laws I seek), and beyond the judgments that once shackled her sex, will in these houses be able to indulge in everything nature prescribes her. She will be received with respect, satisfied in abundance, and when out in society, she will be able to speak as publically of the pleasures she has tasted as today she speaks of balls or walks. Charming sex, you will be free. You will enjoy, like men, all the pleasures that nature prescribes, none will be denied to you. Must the more divine half of humanity be fettered by the other?

Ah, break free, nature wants it! Be reined by nothing but your own tastes, have no laws beyond your own desires, follow no morality besides that of your own nature. Languish no longer under those savage judgments which wither your charms and incarcerate the divine impulses of your hearts...

Is incest more dangerous? No, certainly not. It loosens family bonds and thereby invigorates the love of citizens for their country. We feel within us how it is dictated by the primary laws of nature. And our delight in objects that belong to us always seems more delicious. Primal institutions were favourable to incest; it is found in the origins of society; it is consecrated in all religions, every law favoured it. If we travel the world, we find incest established everywhere. The blacks of the Ivory Coast and Gabon prostitute their wives to their own children; the eldest son in Judah must marry his father's wife; Chileans sleep with both their sisters and their daughters, and often marry mother and daughter at the same time. I boldly maintain, in a word, that incest ought to be the law of every government whose basis is fraternity. How could reasonable men be so foolish as to believe that delighting in one's mother, sister or daughter is criminal? Is it not, I ask you, abominable to judge a man a criminal for delighting in those objects which he is drawn towards by natural affection? It is the same as claiming that we are forbidden to love too greatly those individuals nature enjoins us to love the best, and that the more it gives us a taste for some object, the more it orders us to distance ourselves from it. These contradictions are absurd. Only people stupefied by superstition could believe or embrace them...

Is it possible to imagine that nature gave us the possibility of a crime which would outrage her? Is it possible for her to consent to the destruction by man of her pleasures, such that we thereby become stronger than she? It is astonishing, the depths of stupidity we throw ourselves into when we reason without the use of reason's light! Let us hold to our assuredness that it is as easy to enjoy a woman in one way as in another, that it is absolutely irrelevant whether you enjoy a girl or a boy, and, as soon as it is understood that we can possess no inclinations except those given to us by nature, that she is too wise and too rational to have placed in us anything which could ever offend her.'

97. Are you incomplete?

> Ancient Greek symposia were roisterous, dissolute and multifarious in their delights. These drinking parties consisted of garlanded, perfumed men reclining on couches, playing games, singing, reciting poetry, or being entertained by musicians, dancers, acrobats or courtesans.
>
> One night in the 5th century BCE, however, things took a different turn. As **Plato** (*c.* 429-347 BCE) recounts in *The Symposium*, the attendees, still hung-over from the night before, decided to drink temperately. They dismissed the flute-girl and substituted their typical debauchery for discourses on the nature of love. The following extract is the playwright Aristophanes' contribution.

'In the first place, let me treat of the nature of man and what has happened to it; for the original human nature was not like the present, but different. The sexes were not two as they are now, but originally three in number; there was man, woman, and the union of the two, having a name corresponding to this double nature, which had once a real existence, but is now lost, and the word "Androgynous" is only preserved as a term of reproach. In the second place, the primeval man was round, his back and sides forming a circle; and he had four hands and four feet, one head with two faces, looking opposite ways, set on a round neck and precisely alike; also four ears, two privy members, and the remainder to correspond. He could walk up right as men now do, backwards or forwards as he pleased, and he could also roll over and over at a great pace, turning on his four hands and four feet, eight in all, like tumblers going over and over with their legs in the air; this was when he wanted to run fast. Now the sexes were three, and such as I have described them; because the sun, moon, and earth are three; and the man was originally the child of the sun, the woman of the earth, and the man-woman of the moon, which is made up of sun and earth, and they were all round and moved round and round: like their parents. Terrible was their might and strength, and the thoughts of their hearts were great, and they made an attack upon the gods; of them is told the tale of Otys and Ephialtes who, as Homer says, dared to scale heaven, and would have laid hands upon the gods. Doubt reigned in the celestial councils. Should they kill them and annihilate the race with thunderbolts, as they had done the giants, then there would be an end of the sacrifices and worship which men offered to them; but, on the other hand, the gods could not suffer their insolence to be unrestrained.

At last, after a good deal of reflection, Zeus discovered a way. He said: "Methinks I have a plan which will humble their pride and improve their manners; men shall continue to exist, but I will cut them in two and then they will be diminished in strength and increased in numbers; this will have the advantage of making them more profitable to us. They shall walk upright on two legs, and if they continue insolent and will not be quiet, I will split them again and they shall hop about on a single leg." He spoke and cut men in two, like a sorb-apple which is halved for pickling, or as you might divide an egg with a hair; and as he cut them one after another, he bade Apollo give the face and the half of the neck a turn in order that the man might contemplate the section of himself: he would thus learn a lesson of humility. Apollo was also bidden to heal their wounds and compose their forms. So he gave a turn to the face and pulled the skin from the sides all over that which in our language is called the belly, like the purses which draw in, and he made one mouth at the centre, which he fastened in a knot (the same which is called the navel); he also moulded the breast and took out most of the wrinkles, much as a shoemaker might smooth leather upon a last; he left a few, however, in the region of the belly and navel, as a memorial of the primeval state. After the division the two parts of man, each desiring his other half, came together, and throwing their arms about one another, entwined in mutual embraces, longing to grow into one, they were on the point of dying from hunger and self-neglect, because they did not like to do anything apart; and when one of the halves died and the other survived, the survivor sought another mate, man or woman as we call them, being the sections of entire men or women, and clung to that. They were being destroyed, when Zeus in pity of them invented a new plan: he turned the parts of generation round to the front, for this had not been always their position and they sowed the seed no longer as hitherto like grasshoppers in the ground, but in one another; and after the transposition the male generated in the female in order that by the mutual embraces of man and woman they might breed, and the race might continue; or if man came to man they might be satisfied, and rest, and go their ways to the business of life: so ancient is the desire of one another which is implanted in us, reuniting our original nature, making one of two, and healing the state of man.

Each of us when separated, having one side only, like a flat fish, is but the indenture of a man, and he is always looking for his other half. Men who are a section of that double nature which was once called Androgynous are lovers of women; adulterers are generally of this breed, and also adulterous women who lust after men: the women who are a section of the woman do not care for men, but have female attachments; the female companions are of this sort. But they who are a section of the male follow the male, and while they are young, being slices of the original man, they hang about men and embrace them, and they are themselves the best of boys and youths, because they have the most manly nature. Some indeed assert that they are shameless, but this is not true; for they do not act thus from any want of shame, but because they are valiant and manly, and have a manly countenance, and they embrace that which is like them. And these when they grow up become our statesmen, and these only, which is a great proof of the truth of what I am saving. When they reach manhood they are loves of youth, and are not naturally inclined to marry or beget children,–if at all, they do so only in obedience to the law; but they are satisfied if they may be allowed to live with one another unwedded; and such a nature is prone to love and ready to return love, always embracing that which is akin to him. And when one of them meets with his other half, the actual half of himself, whether he be a lover of youth or a lover of another sort, the pair are lost in an amazement of love and friendship and intimacy, and would not be out of the other's sight, as I may say, even for a moment: these are the people who pass their whole lives together; yet they could not explain what they desire of one another. For the intense yearning which each of them has towards the other does not appear to be the desire of lover's intercourse, but of something else which the soul of either evidently desires and cannot tell, and of which she has only a dark and doubtful presentiment. Suppose Hephaestus, with his instruments, to come to the pair who are lying side, by side and to say to them, "What do you people want of one another?" they would be unable to explain. And suppose further, that when he saw their perplexity he said: "Do you desire to be wholly one; always day and night to be in one another's company? for if this is what you desire, I am ready to melt you into one and let you grow together, so that being two you shall become one, and while you live a common life as if you were a single man, and after your death in the world below still be one departed soul instead of two–I ask whether this is what you lovingly desire, and whether you are satisfied to attain this?" –there is not a man of them who when he heard the proposal would deny or would not acknowledge that this meeting and melting into one another, this becoming one instead of two, was the very expression of his ancient need. And the reason is that human nature was originally one and we were a whole, and the desire and pursuit of the whole is called love.'

For Plato, see Q. 145.

99. Are humans fundamentally selfish?

Facilitated by Scotland's concentration of universities and societies, the Scottish Enlightenment was an 18th century intellectual movement which generated significant developments in a variety of fields, including philosophy, economics, history, medicine and geology. **Francis Hutcheson** (1694-1746) has been called the father of the Scottish Enlightenment and his emphasis on human sociability set the tone.

A trait within the movement's moral philosophy was the rejection of psychological egoism, the view that human action is entirely motivated by self-interest. Thomas Hobbes, a proponent of this view, had written in the previous century, 'no man giveth, but with the intention of Good to himself, because Gift is voluntary, and of all Voluntary acts, the Object is to every man his own Good'.

Hutcheson vehemently disagreed with Hobbes. He believed that humans were naturally benevolent and capable of genuine altruism, as he sought to prove in the following passage from his 'Inaugural Lecture on the Social Nature of Man'.

'What if God said to you, "You will perish imminently, without pain or fear, and your mind will not survive your body, for I, who can do all things, desire it. Know, meanwhile, that anything you ask of for other people, even with your final breath, I will make happen, though no one will be grateful to you no matter how good your request; and no one will despise or curse you for the evils you might invoke. From now on you will gain neither happiness nor sorrow from the fortune of others: being nothing, you will feel nothing. In this situation would you become estranged and indifferent to human matters? I shall make your children, friends, compatriots, as happy or as miserable as you request. They will flourish in virtue, health, friendship, wealth and honour; or else they will dwell in a wretched state of vice, illness, hatred, envy, poverty, dishonour, wickedness and servitude." Faced with these possibilities, is there anyone who would not care either way? No indeed, at the moment of death there are so few who would not desire, with the same passion and resolve, the same things for all those they hold dear as they would at any other moment, even though it is of no profit to them. There are, therefore, within us benevolent affections which principally, and often exclusively, seek the happiness of others.'

For figures of the Scottish Enlightenment, see *Qs*. 1, 25, 113 and 124.

103. Is the fear of death irrational?

Outside the walls of Athens, amid the shaded groves of his garden, **Epicurus** (341-270 BCE) and his band of followers led frugal, civically detached lives devoted to attaining and sustaining ataraxy. The basic tenets of his philosophy were antidotes to disquiet: we are mortal, so death should not be feared; the world is governed by natural forces, so we should not cower before the gods; status and wealth do not offer happiness, so toil and stress are unnecessary. To modern ears and in summary these ideas risk sounding banal, but

Epicurean pith still has the power to challenge, as these two injunctions may attest: *Live unnoticed. Die as if you had never lived.*

Though Epicurus was a prolific writer who authored up to 300 texts, nothing much survives. The following is from his 'Letter to Menoeceus'.

'Accustom yourself to the belief that death is nothing to us. For all good and evil consists in sensation, but death is deprivation of sensation. And therefore a right understanding that death is nothing to us makes the mortality of life enjoyable, not because it adds to it an infinite span of time, but because it takes away the craving for immortality. For there is nothing terrible in life for the man who has truly comprehended that there is nothing terrible in not living. So that the man speaks but idly who says that he fears death not because it will be painful when it comes, but because it is painful in anticipation. For that which gives no trouble, when it comes, is but an empty pain in anticipation. So death, the most terrifying of ills, is nothing to us, since so long as we exist, death is not with us; but when death comes, then we do not exist. It does not then concern either the living or the dead, since for the former it is not, and the latter are no more.

But the many at one moment shun death as the greatest of evils, at another yearn for it as a respite from the evils in life. But the wise man neither seeks to escape life nor fears the cessation of life, for neither does life offend him nor does the absence of life seem to be any evil. And just as with food he does not seek simply the larger share and nothing else, but rather the most pleasant, so he seeks to enjoy not the longest period of time, but the most pleasant.'

For a later Epicurean, see *Qs*. 91 and 243.

105. Is democracy a wonderful thing?

> The French philosopher Gilles Deleuze claimed that democratic states provide the most favourable conditions for philosophers. The ideal society for these 'shadows' and 'hermits' is one that 'exempts the power of thinking from the obligation to obey'.
>
> In the extract below from *On the Sublime,* **Longinus** (*fl.* 1st c) considers similar ideas in relation to oratory. It is suggested that democracy, as a bastion of liberty and equality, is the 'kindly nurse of sublime genius'. Yet, having presented these ideas with considerable eloquence, he ultimately dismisses them: oratorical degradation is not caused by political oppression but moral weakness.

'In consideration of your desire for useful information, my dearest Terentianus, I shall not hesitate to add an elucidation of that remaining question, which was recently proposed by a certain philosopher. I wonder, said he, and not I alone, but doubtless many others also, how it happens that in the age we live in, there are many men eminently endowed with talents for persuasion and public speaking, remarkable for shrewdness and readiness, and, above all, expert in the arts which give grace and sweetness to language; but that there are now none at all, or very few, who are distinguished for loftiness and grandeur of style. So great and universal is the dearth of genuine eloquence that prevails in this age. Must we believe at last, that there is truth in that oft-repeated observation. That democracy is the kindly nurse of sublime genius; with whose strength alone truly powerful orators flourish, and disappear as it declines? For liberty, say they, is able to supply nutriment to the lofty conceptions of great minds, and feed their aspirations, and at the same time to foster the flame of mutual emulation, and stimulate ambition for pre-eminence. Nay further, that the mental excellencies of orators are whetted continually by reason of the rewards proposed in free states; that they are made, as it were, to give out fire by collision, and naturally exhibit the light of liberty in their oratorical efforts. But we of the present day, continued he, seem to be trained from our childhood to absolute slavery, having been all but swathed in its customs and institutes, and never allowed to taste of that most copious fountain of all that is admirable and attractive in eloquence, I mean, liberty; and hence it is that we turn out to be nothing but pompous flatterers. This, he said, was the cause why we see that all other attainments may be found in menials: but never yet a slave become an orator. His spirit being effectually broken, the timorous vassal will still be uppermost; the habit of subjection continually overawes and beats down his genius. For, according to Homer, (*Odyssey*, Book XVII):

> Jove fix'd it certain, that whatever day
> Makes man a slave, takes half his worth away.

As then, said he, (if what I have heard deserves credit,) the cages, in which what are called pigmies are kept, not only prevent the growth of those who are inclined in them, but contract their dimensions by reason of the confinement in which their whole bodies are placed; so slavery of every kind, even the mildest, one might declare to be the cage and common prison of the mind.'

108. Which would you most like to excel in: strength, intelligence, kindness or beauty?

With his belief that we are by nature political animals, **Aristotle** (384-322 BCE) would inevitably consider this question from a political perspective. Contrary to the Epicureans who advocated civic disengagement (see *Q.* 103) and the English philosopher Thomas Hobbes who regarded security as the state's ultimate purpose, Aristotle believed that the state's true end was the good life of its citizens. Indeed, for Aristotle, the good life can only be achieved within a state; only as citizens can we achieve moral and intellectual excellence. To disrupt civic life is to vitiate human flourishing.

From *Politics* –

'Now in all states there are three elements: one class is very rich, another very poor, and a third in a mean. It is admitted that moderation and the mean are best, and therefore it will clearly be best to possess the gifts of fortune in moderation; for in that condition of life men are most ready to follow rational principle. But he who greatly excels in beauty, strength, birth, or wealth, or on the other hand who is very poor, or very weak, or very much disgraced, finds it difficult to follow rational principle. Of these two the one sort grow into violent and great criminals, the others into rogues and petty rascals. And two sorts of offenses correspond to them, the one committed from violence, the other from roguery. Again, the middle class is least likely to shrink from rule, or to be over-ambitious for it; both of which are injuries to the state. Again, those who have too much of the goods of fortune, strength, wealth, friends, and the like, are neither willing nor able to submit to authority. The evil begins at home; for when they are boys, by reason of the luxury in which they are brought up, they never learn, even at school, the habit of obedience. On the other hand, the very poor, who are in the opposite extreme, are too degraded. So that the one class cannot obey, and can only rule despotically; the other knows not how to command and must be ruled like slaves. Thus arises a city, not of freemen, but of masters and slaves, the one despising, the other envying; and nothing can be more fatal to friendship and good fellowship in states than this: for good fellowship springs from friendship; when men are at enmity with one another, they would rather not even share the same path. But a city ought to be composed, as far as possible, of equals and similars; and these are generally the middle classes. Wherefore the city which is composed of middle-class citizens is necessarily best constituted in respect of the elements of which we say the fabric of the state naturally consists. And this is the class of citizens which is most secure in a state, for they do not, like the poor, covet their neighbours' goods; nor do others covet theirs, as the poor covet the goods of the rich; and as they neither plot against others, nor are themselves plotted against, they pass through life safely. Wisely then did Phocylides pray, "Many things are best in the mean; I desire to be of a middle condition in my city."'

109. Is it always wrong to blame other people for our failures?

Epictetus (*c.* 55-135 CE) was an emancipated slave who left Rome for Greece to establish a school of philosophy following Emperor Domitian's edict banishing philosophers from Italy.

The following is from the *Manual*, a book of Epictetus's teachings recorded by his student Arrian.

'It is not the world that troubles us but only our judgments of the world. Death, to be sure, is nothing terrible, for if it were, it would have appeared so to Socrates. Its terror consists only in our notion of it. Therefore, whenever we are thwarted or upset or grieved, let us never blame others but rather ourselves, that is, our own judgments. An uneducated person accuses others for his misfortunes; a person who has started his education accuses himself; an educated person accuses neither someone else nor himself.'

113. Can you know yourself without knowing what other people think of you?

There was once a shepherd from Lydia who discovered a magical ring which bestowed upon its wearer the power of invisibility. Knowing that he could now act with impunity, free from the eyes of judgment, the shepherd used his power to murder the local king and take his throne.

In Plato's *Republic,* Socrates' interlocutor Glaucon uses this parable to illustrate our basic amorality, arguing that we are essentially no different from this shepherd. While we may not share the shepherd's murderous appetites, with the ring in our possession our behaviour would certainly darken. According to Glaucon, we are only moral to the extent that we fear being caught.

The Scottish philosopher and economist **Adam Smith** (1723-1790) would dispute the parable. In Smith's view the ring would not alter our behaviour because invisibility is not enough to occlude the eyes of judgment. Within society, the experience of being seen by others is internalised. Society teaches us to watch ourselves, to evaluate our actions from the standpoint of an imagined spectator. The only way to test Glaucon's hypothesis would be to somehow become invisible to ourselves, to purge the social influence and blind the internal spectator, 'this inmate of the breast, this abstract man, the representative of mankind, and substitute of the Deity'.

From *The Theory of Moral Sentiments* –

'The principle by which we naturally either approve or disapprove of our own conduct, seems to be altogether the same with that by which we exercise the like judgments concerning the conduct of other people. We either approve or disapprove of the conduct of another man, according as we feel that, when we bring his case home to ourselves, we either can or cannot entirely sympathize with the sentiments and motives which directed it. And, in the same manner, we either approve or disapprove of our own conduct, according as we feel that, when we place ourselves in the situation of another man, and view it, as it were, with his eyes and from his station, we either can or cannot entirely enter into and sympathize with the sentiments and motives which influenced it. We can never survey our own sentiments and motives, we can never form any judgment concerning them, unless we remove ourselves, as it were, from our own natural station, and endeavour to view them as at a certain distance from us. But we can do this in no other way than by endeavouring to view them with the eyes of other people, or as other people are likely to view them. Whatever judgment we can form concerning them, accordingly, must always bear some secret reference, either to what are, or to what, upon a certain condition, would be, or to what, we imagine, ought to be the judgment of others. We endeavour to examine our own conduct as we imagine any other fair and impartial spectator would examine it. If, upon placing ourselves in his situation, we thoroughly enter into all the passions and motives which influenced it, we approve of it, by sympathy with the approbation of this supposed equitable judge. If otherwise, we enter into his disapprobation, and condemn it.

Were it possible that a human creature could grow up to manhood in some solitary place, without any communication with his own species, he could no more think of his own character, of the propriety or demerit of his own sentiments and conduct, of the beauty or deformity of his own mind, than of the beauty or deformity of his own face. All these are objects which he cannot easily see, which naturally he does not look at, and with regard to which he is provided with no mirror which can present them to his view. Bring him into society, and he is immediately provided with the mirror which he wanted before.

It is placed in the countenance and behaviour of those he lives with, which always mark when they enter into, and when they disapprove of his sentiments; and it is here that he first views the propriety and impropriety of his own passions, the beauty and deformity of his own mind. To a man who from his birth was a stranger to society, the objects of his passions, the external bodies which either pleased or hurt him, would occupy his whole attention. The passions themselves, the desires or aversions, the joys or sorrows, which those objects excited, though of all things the most immediately present to him, could scarce ever be the objects of his thoughts. The idea of them could never interest him so much as to call upon his attentive consideration. The consideration of his joy could in him excite no new joy, nor that of his sorrow any new sorrow, though the consideration of the causes of those passions might often excite both. Bring him into society, and all his own passions will immediately become the causes of new passions. He will observe that mankind approve of some of them, and are disgusted by others. He will be elevated in the one case, and cast down in the other; his desires and aversions, his joys and sorrows, will now often become the causes of new desires and new aversions, new joys and new sorrows: they will now, therefore, interest him deeply, and often call upon his most attentive consideration.'

114. Can emotions lie?

In 1878 **William James** (1842-1910) was commissioned to write a psychology textbook. His publisher wanted it finished in no longer than six months. James asked for twenty-four months. In the end it took twelve years, not appearing till 1890.

Part of the reason for the delay was that James was not content to write a basic summary of current ideas. *The Principles of Psychology* was itself a significant new addition to the burgeoning field of psychology replete with fresh and startling insights. James, for instance, rejected the idea that our bodies are affected by our emotions. He instead proposed the primacy of the body, claiming that (many) emotions are the mental sensations of bodily events.

For us, then, if James is right, the question needs recasting. To know whether emotions can lie we must determine whether the body can lie.

'Our natural way of thinking about these standard emotions [surprise, curiosity, rapture, fear, anger, lust, greed, and the like] is that the mental perception of some fact excites the mental affection called the emotion, and that this latter state of mind gives rise to the bodily expression. My thesis on the contrary is that the bodily changes follow directly the perception of the exciting fact, and that our feeling of the same changes as they occur IS the emotion. Common sense says, we lose our fortune, are sorry and weep; we meet a bear, are frightened and run; we are insulted by a rival, are angry and strike. The hypothesis here to be defended says that this order of sequence is incorrect, that the one mental state is not immediately induced by the other, that the bodily manifestations must first be interposed between, and that the more rational statement is that we feel sorry because we cry, angry because we strike, afraid because we tremble, and not that we cry, strike, or tremble, because we are sorry, angry, or fearful, as the case may be. Without the bodily states following on the perception, the latter would be purely cognitive in form, pale, colourless, destitute of emotional warmth. We might then see the bear, and judge it best to run, receive the insult and deem it right to strike, but we could not actually feel afraid or angry...

If we fancy some strong emotion, and then try to abstract from our consciousness of it all the feelings of its characteristic bodily symptoms, we find we have nothing left behind, no "mind-stuff" out of which the emotion can be constituted, and that a cold and neutral state of intellectual perception is all that remains. It is true that, although most people, when asked say that their introspection verifies this statement, some persist in saying theirs does not. Many cannot be made to understand the question. When you beg them to imagine away every feeling of laughter and of tendency to laugh from their consciousness of the ludicrousness of an object, and then to tell you what the feeling of its ludicrousness would be like, whether it be anything more than the perception that the object belongs to the class "funny," they persist in replying that the thing proposed is a physical impossibility, and that they always must laugh, if they see a funny object. Of course the task proposed is not the practical one of seeing a ludicrous object and annihilating one's tendency to laugh. It is the purely speculative one of subtracting certain elements of feeling from an emotional state supposed to exist in its fulness, and saying what the residual elements are. I cannot help thinking that all who rightly apprehend this problem will agree with the proposition above laid down. What kind of an emotion of fear would be left, if the feelings neither of quickened heart-beats nor of shallow breathing, neither of trembling lips nor of weakened limbs, neither of goose-flesh nor of visceral stirrings, were present, it is quite impossible to think. Can one fancy the state of rage and picture no ebullition of it in the chest, no flushing of the face, no dilatation of the nostrils, no clenching of the teeth, no impulse to vigorous action, but in their stead limp muscles, calm breathing, and a placid face? The present writer, for one, certainly cannot. The rage is as completely evaporated as the sensation of its so-called manifestations, and the only thing that can possibly be supposed to take its place is some cold-blooded and dispassionate judicial sentence, confined entirely to the intellectual realm, to the effect that a certain person or persons merit chastisement for their sins. In like manner of grief: what would it be without its tears, its sobs, its suffocation of the heart, its pang in the breast-bone? A feelingless cognition that certain circumstances are deplorable, and nothing more. Every passion in turn tells the same story. A purely disembodied human emotion is a nonentity. I do not say that it is a contradiction in the nature of things, or that pure spirits are necessarily condemned to cold intellectual lives; but I say that for us, emotion dissociated from all bodily feeling is inconceivable. The more closely I scrutinise my states, the more persuaded I become, that whatever moods, affections, and passions I have, are in very truth constituted by, and made up of, those bodily changes we ordinarily call their expression or consequence; and the more it seems to me that if I were to become corporeally anaesthetic, I should be excluded from the life of the affections, harsh and tender alike, and drag out an existence of merely cognitive or intellectual form.'

For James, see *Qs*. 121 and 305.

121. Since waking up today, have you had a series of different thoughts or a single continuously changing thought?

In her 1919 essay 'Modern Fiction' Virginia Woolf wrote, 'The mind receives a myriad impressions—trivial, fantastic, evanescent, or engraved with the sharpness of steel. From all sides they come, an incessant shower of innumerable atoms; and… if [the writer] could base his work upon his own feeling and not upon convention, there would be no plot, no comedy, no tragedy, no love interest or catastrophe in the accepted style.'

She was alluding to an approach to writing known as 'stream of consciousness' – a phrase coined by **William James** (1842-1910). James, too, believed that the contents of the mind are akin to an 'incessant shower', though one continuous rather than atomic, 'without breach, crack or division', such that if we were to capture in prose the true fluidity of thought, the full stop would be the first casualty.

From *The Principles of Psychology* –

'Consciousness, then, does not appear to itself chopped up in bits. Such words as "chain" or "train" do not describe it fitly as it presents itself in the first instance. It is nothing jointed; it flows. A "river" or a "stream" are the metaphors by which it is most naturally described. *In talking of it hereafter, let us call it the stream of thought, of consciousness, or of subjective life.*

But now there appears, even within the limits of the same self, and between thoughts all of which alike have this same sense of belonging together, a kind of jointing and separateness among the parts, of which this statement seems to take no account. I refer to the breaks that are produced by sudden contrasts in the quality of the successive segments of the stream of thought. If the words "chain" and "train" had no natural fitness in them, how came such words to be used at all? Does not a loud explosion rend the consciousness upon which it abruptly breaks, in twain? Does not every sudden shock, appearance of a new object, or change in a sensation, create a real interruption, sensibly felt as such, which cuts the conscious stream across at the moment at which it appears? Do not such interruptions smite us every hour of our lives, and have we the right, in their presence, still to call our consciousness a continuous stream?

This objection is based partly on a confusion and partly on a superficial introspective view.

The confusion is between the thoughts themselves, taken as subjective facts, and the things of which they are aware. It is natural to make this confusion, but easy to avoid it when once put on one's guard. The things are discrete and discontinuous; they do pass before us in a train or chain, making often explosive appearances and rending each other in twain. But their comings and goings and contrasts no more break the flow of the thought that thinks them than they break the time and the space in which they lie. A silence may be broken by a thunder-clap, and we may be so stunned and confused for a moment by the shock as to give no instant account to ourselves of what has happened. But that very confusion is a mental state, and a state that passes us straight over from the silence to the sound. The transition between the thought of one object and the thought of another is no more a break in the *thought* than a joint in a bamboo is a break in the wood. It is a part of the *consciousness* as much as the joint is a part of the *bamboo*.

The superficial introspective view is the overlooking, even when the things are contrasted with each other most violently, of the large amount of affinity that may still remain between the thoughts by whose means they are cognized. Into the awareness of the thunder itself the awareness of the previous silence creeps and continues; for what we hear when the thunder crashes is not thunder *pure,* but thunder-breaking-upon-silence-and-contrasting-with-it. Our feeling of the same objective thunder, coming in this way, is quite different from what it would be were the thunder a continuation of previous thunder. The thunder itself we believe to abolish and exclude the silence; but the *feeling* of the thunder is also a feeling of the silence as just gone; and it would be difficult to find in the actual concrete consciousness of man a feeling so limited to the present as not to have an inkling of anything that went before. Here, again, language works against our perception of the truth. We name our thoughts simply, each after its thing, as if each knew its own thing and nothing else. What each really knows is clearly the thing it is named for, with dimly perhaps a thousand other things. It ought to be named after all of them, but it never is.'

For James, see *Qs*. 114 and 305.

122. Thoughts, they say, are in the head. Try to imagine instead that they are on the surface of your eyes or within the cavity of your mouth. Can you?

In his bid to become a student of philosophy, **Zeno of Citium** (*c.* 334-262 BCE) asked a bookseller in Athens where he might find a man like Socrates. At that moment the Cynic philosopher (see *Q.* 138) Crates walked by (possibly masturbating) and Zeno was advised to follow him. It was thus that he became Crates' student. He was, however, too modest for Cynic shamelessness and eventually established his own school of philosophy known as Stoicism.

The brief argument below was documented by Galen in *On the Doctrines of Hippocrates and Plato*.

'The voice comes through the windpipe. If it were coming from the brain, it would not pass through the windpipe. Now the voice comes from the same place as language (*logos*). But language comes from thought, so thought is not in the brain.'

124. When you wince I see your pain.
When you wince I see the effect of your pain.
Which statement is correct?

Thomas Reid (1710-1796) argued that it is impossible to feel anything beyond the bounds of your body. Everything you feel is a sensation within the mind, but sensations are entirely different in nature from the external world objects that cause them. When you take a bowling ball in both hands, the sensation you feel is nothing like the ball itself. Though the ball is round and heavy, your sensation is neither – it makes no sense to speak of round and heavy sensations. A sensation cannot roll away. It cannot weigh you down. As such, we cannot infer the existence of a bowling ball from the sensation we feel while holding it. Nevertheless, something within your nature ensures that this sensation leads to the belief that there is a round and heavy ball in your hands. The sensation is a *sign* of the ball's presence, one that you seemingly understand without deliberation or reason.

Reid claimed it was through a similar mechanism that we are able to form the understanding that a wince *means* pain. Wincing is certainly a *sign* of pain, but since pain, as a state of mind, is invisible – to see a man's pain would require us to see his mind, but the mind is neither coloured nor illuminable – it is impossible that we should have learnt of the connection between wincing and pain from experience. Indeed, Reid argues that there are connections between states of mind and physical behaviour that we are aware of from birth. Experience cannot explain our understanding of their connection. It must be attributable to the basic constitution of our nature.

From *Essays on the Intellectual Powers of the Human Mind* –

'That many operations of the mind have their natural signs in the countenance, voice, and gesture, I suppose every man will admit. *Omnis enim motus animi*, says Cicero, *suum quemdam habet a natura vultum, et vocem, et gestum* [To every emotion nature has assigned a particular look, tone of voice, and bearing]. The only question is whether we understand the signification of those signs by the constitution of our nature, by a kind of natural perception similar to the perceptions of sense; or whether we gradually learn the signification of such signs from experience, as we learn that smoke is a sign of fire or that freezing of water is a sign of cold. I take the first to be the truth.

It seems to me incredible that the notions men have of the expression of features, voice, and gesture are entirely the fruit of experience. Children, almost as soon as born, may be frighted and thrown into fits by a threatening or angry tone of voice...

The countenance and gesture have an expression no less strong and natural than the voice. The first time one sees a stern and fierce look, a contracted brow, and a menacing posture, he concludes that the person is inflamed with anger. Shall we say that, previous to experience, the most hostile countenance has as agreeable an appearance as the most gentle and benign? This surely would contradict all experience, for we know that an angry countenance will fright a child in the cradle. Who has not observed that children, very early, are able to distinguish what is said to them in jest from what is said in earnest, by the tone of the voice and the features of the face? They judge by these natural signs, even when they seem to contradict the artificial.

If it were by experience that we learn the meaning of features, and sound, and gesture, it might be expected that we should recollect the time when we first learned those lessons, or at least some of such a multitude.

Those who give attention to the operations of children can easily discover the time when they have their earliest notices from experience such as that flame will burn or that knives will cut. But no man is able to recollect in himself, or to observe in others, the time when the expression of the face, voice, and gesture were learned.

Nay, I apprehend that it is impossible that this should be learned from experience.

When we see the sign, and see the thing signified always conjoined with it, experience may be the instructor and teach us how that sign is to be interpreted. But how shall experience instruct us when we see the sign only, when the thing signified is invisible? Now, this is the case here: the thoughts and passions of the mind, as well as the mind itself, are invisible, and therefore their connection with any sensible sign cannot be first discovered by experience; there must be some earlier source of this knowledge.

Nature seems to have given to men a faculty or sense by

which this connection is perceived. And the operation of this sense is very analogous to that of the external senses.

When I grasp an ivory ball in my hand, I feel a certain sensation of touch. In the sensation there is nothing external, nothing corporeal. The sensation is neither round nor hard; it is an act of feeling of the mind from which I cannot, by reasoning, infer the existence of any body. But by the constitution of my nature, the sensation carries along with it the conception and belief of a round hard body really existing in my hand.

In like manner when I see the features of an expressive face, I see only figure and colour variously modified. But by the constitution of my nature the visible object brings along with it the conception and belief of a certain passion or sentiment in the mind of the person.

In the former case a sensation of touch is the sign, and the hardness and roundness of the body I grasp is signified by that sensation. In the latter case the features of the person is the sign, and the passion or sentiment is signified by it.'

For Reid, see Q. 267.

126. Are you performing an action when you dream?

In Greek mythology, the god of sleep (Hypnos) was thought to be the brother of the god of death (Thanatos), which is somewhat puzzling. Why regard Hypnos and Thanatos as kindred? If death is the negation of life, how can a state within life bear any relation to death?

We may be inclined to answer that both sleep and death are similarly impervious to the world, but **Henri Bergson** (1859-1941) would disagree. He claimed that the sleeping mind is porous and sensitive, and that dreams are in fact fabricated from the sensations – buzzing mosquitoes, creeping spiders and whatnot – we experience while asleep. Dreams occur when these sensations evoke our memories, memories we may not even know we possess since 'nothing is forgotten'.

In waking life we also use memories to interpret our current sensations. The difference, however, is that in waking life we restrict our memories to suit the practical requirements of the present moment. Dreams arise when our memories are liberated from the narrow focus of our worldly concerns.

Here then, perhaps, lies the kinship between sleep and death. Dreams are the passive detachment from the concerns of life, a letting go of life. In death we cannot will, and in dreaming, as Bergson states, we cease to will.

From *Mind-Energy* –

'The dream is not something fantastic hovering above and additional to the reality of being awake; on the contrary, that reality of the waking state is gained by limitation, by concentration and by tension of a diffuse psychical life, which is the dream-life. In a sense, the perception and memory we exercise in the dream-state are more natural than those in the waking state: there does consciousness disport itself, perceiving just to perceive, remembering just to remember, with no care for life, that is, for the action to be accomplished. But the waking state consists in eliminating, in choosing, in concentrating unceasingly the totality of the diffuse dream-life at the point where a practical problem is presented. To be awake means to will. Cease to will, detach yourself from life, disinterest yourself, and by that mere abstention you pass from the awake-self to the dream-self — less *tense* but more *extended*…

Your life in the waking state is, then, a life of toil, even when you suppose you are doing nothing, for at every moment you must choose and at every moment you have to exclude. You choose among your sensations, since you reject from consciousness a host of "subjective" sensations which reappear when you sleep. You choose among your memories, since you reject every recollection which does not mould itself on your present state. This choice which you are continually accomplishing, this adaptation ceaselessly renewed, is the essential condition of what you call common sense. But such adaptation and choice keeps you in a state of uninterrupted tension. You take no account of it at the time, any more than you feel the weight of the atmosphere. But it fatigues you in the long run. Common sense is very tiring.

"Now, let me repeat it, I differ from you precisely in that I do nothing. The effort you are called on to make without cessation, I simply abstain from. You are attached to life, I am detached from it. Everything is indifferent to me. I am disinterested in everything. To sleep is to be disinterested. We sleep to the exact extent to which we are disinterested. A mother asleep by the side of her child will not hear the thunder, but the child's sob will wake her. Is she, then, really asleep in regard to her child? We do not sleep in regard to anything which continues to interest us.

"You ask me what I do when I dream? Let me tell you what you do when you wake. I, your dream-self, am the totality of your past – you take me and bring me, from contraction to contraction, to shut myself into the very small circle you trace around your present action. This is being awake, this is living the normal psychical life, and this is striving and willing. As to dreaming, need I explain it? It is the state into which you naturally fall when you let yourself go, when you no longer care to concentrate, yourself on a single point, when you cease to will. If you still insist and require explanation, ask how your will contrives, at every moment of waking life, to obtain instantaneously and almost unconsciously the concentration of all that you have within you on the one point which interests you. But address your inquiry to the psychology of waking. Its main function is to reply to you, for waking and willing are one and the same."

This is what the dream-self would say. It might tell us much more would we let it. But I must conclude. What is then the essential difference between being in a dream and being awake? I will sum it up by saying that the same faculties are being exercised whether we are awake or dreaming, but they are in tension in the one case, and relaxed in the other. The dream is the entire mental life, minus the effort of concentration. We still perceive, still remember, still reason. Perceptions, memories, reasonings may abound in a dreamer, for abundance, in the mental domain, does not mean effort. What requires effort is the *precision of adjustment*. For the barking of a dog, while it is going on, to detach from my memory the recollection of an uproarious assembly simply because that recollection happens to be on its way, I need not do anything. But that the barking should go and choose, in preference to all recollections, the recollection of a bark, and thereupon, coalescing with it, be interpreted, — I mean, actually perceived as a bark, — requires a positive effort. The dreamer has no longer the force to make it. This, and this alone, distinguishes him from the man who is awake.'

For Bergson, see *Qs*. 19, 213, 265 and 389.

130. Can music enhance our perception of reality?

Arthur Schopenhauer (1788-1860) believed that music is uniquely capable of taking us closer to reality.

The world is ultimately Will, a single universal striving which becomes manifest in us through our individual impulses. We cannot (fully) perceive the Will itself, partly because our perceptions are conditioned by time. Our access is more or less limited to the phenomenal world, the world of appearance, or representation.

Schopenhauer believed that like the other arts music is representational, however, unlike the other arts it does not represent the phenomenal world. Music represents Will, reality's essence, the imperceptible truth, and this is why it affects us so profoundly. The motions of music – its tensions, frustrations and resolutions – replicate the motions of Will. For Schopenhauer, himself a flautist, listening to music is no frivolity. It effects a metaphysical attunement to the world far beyond the powers of scientific observation or philosophical reasoning.

From *The World as Will and Representation* –

'[Music] stands alone, quite cut off from all the other arts. In it we do not recognise the copy or repetition of any Idea of existence in the world. Yet it is such a great and exceedingly noble art, its effect on the inmost nature of man is so powerful, and it is so entirely and deeply understood by him in his inmost consciousness as a perfectly universal language, the distinctness of which surpasses even that of the perceptible world itself, that we certainly have more to look for in it than *an exercitum arithmeticoe occultum nescientis se numerare animi* [a hidden arithmetic exercise of the soul, which doesn't know that it is counting], which Leibniz called it. Yet he was perfectly right, as he considered only its immediate external significance, its form. But if it were nothing more, the satisfaction which it affords would be like that which we feel when a sum in arithmetic comes out right, and could not be that intense pleasure with which we see the deepest recesses of our nature find utterance. From our standpoint, therefore, at which the aesthetic effect is the criterion, we must attribute to music a far more serious and deep significance, connected with the inmost nature of the world and our own self, and in reference to which the arithmetical proportions, to which it may be reduced, are related, not as the thing signified, but merely as the sign. That in some sense music must be related to the world as the representation to the thing represented, as the copy to the original, we may conclude from the analogy of the other arts, all of which possess this character, and affect us on the whole in the same way as it does, only that the effect of music is stronger, quicker, more necessary and infallible. Further, its representative relation to the world must be very deep, absolutely true, and strikingly accurate, because it is instantly understood by everyone, and has the appearance of a certain infallibility, because its form may be reduced to perfectly definite rules expressed in numbers, from which it cannot free itself without entirely ceasing to be music...

Music is entirely independent of the phenomenal world, ignores it altogether, and could to a certain extent exist if there was no world at all, which cannot be said of the other arts. Music is as *direct* an objectification and copy of the whole *will* as the world itself, nay, even as the Ideas, whose multiplied manifestation constitutes the world of individual things. Music is thus by no means like the other arts, the copy of the Ideas, but *the copy of the will itself,* whose objectivity the Ideas are. This is why the effect of music is so much more powerful and penetrating than that of the other arts, for they speak only of shadows, but it speaks of the thing itself...

Now the nature of man consists in this, that his will strives, is satisfied and strives anew, and so on forever. Indeed, his happiness and well-being consist simply in the quick transition from wish to satisfaction, and from satisfaction to a new wish. For the absence of satisfaction is suffering, the empty longing for a new wish, languor, ennui. And corresponding to this the nature of melody is a constant digression and deviation from the keynote in a thousand ways, not only to the harmonious intervals to the third and dominant, but to every tone, to the dissonant sevenths and to the superfluous degrees; yet there always follows a constant return to the keynote. In all these deviations melody expresses the multifarious efforts of will, but always its satisfaction also by the final return to a harmonious interval, and still more, to the keynote. The composition of melody, the disclosure in it of all the deepest secrets of human willing and feeling, is the work of genius, whose action, which is more apparent here than anywhere else, lies far from all reflection and conscious intention, and may be called an inspiration… As quick transition from wish to satisfaction, and from satisfaction to a new wish, is happiness and well-being, so quick melodies without great deviations are cheerful; slow melodies, striking painful discords, and only winding back through many bars to the keynote are, as analogous to the delayed and hardly won satisfaction, sad. The delay of the new excitement of will, languor, could have no other expression than the sustained keynote, the effect of which would soon be unbearable; very monotonous and unmeaning melodies approach this effect. The short intelligible subjects of quick dance-music seem to speak only of easily attained common pleasure. On the other hand, the *Allegro maestoso,* in elaborate movements, long passages, and wide deviations, signifies a greater, nobler effort towards a more distant end, and its final attainment. The *Adagio* speaks of the pain of a great and noble effort which despises all trifling happiness. But how wonderful is the effect of the *minor* and *major!* How astounding that the change of half a tone, the entrance of a minor third instead of a major, at once and inevitably forces upon us an anxious painful feeling, from which again we are just as instantaneously delivered by the major. The *Adagio* lengthens in the minor the expression of the keenest pain, and becomes even a convulsive wail…

Music does not therefore express this or that particular and definite joy, this or that sorrow, or pain, or horror, or delight, or merriment, or peace of mind; but joy, sorrow, pain, horror, delight, merriment, peace of mind themselves, to a certain extent in the abstract, their essential nature, without accessories, and therefore without their motives.'

For Schopenhauer, see *Q*. 70.

134. 'One has renounced the great life when one renounces war,' wrote the philosopher Friedrich Nietzsche. Do you agree?

The English essayist **William Hazlitt** (1778-1830) had a tendency to rub people the wrong way. During his lifetime he was derided by critics as an infidel, a Bonapartist, a whoremonger, a slanderer of the human race, an incendiary, a Cockney Aristotle, a pimpled slang-whanger, and a saboteur intent on destroying the very foundations of modesty and decorum. His own friend Samuel Taylor Coleridge was scarcely less damning, describing him as 'jealous, gloomy, and of an irritable pride – addicted to women.'

The nature and distinctness of these impressions is somewhat surprising given the diaphanous existence he valorises below. Contrary to the tumultuous appetites of Nietzsche, Hazlitt favours contemplation over action and distance over immersion. Yet his preference seems predicated on a questionable dichotomy, namely, that we must choose to live either as frustrated egotists or contented ghosts.

From 'On Living to One's-Self' –

'What I mean by living to one's-self is living in the world, as in it, not of it: it is as if no one knew there was such a person, and you wished no one to know it: it is to be a silent spectator of the mighty scene of things, not an object of attention or curiosity in it; to take a thoughtful, anxious interest in what is passing in the world, but not to feel the slightest inclination to make or meddle with it. It is such a life as a pure spirit might be supposed to lead, such an interest as it might take in the affairs of men, calm, contemplative, passive, distant, touched with pity for their sorrows, smiling at their follies without bitterness, sharing their affections, but not troubled by their passions, not seeking their notice, nor once dreamt of by them. He who lives wisely to himself and to his own heart, looks at the busy world through the loop-holes of retreat, and does not want to mingle in the fray. "He hears the tumult, and is still." He is not able to mend it. He sees enough in the universe to interest him without putting himself forward to try what he can do to fix the eyes of the universe upon him. Vain the attempt! He reads the clouds, he looks at the stars, he watches the return of the seasons, the falling leaves of autumn, the perfumed breath of spring, starts with delight at the note of the thrush in a copse near him, sits by the fire, listens to the moaning of the wind, pores upon a book, or discourses the freezing hours away, or melts down hours to minutes in pleasing thought. All this while he is taken up with other things, forgetting himself. He relishes an author's style without thinking of turning author. He is fond of looking at a print from an old picture in the room, without teasing himself to copy it. He does not fret himself to death with trying to be what he is not, or do what he cannot. He hardly knows what he is capable of, and is not in the least concerned whether he shall ever make a figure in the world. He feels the truth of the lines –

> The man whose eye is ever on himself,
> Doth look one, the least of nature's works;
> One who might move the wise man to that scorn
> Which wisdom holds unlawful ever -

he looks out of himself at the wide extended prospect of nature, and takes an interest beyond his narrow pretensions in general humanity. He is free as air, and independent as the wind. Woe be to him when he first begins to think what others say of him. While a man is contented with himself and his own resources, all is well. When he undertakes to play a part on the stage, and to persuade the world to think more about him than they do about themselves, he is got into a track where he will find nothing but briars and thorns, vexation and disappointment. I can speak a little to this point. For many years of my life I did nothing but think. I had nothing else to do but solve some knotty point, or dip in some abstruse author, or look at the sky or wander by the pebbled sea-side –

> To see the children sporting on the shore,
> And hear the mighty waters rolling evermore.

I cared for nothing, I wanted nothing... I wished well to the world, and believed as favourable of it as I could. I was like a stranger in a foreign land, at which I looked with wonder, curiosity, and delight, without expecting to be an object of attention in return. I had no relations to the state, no duty to perform, no ties to bind me to others: I had neither friend nor mistress, wife nor child. I lived in a world of contemplation, and not of action.

This sort of dreaming existence is the best. He who quits it to go in search of realities, generally barters repose for repeated disappointments and vain regrets. His time, thoughts, and feelings are no longer at his own disposal. From that instant he does not survey the objects of nature as they are in themselves, but looks asquint at them to see whether he cannot make them the instruments of his ambition, interest, or pleasure; for a candid, undesigning, undisguised simplicity of character, his views become jaundiced, sinister, and double: he takes no farther interest in the great changes of the world but as he has a paltry share in producing them: instead of opening his senses, his understanding, and his heart to the resplendent fabric of the universe, he holds a crooked mirror before his face, in which he may admire his own person and pretensions, and just glance his eye aside to see whether others are not admiring him too.'

For Hazlitt, see *Q*. 328.

138. What do you most want: wealth, fame, power or love?

Cynics were a familiar sight on the streets of ancient Greek cities. Mendicant, uncouth and shameless, these derelicts held a philosophy characterised by a rejection of civilised society and its affectations. Like animals, they were indifferent to social norms and lived in accordance with their natural inclinations. They regarded this as the path to freedom and self-sufficiency.

Diogenes of Sinope (*c.* 404-323 BCE) was one of the founders of Cynicism. Since his works are lost we only know of his ideas through the tales of what he said and did. We are told, for instance, that he freely masturbated in public whenever the need arose. We are also told of a dinner party where the guests were tossing him scraps of food and calling him a dog, to which he responded by urinating over them.

Though the term Cynic means dog-like, Diogenes was actually first inspired by a mouse, as the following passage from Claudius Aelianus's *Various Histories* recounts. The second extract is from Diogenes Laertius's *Lives of the Eminent Philosophers*.

'Diogenes was a loner. No one liked him. He was too poor to entertain guests and he was never invited anywhere. People avoided him because he was always so critical and dissatisfied with everything they said. Miserably, then, he dined alone, eating bread and leaves, for this was all that he had. But one day a mouse came scurrying along to eat his crumbs. Diogenes watched the little creature at work, and he smiled, becoming more cheerful, and said, "This mouse doesn't need any of the luxuries of the Athenians, but you, Diogenes, are upset at not dining with the Athenians." And this thought comforted him greatly.'

* * *

'Cynics believe that we should live frugally, eating food for nourishment only and wearing a single garment. Wealth and fame and high birth they despise. Some at all events are vegetarians and drink cold water only and are content with any kind of shelter or tubs, like Diogenes, who used to say that it was the privilege of the gods to need nothing and god-like humans to want but little.'

139. Do you want a revolution?

> Do you believe in the Supreme Being, Miss Goodman?
> No, sir, I do not.
> Is there any government on earth whose laws you approve?
> No, sir, for they are all against the people.
> Why don't you leave this country if you don't like its laws?
> Where shall I go? Everywhere on earth the laws are against the poor, and they tell me I cannot go to heaven, nor do I want to go there.

This exchange took place during the trial of the anarchist **Emma Goldman** (1869-1940) in 1893. Having exhorted the unemployed to take food by force, she was tried for inciting a riot. When the arresting officer offered to drop the charges if she agreed to inform on her comrades, she threw a glass of water in his face. She was sentenced to one year in prison.

This was not her only confrontation with the law. In 1916 she was jailed for distributing birth control literature. Then in 1917, during the First World War, she was sentenced to two years for conspiracy to obstruct the draft.

J. Edgar Hoover described Goldman as 'one of the most dangerous women in America'. To her mind she was simply fighting for the very thing America prides itself on: freedom.

Nevertheless, in 1919 she was stripped of her citizenship and deported.

From her essay 'Anarchism: What It Really Stands For' –

'Oscar Wilde defines a perfect personality as "one who develops under perfect conditions, who is not wounded, maimed, or in danger." A perfect personality, then, is only possible in a state of society where man is free to choose the mode of work, the conditions of work, and the freedom to work. One to whom the making of a table, the building of a house, or the tilling of the soil, is what the painting is to the artist and the discovery to the scientist – the result of inspiration, of intense longing, and deep interest in work as a creative force. That being the ideal of Anarchism, its economic arrangements must consist of voluntary productive and distributive associations, gradually developing into free communism, as the best means of producing with the least waste of human energy. Anarchism, however, also recognizes the right of the individual, or numbers of individuals, to arrange at all times for other forms of work, in harmony with their tastes and desires.

Such free display of human energy being possible only under complete individual and social freedom, Anarchism directs its forces against the third and greatest foe of all social equality; namely, the State, organized authority, or statutory law,– the dominion of human conduct.

Just as religion has fettered the human mind, and as property, or the monopoly of things, has subdued and stifled man's needs, so has the State enslaved his spirit, dictating every phase of conduct. "All government in essence," says Emerson, "is tyranny." It matters not whether it is government by divine right or majority rule. In every instance its aim is the absolute subordination of the individual...

With the arrogance and self-sufficiency of the King who could do no wrong, governments ordain, judge, condemn, and punish the most insignificant offenses, while maintaining themselves by the greatest of all offenses, the annihilation of individual liberty... The most absurd apology for authority and law is that they serve to diminish crime. Aside from the fact that the State is itself the greatest criminal, breaking every written and natural law, stealing in the form of taxes, killing in the form of war and capital punishment, it has come to an absolute standstill in coping with crime. It has failed utterly to destroy or even minimize the horrible scourge of its own creation.

Crime is naught but misdirected energy. So long as every institution of today, economic, political, social, and moral, conspires to misdirect human energy into wrong channels; so long as most people are out of place doing the things they hate to do, living a life they loathe to live, crime will be inevitable, and all the laws on the statutes can only increase, but never do away with, crime...

Anarchism aims to strip labor of its deadening, dulling aspect, of its gloom and compulsion. It aims to make work an instrument of joy, of strength, of color, of real harmony, so that the poorest sort of a man should find in work both recreation and hope.

To achieve such an arrangement of life, government, with its unjust, arbitrary, repressive measures, must be done away with. At best it has but imposed one single mode of life upon all, without regard to individual and social variations and needs. In destroying government and statutory laws, Anarchism proposes to rescue the self-respect and independence of the individual from all restraint and invasion by authority. Only in freedom can man grow to his full stature. Only in freedom will he learn to think and move, and give the very best in him. Only in freedom will he realize the true force of the social bonds which knit men together, and which are the true foundation of a normal social life.'

143. Is blind faith admirable or foolish?

> Thomas, one of the twelve, called Didymus, was not with them when Jesus came. The other disciples therefore said unto him, We have seen the Lord. But he said unto them, Except I shall see in his hands the print of the nails, and put my finger into the print of the nails, and thrust my hand into his side, I will not believe.
>
> And after eight days again his disciples were within, and Thomas with them: then came Jesus, the doors being shut, and stood in the midst, and said, Peace be unto you. Then saith he to Thomas, Reach hither thy finger, and behold my hands; and reach hither thy hand, and thrust it into my side: and be not faithless, but believing.
>
> And Thomas answered and said unto him, My Lord and my God.
>
> Jesus saith unto him, Thomas, because thou hast seen me, thou hast believed: blessed are they that have not seen, and yet have believed.

In this passage from the Gospel of John, Jesus focuses his praise on the method rather than the content of belief. He sees a difference between believing well and believing badly. In this respect, the English mathematician **W. K. Clifford** (1845-1879) was the precise reflection of Jesus, that is to say, identical but opposite. Like Jesus, Clifford thought that *how* we form our beliefs is of immense importance. However, unlike Jesus, Clifford argued that beliefs ought to be supported and fully justified; Thomas's scepticism was in fact highly commendable. Beliefs should be earned through the hard currency of evidence. To believe without seeing is akin to theft, assuming that which is not rightfully ours.

From 'The Ethics of Belief' –

'A shipowner was about to send to sea an emigrant-ship. He knew that she was old, and not over-well built at the first; that she had seen many seas and climes, and often had needed repairs. Doubts had been suggested to him that possibly she was not seaworthy. These doubts preyed upon his mind and made him unhappy; he thought that perhaps he ought to have her thoroughly overhauled and refitted, even though this should put him to great expense. Before the ship sailed, however, he succeeded in overcoming these melancholy reflections. He said to himself that she had gone safely through so many voyages and weathered so many storms that it was idle to suppose she would not come safely home from this trip also. He would put his trust in Providence, which could hardly fail to protect all these unhappy families that were leaving their fatherland to seek for better times elsewhere. He would dismiss from his mind all ungenerous suspicions about the honesty of builders and contractors. In such ways he acquired a sincere and comfortable conviction that his vessel was thoroughly safe and seaworthy; he watched her departure with a light heart, and benevolent wishes for the success of the exiles in their strange new home that was to be; and he got his insurance-money when she went down in mid-ocean and told no tales.

What shall we say of him? Surely this, that he was verily guilty of the death of those men. It is admitted that he did sincerely believe in the soundness of his ship; but the sincerity of his conviction can in no wise help him, because *he had no right to believe on such evidence as was before him*. He had acquired his belief not by honestly earning it in patient investigation, but by stifling his doubts. And although in the end he may have felt so sure about it that he could not think otherwise, yet inasmuch as he had knowingly and willingly worked himself into that frame of mind, he must be held responsible for it...

Belief, that sacred faculty which prompts the decisions of our will, and knits into harmonious working all the compacted energies of our being, is ours not for ourselves but for humanity. It is rightly used on truths which have been established by long experience and waiting toil, and which have stood in the fierce light of free and fearless questioning. Then it helps to bind men together, and to strengthen and direct their common action. It is desecrated when given to unproved and unquestioned statements, for the solace and private pleasure of the believer...

We all suffer severely enough from the maintenance and support of false beliefs and the fatally wrong actions which they lead to, and the evil born when one such belief is entertained is great and wide. But a greater and wider evil arises when the credulous character is maintained and supported, when a habit of believing for unworthy reasons is fostered and made permanent. If I steal money from any person, there may be no harm done from the mere transfer of possession; he may not feel the loss, or it may prevent him from using the money badly. But I cannot help doing this great wrong towards Man, that I make myself dishonest. What hurts society is not that it should lose its property, but that it should become a den of thieves, for then it must cease to be society. This is why we ought not to do evil, that good may come; for at any rate this great evil has come, that we have done evil and are made wicked thereby. In like manner, if I let myself believe anything on insufficient evidence, there may be no great harm done by the mere belief; it may be true after all, or I may never have occasion to exhibit it in outward acts. But I cannot help doing this great wrong towards Man, that I make myself credulous. The danger to society is not merely that it should believe wrong things, though that is great enough; but that it should become credulous, and lose the habit of testing things and inquiring into them; for then it must sink back into savagery...

To sum up: it is wrong always, everywhere, and for anyone, to believe anything upon insufficient evidence.

If a man, holding a belief which he was taught in childhood

or persuaded of afterwards, keeps down and pushes away any doubts which arise about it in his mind, purposely avoids the reading of books and the company of men that call into question or discuss it, and regards as impious those questions which cannot easily be asked without disturbing it—the life of that man is one long sin against mankind...

"But," says one, "I am a busy man; I have no time for the long course of study which would be necessary to make me in any degree a competent judge of certain questions, or even able to understand the nature of the arguments."

Then he should have no time to believe.'

144. Is the willingness to die for one's country absurd?

On a warm summer's day in 1749 **Jean-Jacques Rousseau** (1712-1778) suffered an unprecedented bout of philosophical excitement. Assailed by a rapid build-up of ideas, with pen and paper in hand he had no choice but to relieve himself beneath an oak tree.

The episode occurred while he was walking to visit his friend Denis Diderot in prison. Unable to afford a cab, he had taken a magazine to accompany him on the six mile journey from Paris to Vincennes. Reading as he walked, he came across the question for an essay competition: Has the progress of the sciences and arts contributed to the corruption or improvement of morals? As Rousseau recounts, 'The moment I read this, I seemed to behold another world, and became a different man.'

Arriving at the prison, he showed Diderot everything he had scribbled down beneath the tree. Diderot encouraged him to pursue his ideas and enter the competition, which he did, and took first prize: 'All the rest of my life and of my misfortunes followed inevitably as a result of that moment's madness.'

In the passage below from *A Discourse on Political Economy*, Rousseau, a proud though not always welcome Genevan, discusses the virtues of patriotism.

'It appears that the feeling of humanity evaporates and grows feeble in embracing all mankind, and that we cannot be affected by the calamities of Tartary or Japan, in the same manner as we are by those of European nations. It is necessary in some degree to confine and limit our interest and compassion in order to make it active. Now, as this sentiment can be useful only to those with whom we have to live, it is proper that our humanity should confine itself to our fellow-citizens, and should receive a new force because we are in the habit of seeing them, and by reason of the common interest which unites them. It is certain that the greatest miracles of virtue have been produced by patriotism: this fine and lively feeling, which gives to the force of self-love all the beauty of virtue, lends it an energy which, without disfiguring it, makes it the most heroic of all passions. This it is that produces so many immortal actions, the glory of which dazzles our feeble eyes; and so many great men, whose old-world virtues pass for fables now that patriotism is made mock of. This is not surprising; the transports of susceptible hearts appear altogether fanciful to any one who has never felt them; and the love of one's country, which is a hundred times more lively and delightful than the love of a mistress, cannot be conceived except by experiencing it. But it is easy to perceive in every heart that is warmed by it, in all the actions it inspires, a glowing and sublime ardour which does not attend the purest virtue, when separated from it. Contrast Socrates even with Cato; the one was the greater philosopher, the other more of the citizen. Athens was already ruined in the time of Socrates, and he had no other country than the world at large. Cato had the cause of his country always at heart; he lived for it alone, and could not bear to outlive it. The virtue of Socrates was that of the wisest of men; but, compared with Caesar and Pompey, Cato seems a God among mortals. Socrates instructed a few individuals, opposed the Sophists, and died for truth: but Cato defended his country, its liberty and its laws, against the conquerors of the world, and at length departed from the earth, when he had no longer a country to serve. A worthy pupil of Socrates would be the most virtuous of his contemporaries; but a worthy follower of Cato would be one of the greatest. The virtue of the former would be his happiness; the latter would seek his happiness in that of all. We should be taught by the one, and led by the other; and this alone is enough to determine which to prefer: for no people has ever been made into a nation of philosophers, but it is not impossible to make a people happy.'

For Rousseau, see *Q.* 190.

145. 'There is great joy in darkness,' wrote the Persian poet Sana'i. Do you agree?

While the Persian Wars took place over 1000 years before the life of Sana'i, between his tenebrous yearnings and the heliotropism of **Plato** (*c.* 429-347 BCE) we find a trace of the ancient conflict.

In the *Republic* Plato characterises education as the process of turning away from illusion, the transition from darkness to light, ignorance to knowledge. Though the symbolic identification of redemption with light is hardly unique ('I am the light of the world. Whoever follows me will never walk in darkness, but will have the light of life,' John 8:12), Plato goes further by describing the discomforture of leaving the subterranean gloom. When we first step out into the sunlight, our eyes are pained by the glare. Accustomed to our abiding ignorance, we resist and resent the initial strangeness of truth. But once the pain subsides and our eyes adjust, we wish to remain and are loath to return to the darkness below.

'And now, I said, let me show in a figure how far our nature is enlightened or unenlightened:—Behold! human beings living in a underground cave, which has a mouth open towards the light and reaching all along the cave; here they have been from their childhood, and have their legs and necks chained so that they cannot move, and can only see before them, being prevented by the chains from turning round their heads. Above and behind them a fire is blazing at a distance, and between the fire and the prisoners there is a raised way; and you will see, if you look, a low wall built along the way, like the screen which marionette players have in front of them, over which they show the puppets.

I see.

And do you see, I said, men passing along the wall carrying all sorts of vessels, and statues and figures of animals made of wood and stone and various materials, which appear over the wall? Some of them are talking, others silent.

You have shown me a strange image, and they are strange prisoners.

Like ourselves, I replied; and they see only their own shadows, or the shadows of one another, which the fire throws on the opposite wall of the cave?

True, he said; how could they see anything but the shadows if they were never allowed to move their heads?

And of the objects which are being carried in like manner they would only see the shadows?

Yes, he said.

And if they were able to converse with one another, would they not suppose that they were naming what was actually before them?

Very true.

And suppose further that the prison had an echo which came

from the other side, would they not be sure to fancy when one of the passers-by spoke that the voice which they heard came from the passing shadow?

No question, he replied.

To them, I said, the truth would be literally nothing but the shadows of the images.

That is certain.

And now look again, and see what will naturally follow if the prisoners are released and disabused of their error. At first, when any of them is liberated and compelled suddenly to stand up and turn his neck round and walk and look towards the light, he will suffer sharp pains; the glare will distress him, and he will be unable to see the realities of which in his former state he had seen the shadows; and then conceive some one saying to him, that what he saw before was an illusion, but that now, when he is approaching nearer to being and his eye is turned towards more real existence, he has a clearer vision,—what will be his reply? And you may further imagine that his instructor is pointing to the objects as they pass and requiring him to name them,—will he not be perplexed? Will he not fancy that the shadows which he formerly saw are truer than the objects which are now shown to him?

Far truer.

And if he is compelled to look straight at the light, will he not have a pain in his eyes which will make him turn away to take refuge in the objects of vision which he can see, and which he will conceive to be in reality clearer than the things which are now being shown to him?

True, he said.

And suppose once more, that he is reluctantly dragged up a steep and rugged ascent, and held fast until he is forced into the presence of the sun himself, is he not likely to be pained and irritated? When he approaches the light his eyes will be dazzled, and he will not be able to see anything at all of what are now called realities.

Not all in a moment, he said.

He will require to grow accustomed to the sight of the upper world. And first he will see the shadows best, next the reflections of men and other objects in the water, and then the objects themselves; then he will gaze upon the light of the moon and the stars and the spangled heaven; and he will see the sky and the stars by night better than the sun or the light of the sun by day?

Certainly.

Last of all he will be able to see the sun, and not mere reflections of him in the water, but he will see him in his own proper place, and not in another; and he will contemplate him as he is.

Certainly.

He will then proceed to argue that this is he who gives the season and the years, and is the guardian of all that is in the visible world, and in a certain way the cause of all things which he and his fellows have been accustomed to behold?

Clearly, he said, he would first see the sun and then reason about him.

And when he remembered his old habitation, and the wisdom of the cave and his fellow-prisoners, do you not suppose that he would felicitate himself on the change, and pity them?

Certainly, he would.

And if they were in the habit of conferring honours among themselves on those who were quickest to observe the passing shadows and to remark which of them went before, and which followed after, and which were together; and who were therefore best able to draw conclusions as to the future, do you think that he would care for such honours and glories, or envy the possessors of them? Would he not say with Homer, "Better to be the poor servant of a poor master," and to endure anything, rather than think as they do and live after their manner?

Yes, he said, I think that he would rather suffer anything than entertain these false notions and live in this miserable manner.

Imagine once more, I said, such an one coming suddenly out of the sun to be replaced in his old situation; would he not be certain to have his eyes full of darkness?

To be sure, he said.

And if there were a contest, and he had to compete in measuring the shadows with the prisoners who had never moved out of the cave, while his sight was still weak, and before his eyes had become steady (and the time which would be needed to acquire this new habit of sight might be very considerable), would he not be ridiculous? Men would say of him that up he went and down he came without his eyes; and that it was better not even to think of ascending; and if any one tried to loose another and lead him up to the light, let them only catch the offender, and they would put him to death.

No question, he said.

This entire allegory, I said, you may now append, dear Glaucon, to the previous argument; the prison-house is the world of sight, the light of the fire is the sun, and you will not misapprehend me if you interpret the journey upwards to be the ascent of the soul into the intellectual world according to my poor belief, which, at your desire, I have expressed—whether rightly or wrongly God knows. But, whether true or false, my opinion is that in the world of knowledge the idea of good appears last of all, and is seen only with an effort; and, when seen, is also inferred to be the universal author of all things beautiful and right, parent of light and of the lord of light in this visible world, and the immediate source of reason and truth in the intellectual; and that this is the power upon which he who would act rationally either in public or private life must have his eye fixed.

I agree, he said, as far as I am able to understand you.

Moreover, I said, you must not wonder that those who attain to this beatific vision are unwilling to descend to human affairs; for their souls are ever hastening into the upper world where they desire to dwell; which desire of theirs is very natural, if our allegory may be trusted.

Yes, very natural.

And is there anything surprising in one who passes from divine contemplations to the evil state of man, misbehaving himself in a ridiculous manner; if, while his eyes are blinking and before he has become accustomed to the surrounding darkness, he is compelled to fight in courts of law, or in other places, about the images or the shadows of images of justice, and is endeavouring to meet the conceptions of those who have never yet seen absolute justice?

Anything but surprising, he replied.

Any one who has common sense will remember that the bewilderments of the eyes are of two kinds, and arise from two causes, either from coming out of the light or from going into the light, which is true of the mind's eye, quite as much as of the bodily eye; and he who remembers this when he sees any one whose vision is perplexed and weak, will not be too ready to laugh; he will first ask whether that soul of man has come out of the brighter life, and is unable to see because unaccustomed to the dark, or having turned from darkness to the day is dazzled by excess of light. And he will count the one happy in his condition and state of being, and he will pity the other; or, if he have a mind to laugh at the soul which comes from below into the light, there will be more reason in this than in the laugh which greets him who returns from above out of the light into the cave.'

For Plato, see *Q*. 97.

146. If you knew that you were destined to repeat your life endlessly, would you live it differently?

Friedrich Nietzsche (1844-1900) described the ability to will the eternal return of all things as the highest affirmation of life. Within this eternally revolving world there is no ultimate purpose, no end-point, no transcendent beyond. The passing seconds take us closer to nothing but their own return.

To affirm the eternal return of life is to 'redeem the past and transform every "It was" into "I wanted it thus!"' It is to have attained what Nietzsche called *amor fati*, the love of one's fate: not wanting your life to be other than it is, was, or will be. This is the great embrace, to say *Yes* to the whole of life: *Yes* to pleasure. *Yes* to pain. *Yes* to the past. *Yes* to the future. *Yes* to chaos. *Yes* to death. *Yes* to war. *Yes* to the body. *Yes* to the earth. *Yes* to longing. *Yes* to hardship. *Yes* to struggle. *Yes* to beauty. *Yes* to change. *Yes* to now. *Yes* to eternity.

From *The Gay Science* –

'What if some day or night a demon were to creep into your loneliest loneliness and say to you: "This life as you now live it, and have lived it, you will have to live once again and innumerable times again; and there will be nothing new in it, but every pain and every joy and every thought and sigh and everything unspeakably small or great in your life must return to you, all in the same series and sequence – even this spider and this moonlight among the trees, and even this moment and I myself. The eternal hourglass of existence will ever be turned once more, and you with it, speck of dust!" Would you not throw yourself down and gnash your teeth and curse the demon who spoke thus? Or have you once experienced a tremendous moment when you would have answered him: "You are a god, and never did I hear anything so divine!" If this thought acquired power over you as you are, it would transform you, and possibly crush you; the question with regard to all and everything, "Do you want this and innumerable times again?" would lie as the heaviest burden on your actions. Or how would you have to become favourably inclined to yourself and to life in order to long for nothing more ardently than for this eternal confirmation and seal?'

For Nietzsche, see *Qs*. 44 and 295.

147. Do you believe in salvation?

D. H. Lawrence (1885-1930) lived impecuniously, nomadically, intensely and rather briefly.

From *Studies in Classical American Literature* –

'The Open Road. The great home of the Soul is the open road. Not heaven, not paradise. Nor "above". Not even "within". The soul is neither "above" nor "within". It is a wayfarer down the open road.

Not by meditating. Not by fasting. Not by exploring heaven after heaven, inwardly, in the manner of the great mystics. Not by exaltation. Not by ecstasy. Not by any of those ways does the soul come into her own.

Only by taking the open road.

Not through charity. Not through sacrifice. Not even through love. Not through good works. Not through these does the soul accomplish herself.

Only through the journey down the open road.

The journey itself, down the open road. Exposed to full contact. On two slow feet. Meeting whatever comes down the open road. In company with those that drift in the same measure along the same way. Towards no goal. Always the open road.

Having no known direction even. Only the soul remaining true to herself in her going.

Meeting all the other wayfarers along the road. And how? How meet them, and how pass? With sympathy, says Whitman. Sympathy. He does not say love. He says sympathy. Feeling with. Feel with them as they feel with themselves. Catching the vibration of their soul and flesh as we pass.

It is a new great doctrine. A doctrine of life. A new great morality. A morality of actual living, not of salvation. Europe has never got beyond the morality of salvation. America to this day is deathly sick with saviourism. But Whitman, the greatest and the first and the only American teacher, was no Saviour. His morality was no morality of salvation. His was a morality of the soul living her life, not saving herself. Accepting the contact with other souls along the open way, as they lived their lives. Never trying to save them. The soul living her life along the incarnate mystery of the open road.

This was Whitman. And the true rhythm of the American continent speaking out in him. He is the first white aboriginal.

"In my Father's house are many mansions."

"No," said Whitman. "Keep out of mansions. A mansion may be heaven on earth, but you might as well be dead. Strictly avoid mansions. The soul is herself when she is going on foot down the open road."'

For Lawrence, see *Q*. 330.

149. Does perfection exist?

Giorgio Vasari despised Gothic architecture. He described it as 'monstrous and barbarous, and lacking everything that can be called order'. The English art critic **John Ruskin** (1819-1900) entirely agreed with Vasari's description, but these supposed vices he regarded as great virtues. His ire was rather directed towards the purity and order of classical architecture, which he thought 'devoid of all life... base, unnatural, unfruitful, unenjoyable, and impious'. The glory of the Gothic is the glory of freedom, and the glory of freedom is the aureole of imperfection. Where builders and artisans are free to express their creativity, imperfection is inevitable. The uniformity and orderliness of classical architecture stifles the joy of creation. It turns architects into plagiarists and workers into slaves.

From *The Stones of Venice* –

'Men were not intended to work with the accuracy of tools, to be precise and perfect in all their actions. If you will have that precision out of them, and make their fingers measure degrees like cog-wheels, and their strike curves like compasses, you must unhumanise them. All the energy of their spirits must be given to make cogs and compasses of themselves. All their attention and strength must go to the accomplishment of the mean act. The eye of the soul must be bent upon the finger-point, and the soul's force must fill all the invisible nerves that guide it, ten hours a day, that it may not err from its steely precision, and so soul and sight be worn away, and the whole human being be lost at last—a heap of sawdust, so far as its intellectual work in this world is concerned; saved only by its Heart, which cannot go into the form of cogs and compasses, but expands, after the ten hours are over, into fireside humanity. On the other hand, if you will make a man of the working creature, you cannot make a tool. Let him but begin to imagine, to think, to try to anything worth doing; and the engine-turned precision is lost at once. Out come all his roughness, all his dullness, all his incapability; shame upon shame, failure upon failure, pause after pause: but out comes the whole majesty of him also…

[G]o forth again and gaze upon the old cathedral front, where you have smiled so often at the fantastic ignorance of the old sculptors: examine once more those ugly goblins, and formless monsters, and stern statues, anatomiless and rigid; but do not mock at them, for they are signs of the life and liberty of every workman who struck the stone; a freedom of thought, and rank in scale of being, such as no laws, no charters, no charities can secure…

[I]mperfection is in some sort essential to all that we know of life. It is the sign of life in a mortal body, that is to say, a state of progress and change. Nothing that lives is, or can be, rigidly perfect; part of it is decaying, part nascent. The foxglove blossom,– a third part bud, a third part past, a third part in full bloom,– is a type of the life of this world. And in all things that live there are certain irregularities and deficiencies which are not only signs of life, but sources of beauty. No human face is exactly the same in its lines on each side, no leaf perfect in its lobe, no branch in its symmetry. All admit irregularity as they imply change; and to banish imperfection is to destroy expression, to check exertion, to paralyse vitality. All things are literally better, lovelier, and more beloved for the imperfections which have been divinely appointed, that the law of human life may be Effort, and the law of human judgment, Mercy.'

For Ruskin, see *Q*. 371.

152. Can one master life?

> The word 'master' originates from *magis*, which is Latin for 'more'. Mastering life, then, may require becoming more than life. But is this possible? Is it conceivable?
>
> For **Zhuangzi** (*c.* 396-286 BCE), it seems, life's project was not to become more but less, empty rather than whole.

'Suppose a boat is crossing a river, and another empty boat is about to collide with it. Even an irritable man would not lose his temper. But supposing there was someone in the second boat. Then the occupant of the first would shout to him to keep clear. And if the other did not hear the first time, nor even when called to three times, bad language would inevitably follow. In the first case there was no anger, in the second there was; because in the first case the boat was empty, and in the second it was occupied. And so it is with man. If he could only roam empty through life, who would be able to injure him?'

For Zhuangzi, see *Q*. 6.

160. Is anyone in a position to tell you how you should live your life?

The early Muslim scholar al-Tabari described an alleged episode in the formation of the Qur'an in which Muhammad, under the influence of Satan, made a proclamation recognising the divine status of three Meccan goddesses. He was subsequently chided by the angel Gabriel and the so-called Satanic verses were repealed.

Had Allah unwisely elected **Ralph Waldo Emerson** (1803-1882) as his earthly medium, this sequence of events would have ended quite differently. Gabriel would have been roundly shunned and the verses would have certainly remained.

This is because Emerson believed that we should trust our own natures, experiences and inclinations above all else, even if, as he argues below, we are under the influence of the Devil. Better to defy God than betray ourselves.

From 'Self-Reliance' –

'Whoso would be a man must be a nonconformist. He who would gather immortal palms must not be hindered by the name of goodness, but must explore if it be goodness. Nothing is at last sacred but the integrity of your own mind. Absolve you to yourself, and you shall have the suffrage of the world. I remember an answer which when quite young I was prompted to make to a valued adviser, who was wont to importune me with the dear old doctrines of the church. On my saying, What have I to do with the sacredness of traditions, if I live wholly from within? my friend suggested, — "But these impulses may be from below, not from above." I replied, "They do not seem to me to be such; but if I am the Devil's child, I will live then from the Devil." No law can be sacred to me but that of my nature. Good and bad are but names very readily transferable to that or this; the only right is what is after my constitution, the only wrong what is against it. A man is to carry himself in the presence of all opposition, as if every thing were titular and ephemeral but he. I am ashamed to think how easily we capitulate to badges and names, to large societies and dead institutions... Man is timid and apologetic; he is no longer upright; he dares not say "I think," "I am," but quotes some saint or sage.'

For Emerson, see *Q*. 39.

162. Can intelligence ever be excessive?

Thomas De Quincey (1785-1859) did not fit comfortably into academic institutions. At the age of 16 he ran away from Manchester Grammar School to the 'boundless ocean of London', preferring the company of prostitutes and the bellyaches of penury to the 'slavish routine of study amongst books grim with dust'. Later, without taking his degree, he fled Oxford, a city so void of spirited conversation he effectively became mute.

De Quincey's discomfort was possibly and in part attributable to the tendency of such institutions to indulge the lower faculties of the mind. Like Henri Bergson (see *Q*. 265), who believed that the intellect was liable to interfere with the insights of intuition, De Quincey thought that the 'understanding' blinds us to our actual experience of the world. Below he cites the example of perspective. Another apparent example would be the gap between earth and sky found in children's drawings. Knowing that the sky is overhead the understanding demands a space and thereby overrides what we actually see: the sky meeting the horizon.

From 'On the Knocking at the Gate in Macbeth' –

'Here I pause for one moment, to exhort the reader never to pay any attention to his understanding when it stands in opposition to any other faculty of his mind. The mere understanding, however useful and indispensable, is the meanest faculty in the human mind, and the most to be distrusted; and yet the great majority of people trust to nothing else; which may do for ordinary life, but not for philosophical purposes. Of this out of ten thousand instances that I might produce, I will cite one. Ask of any person whatsoever, who is not previously prepared for the demand by a knowledge of perspective, to draw in the rudest way the commonest appearance which depends upon the laws of that science; as for instance, to represent the effect of two walls standing at right angles to each other, or the appearance of the houses on each side of a street, as seen by a person looking down the street from one extremity. Now in all cases, unless the person has happened to observe in pictures how it is that artists produce these effects, he will be utterly unable to make the smallest approximation to it. Yet why? For he has actually seen the effect every day of his life. The reason is that he allows his understanding to overrule his eyes. His understanding, which includes no intuitive knowledge of the laws of vision, can furnish him with no reason why a line which is known and can be proved to be a horizontal line, should not appear a horizontal line; a line that made any angle with the perpendicular less than a right angle, would seem to him to indicate that his houses were all tumbling down together. Accordingly he makes the line of his houses a horizontal line, and fails of course to produce the effect demanded. Here then is one instance out of many, in which not only the understanding is allowed to overrule the eyes, but where the understanding is positively allowed to obliterate the eyes as it were, for not only does the man believe the evidence of his understanding in opposition to that of his eyes, but, (what is monstrous!) the idiot is not aware that his eyes ever gave such evidence. He does not know that he has seen (and therefore quoad his consciousness has not seen) that which he has seen every day of his life.'

For De Quincey, see *Q*. 315.

164. Is effort necessary for a good life?

There exists an alternative world in which the term 'Herculean' is ubiquitous in advertising. *Herculean Holidays. Herculean Hammocks. Herculean Hot Tubs.* This is a world in which the valiant hero did not become an emblem of strength and virility but instead became a byword for idleness. As **Prodicus** (*c.* 460-395 BCE) relates, this is a world he could so easily have chosen.

We are told that while a youth Hercules (or Heracles, as the Greeks called him) was contemplating how he should live his life when he was confronted by two women, Virtue and Vice, who presented him with two paths through life, one of effort and the other of ease.

The story was recorded by Xenophon in his *Memorabilia* –

'When Heracles was emerging from boyhood into the bloom of youth, having reached that season in which the young man, now standing upon the verge of independence, shows plainly whether he will enter upon the path of virtue or of vice, he went forth into a quiet place, and sat debating with himself which of those two paths he should pursue; and as he there sat musing, there appeared to him two women of great stature which drew nigh to him…

Now when these two had drawn near to Heracles, she who was first named advanced at an even pace towards him, but the other, in her eagerness to outstrip her, ran forward to the youth, exclaiming, "I see you, Heracles, in doubt and difficulty what path of life to choose; make me your friend, and I will lead you to the pleasantest road and easiest. This I promise you: you shall taste all of life's sweets and escape all bitters. In the first place, you shall not trouble your brain with war or business; other topics shall engage your mind; your only speculation, what meat or drink you shall find agreeable to your palate; what delight of ear or eye; what pleasure of smell or touch; what darling lover's intercourse shall most enrapture you; how you shall pillow your limbs in softest slumber; how cull each individual pleasure without alloy of pain; and if ever the suspicion steal upon you that the stream of joys will one day dwindle, trust me I will not lead you where you shall replenish the store by toil of body and trouble of soul. No! others shall labour, but you shall reap the fruit of their labours; you shall withhold your hand from nought which shall bring you gain. For to all my followers I give authority and power to help themselves freely from every side."

Heracles hearing these words made answer: "What, O lady, is the name you bear?" To which she: "Know that my friends call be Happiness, but they that hate me have their own nicknames for me, Vice and Naughtiness."

But just then the other of those fair women approached and spoke: "Heracles… I will not cheat you with preludings of pleasure, but I will relate to you the things that are according to the ordinances of God in very truth. Know then that among things that are lovely and of good report, not one have the gods bestowed upon mortal men apart from toil and pains. Would you obtain the favour of the gods, then must you pay these same gods service; would you be loved by your friends, you must benefit these friends; do you desire to be honoured by the state, you must give the state your aid; do you claim admiration for your virtue from all Hellas, you must strive to do some good to Hellas; do you wish earth to yield her fruits to you abundantly, to earth must you pay your court; do you seek to amass riches from your flocks and herds, on them must you bestow your labour; or is it your ambition to be potent as a warrior, able to save your friends and to subdue your foes, then must you learn the arts of war from those who have the knowledge, and practise their application in the field when learned; or would you e'en be powerful of limb and body, then must you habituate limbs and body to obey the mind, and exercise yourself with toil and sweat."

At this point, (as Prodicus relates) Vice broke in exclaiming: "See you, Heracles, how hard and long the road is by which yonder woman would escort you to her festal joys. But I will guide you by a short and easy road to happiness."

Then spoke Virtue: "Nay, wretched one, what good thing hast thou? or what sweet thing art thou acquainted with—that wilt stir neither hand nor foot to gain it? Thou, that mayest not even await the desire of pleasure, but, or ever that desire springs up, art already satiated; eating before thou hungerest, and drinking before thou thirsteth; who to eke out an appetite must invent an army of cooks and confectioners; and to whet thy thirst must lay down costliest wines, and run up and down in search of ice in summer-time; to help thy slumbers soft coverlets suffice not, but couches and feather-beds must be prepared thee and rockers to rock thee to rest; since desire for sleep in thy case springs not from toil but from vacuity and nothing in the world to do."'

165. Do some people understand life better than others?

For two years **Henry David Thoreau** (1817-1862) lived a life of self-sufficiency and solitude. Though he was not far from society – two miles from the nearest town – he was very much outside of it. In a small hut by the edge of a lake, amid the fellowship of nature, deaf to the strictures of the ticking clock, he found a slower pace, a contended indolence, and delighted in the simplicity of his feral life.

Yet, despite the pleasures of this life, he did not wish for it to become an example to others: 'I desire that there may be as many different persons in the world as possible; but I would have each one be very careful to find out and pursue his own way, and not his father's or his mother's or his neighbor's instead.'

From *Walden* –

'It is never too late to give up our prejudices. No way of thinking or doing, however ancient, can be trusted without proof. What everybody echoes or in silence passes by as true to-day may turn out to be falsehood to-morrow, mere smoke of opinion, which some had trusted for a cloud that would sprinkle fertilizing rain on their fields. What old people say you cannot do, you try and find that you can. Old deeds for old people, and new deeds for new. Old people did not know enough once, perchance, to fetch fresh fuel to keep the fire a-going; new people put a little dry wood under a pot, and are whirled round the globe with the speed of birds, in a way to kill old people, as the phrase is. Age is no better, hardly so well, qualified for an instructor as youth, for it has not profited so much as it has lost. One may almost doubt if the wisest man has learned anything of absolute value by living. Practically, the old have no very important advice to give the young, their own experience has been so partial, and their lives have been such miserable failures, for private reasons, as they must believe; and it may be that they have some faith left which belies that experience, and they are only less young than they were. I have lived some thirty years on this planet, and I have yet to hear the first syllable of valuable or even earnest advice from my seniors. They have told me nothing, and probably cannot tell me anything to the purpose. Here is life, an experiment to a great extent untried by me; but it does not avail me that they have tried it. If I have any experience which I think valuable, I am sure to reflect that this my Mentors said nothing about.'

For Thoreau's friend and fellow New Englander, see *Qs.* 39 and 160.

168. Can bad people have good lives?

Anthony Ashley Cooper, 3rd Earl of Shaftesbury (1671-1713) was a major influence on the philosophy of Francis Hutcheson (see *Q*. 99). Hutcheson took from Shaftesbury the view that human nature is sociable. He believed that we are naturally drawn towards the pleasures of friendship and kindness. A virtuous life, one that honours these natural affections, is a life of happiness. A life of envy, selfishness and spite, however, is one of despair. As Shaftesbury wrote, 'To be wicked or vicious is to be miserable and unhappy'.

(Before proceeding, be warned: in the considered opinion of the 18th century rhetorician Hugh Blair, Shaftesbury is 'fond, to excess, of the pomp and parade and language' and his 'superfluity of words is disgustful to every reader of correct taste'.)

From *An Inquiry Concerning Virtue, or Merit* –

'To love, and to be kind; to have social or natural affection, complacency, and good-will, is to feel immediate satisfaction and genuine content. 'Tis in itself original joy, depending on no preceding pain or uneasiness, and producing nothing beside satisfaction merely. On the other side, animosity, hatred, and bitterness, is original misery and torment, producing no other pleasure or satisfaction than as the unnatural desire is for the instant satisfied by something which appeases it. How strong soever this pleasure therefore may appear, it only the more implies the misery of that state which produces it...

What enjoyment or rest is there for one who is not conscious of the merited affection or love, but, on the contrary, of the ill-will and hatred of every human soul? Wherever such a creature turns himself, whichever way he cast his eye, everything around must appear ghastly and horrid; everything hostile and, as it were, bent against a private and single being, who is thus divided from everything, and at defiance and war with the rest of Nature.

'Tis thus, at last, that a mind becomes a wilderness, where all is laid waste, everything fair and goodly removed, and nothing extant beside what is savage and deformed. Now if banishment from one's country, removal to a foreign place, or anything which looks like solitude or desertion, be so heavy to endure, what must it be to feel this inward banishment, this real estrangement from human commerce, and to be after this manner in a desert, and in the horridest of solitudes even when in the midst of society? What must it be to live in this disagreement with everything, this irreconcilableness and opposition to the order and government of the universe? Hence it appears that the greatest of miseries accompanies that state which is consequent to the loss of natural affection; and that to have those horrid, monstrous, and unnatural affections is to be miserable in the highest degree...

Thus the wisdom of what rules, and is first and chief in Nature, has made it to be according to the private interest and good of everyone to work towards the general good, which if a creature ceases to promote, he is actually so far wanting to himself, and ceases to promote his own happiness and welfare. He is on this account directly his own enemy, nor can he any otherwise be good or useful to himself than as he continues good to society, and to that whole of which he is himself a part. So that virtue, which of all excellencies and beauties is the chief and most amiable, that which is the prop and ornament of human affairs, which upholds communities, maintains union, friendship, and correspondence amongst men, that by which countries, as well as private families, flourish and are happy, and for want of which everything comely, conspicuous, great, and worthy, must perish and go to ruin – that single quality, thus beneficial to all society, and to mankind in general, is found equally a happiness and good to each creature in particular, and is that by which alone man can be happy, and without which he must be miserable.'

169. Would a life without other people be worth living?

Richard Rorty once wrote, 'Nothing politically useful happens until people begin saying things never said before.' Just as important, however, is that these things are said well, with the eloquence to inspire. Indeed, the American War of Independence was in no small measure impelled by the force of **Thomas Paine's** (1737-1809) prose. His pamphlet *Common Sense* turned American independence from a prospect regarded with widespread circumspection to one embraced by a galvanised populace. 'We have it in our power to begin the world over again,' he declared, and his confidence proved infectious.

Of course, with the power to attract comes an equal and opposite power to repel, and given the range of Paine's targets – monarchy, aristocracy, poverty, slavery, capital punishment and religion – he was ultimately left with few allies. His funeral was a desolate affair.

From *Rights of Man* –

'Great part of that order which reigns among mankind is not the effect of government. It has its origin in the principles of society and the natural constitution of man. It existed prior to government, and would if the formality of government was abolished. The mutual dependence and reciprocal interest which man has upon man, and all the parts of a civilised community with each other, create that great chain of connexion which holds it together. The landholder, the farmer, the manufacturer, the merchant, the tradesman, and every occupation, prospers by the aid which each receives from the other, and from the whole. Common interest regulates their concerns, and forms their law...

To understand the nature and quantity of government proper for man, it is necessary to attend to this character. As Nature created him for social life, she fitted him for the situation she intended. In all cases she made his natural wants greater than his individual powers. No one man is capable, without the aid of society, of supplying his own wants; and those wants, acting upon every individual, impel the whole of them into society, as naturally as gravitation acts to a centre.

But she has gone further. She has not only forced man into a society, by a diversity of wants, which the reciprocal aid of each other can supply, but she has implanted in him a system of social affections, which, though not necessary to his existence, are essential to his happiness. There is no period in life when this love for society ceases to act. It begins and ends with our being.'

171. Should we follow laws we don't agree with?

Marcus Tullius Cicero (106-43 BCE) was a Roman statesman and orator who became embroiled in the power struggles that followed Julius Caesar's assassination and was ultimately decapitated. Such was the rancour of the time that one of his enemies remained unsatisfied by his death and proceeded to jab hairpins into the decaying tongue.

In *De re publica* Cicero wrote that our duty is not to the state's laws but to natural law. If the former conflicts with the latter, if we are ordered to act against our nature, then we should embrace criminality. The legitimacy of state law is contingent on its correlation with nature.

'There is in fact a true law – namely, right reason – which is in accordance with nature, applies to all men, and is unchangeable and eternal. By its commands this law summons men to the performance of their duties; by its prohibitions it restrains them from doing wrong. Its commands and prohibitions always influence good men, but are without effect upon the bad. To invalidate this law by human legislation is never morally right, nor is it permissible ever to restrict its operations, and to annul it wholly is impossible. Neither the senate nor the people can absolve us from our obligation to obey this law, and it requires no Sextus Aelius to expound and interpret it. It will not lay down one rule at Rome and another at Athens, nor will be one rule today and another tomorrow. But there will be one law, eternal and unchangeable, binding at all times upon all peoples; and there will be, as it were, one common master and ruler of men, namely God, who is the author this law, its interpreter and its sponsor. The man who will not obey it will abandon his better self, and, in treating his human nature with contempt, will by this very fact pay the heaviest penalties, even if he escapes all conventional punishments.'

178. We are sometimes punished for mistreating others. Should we ever be punished for mistreating ourselves?

Though **John Stuart Mill's** (1806-1873) *On Liberty* is a pantheonic work of liberalism, though he boldly proclaims that the individual is sovereign, and though his answer to the present question would be a resounding no, he would nevertheless be quick to qualify that answer.

Yes, the individual is sovereign, but according to Mill not everyone is an individual. Individuals are only those in the 'maturity of their faculties'. Children are not individuals. 'Barbarians' are not individuals. Those 'in a state to require being taken care of by others' are not individuals. For these groups, unable to engage in 'free and equal discussion', coercion is legitimate. Indeed, despite his liberalism, Mill, a dutiful employee of the East India Company, was also an imperialist. He believed that certain populations – Asian, African, Irish – require 'good stout despotism'.

'The object of this Essay is to assert one very simple principle, as entitled to govern absolutely the dealings of society with the individual in the way of compulsion and control, whether the means used be physical force in the form of legal penalties, or the moral coercion of public opinion. That principle is, that the sole end for which mankind are warranted, individually or collectively, in interfering with the liberty of action of any of their number, is self-protection. That the only purpose for which power can be rightfully exercised over any member of a civilised community, against his will, is to prevent harm to others. His own good, either physical or moral, is not a sufficient warrant. He cannot rightfully be compelled to do or forbear because it will be better for him to do so, because it will make him happier, because, in the opinions of others, to do so would be wise, or even right. These are good reasons for remonstrating with him, or reasoning with him, or persuading him, or entreating him, but not for compelling him, or visiting him with any evil in case he do otherwise. To justify that, the conduct from which it is desired to deter him must be calculated to produce evil to some one else. The only part of the conduct of any one, for which he is amenable to society, is that which concerns others. In the part which merely concerns himself, his independence is, of right, absolute. Over himself, over his own body and mind, the individual is sovereign.'

For Mill, see *Q*. 10.

185. Is humanity flawed?

Despite stints in prison and exile, on the whole **Voltaire** (1694-1778) had a lot of fun.

The entry for 'Wicked' from his *Philosophical Dictionary* –

'We are told that human nature is essentially perverse; that man is born a child of the devil, and wicked. Nothing can be more injudicious; for thou, my friend, who preachest to me that all the world is born perverse, warnest me that thou art born such also, and that I must mistrust thee as I would a fox or a crocodile. Oh, no! sayest thou; I am regenerated; I am neither a heretic nor an infidel; you may trust in me. But the rest of mankind, which are either heretic, or what thou callest infidel, will be an assemblage of monsters, and every time that thou speakest to a Lutheran or a Turk, thou mayest be sure that they will rob and murder thee, for they are children of the devil, they are born wicked; the one is not regenerated, the other is degenerated. It would be much more reasonable, much more noble, to say to men: "You are all born good; see how dreadful it is to corrupt the purity of your being. All mankind should be dealt with as are all men individually." If a canon leads a scandalous life, we say to him: "Is it possible that you would dishonour the dignity of canon?" We remind a lawyer that he has the honour of being a counsellor to the king, and that he should set an example. We say to a soldier to encourage him: "Remember that thou art of the regiment of Champagne." We should say to every individual: "Remember thy dignity as a man." …

Man is not born wicked; he becomes so, as he becomes sick. Physicians present themselves and say to him: "You are born sick." It is very certain these doctors, whatever they may say or do, will not cure him, if the malady is inherent in his nature; besides, these logicians are often very ailing themselves.

Assemble all the children of the universe; you will see in them only innocence, mildness, and fear; if they were born wicked, mischievous, and cruel, they would show some signs of it, as little serpents try to bite, and little tigers to tear. But nature not having given to men more offensive arms than to pigeons and rabbits, she cannot have given them an instinct leading them to destroy...

If men were essentially wicked—if they were all born submissive to a being as mischievous as unfortunate, who, to revenge himself for his punishment, inspired them with all his passions—we should every morning see husbands assassinated by their wives, and fathers by their children; as at break of day we see fowls strangled by a weasel who comes to suck their blood...

There is, therefore, infinitely less wickedness on the earth than we are told and believe there is. There is still too much, no doubt; we see misfortunes and horrible crimes; but the pleasure of complaining of and exaggerating them is so great, that at the least scratch we say that the earth flows with blood. Have you been deceived?—all men are perjured. A melancholy mind which has suffered injustice, sees the earth covered with damned people: as a young rake, supping with his lady, on coming from the opera, imagines that there are no unfortunates.'

187. Are humans fundamentally barbaric?

Sigmund Freud (1856-1939) believed that life is a war between the forces of growth and decomposition. We are all possessed of two basic conflicting instincts: the life instinct (Eros) and the death instinct. The life instinct drives us towards the renewal and preservation of life, while the death instinct draws us towards the annihilation and stasis of death. Within the alchemy of masochism, where pain becomes pleasure, we find the instincts entwined. This union is also apparent in our libidinal longing for violence. Here the death instinct, alloyed with Eros, is externalised and inflicted on others.

From *Civilization and Its Discontents* –

'Human beings are not gentle, friendly creatures wishing for love, who simply defend themselves if they are attacked, but that a powerful measure of desire for aggression has to be reckoned as part of their instinctual endowment. The result is that their neighbour is to them not only a possible helper or sexual object, but also a temptation to them to gratify their aggressiveness on him, to exploit his capacity for work without recompense, to use him sexually without his consent, to seize his possessions, to humiliate him, to cause him pain, to torture and to kill him. *Homo homini lupus* [Man is a wolf to man]. Who has the courage to dispute it in the face of all the evidence in his own life and in history? This aggressive cruelty usually lies in wait for some provocation, or else it steps into the service of some other purpose, the aim of which might as well have been achieved by milder measures. In circumstances that favour it, when those forces in the mind which ordinarily inhibit it cease to operate, it also manifests itself spontaneously and reveals men as savage beasts to whom the thought of sparing their own kind is alien. Anyone who calls to mind the atrocities of the early migrations, of the invasion by the Huns or by the so-called Mongols under Genghis Khan and Tamerlane, of the sack of Jerusalem by the pious Crusaders, even indeed the horrors of the Great War, will have to bow his head humbly before the truth of this view of man.'

For Freud, see *Q*. 57.

188. Are you more dignified than a pig?

Pyrrho (*c.* 365-275 BCE) was the founder of the Hellenistic school of Scepticism. He eschewed dogma, conviction and certainty, believing instead that peace of mind, or ataraxy, resided in a total suspension of judgment. This wasn't merely academic. He practised what he preached, carrying on as if he knew nothing of the dangers of precipices or oncoming traffic. Fortunately, he was blessed with attentive friends who kept a watchful eye on him.

In *Lives of the Eminent Philosophers,* Diogenes Laertius records this brief anecdote –

'When his fellow passengers on board a ship were all unnerved by a storm, he kept calm and confident, pointing to a little pig in the ship that went on eating, and telling that such was the unperturbed state in which the wise man should keep himself.'

For a fellow Sceptic, see *Q.* 349.

189. Are you more civilised than a rat?

In book 10 of Homer's *Odyssey,* Odysseus's crewmen are drugged and turned into swine by the enchantress Circe. According to the original poem Odysseus managed to have the spell reversed, but in **Plutarch's** (*c.* 46-120 CE) reimagining Odysseus is shocked to learn that his crewmen wish to remain in their bestial state.

Here, from a dialogue entitled 'Gryllus', the eponymous crewman attempts to justify his decision.

'Wild beasts are guileless and artless in their struggles, whether against one another or against you, and conduct their battles with unmistakably naked courage under the impulse of genuine valour. No edict summons them, nor do they fear a writ of desertion. No, it is their nature to flee subjection; with a stout heart they maintain an indomitable spirit to the very end. Nor are they conquered even when physically overpowered; they never give up in their hearts, even while perishing in the fray. In many cases, when beasts are dying, their valour withdraws together with the fighting spirit to some point where it is concentrated in one member and resists the slayer with convulsive movements and fierce anger until, like a fire, it is completely extinguished and departs.

Beasts never beg or sue for pity or acknowledge defeat: lion is never slave to lion, or horse to horse through cowardice, as man is to man when he unprotestingly accepts the name whose root is cowardice. And when men have subdued beasts by snares and tricks, such of them as are full grown refuse food and endure the pangs of thirst until they induce and embrace death in place of slavery...

These facts make it perfectly obvious that bravery is an innate characteristic of beasts, while in human beings an independent spirit is actually contrary to nature. When you face toils and dangers, you do so not because you are courageous, but because you are more afraid of some alternative. For just as that one of your companions who is the first to board ship stands up to the light oar, not because he thinks nothing of it, but because he fears and shuns the heavier one; just so he who accepts the lash to escape the sword, or meets a foe in battle rather than be tortured or killed, does so not from courage to face the one situation, but from fear of the other. So it is clear that all your courage is merely the cowardice of prudence and all your valour merely fear that has the good sense to escape one course by taking another. And, to sum up, if you think that you are better in courage than beasts, why do your poets call the doughtiest fighters "wolf-minded" and "lion-hearted" and "like a boar in valour," though no poet ever called a lion "man-hearted" or a boar "like a man in valour"? ...

Certainly there was a time when I myself, no less than you now, was dazzled by gold and held it to be an incomparable possession; so likewise I was caught by the lure of silver and ivory and the man who had most property of this sort seemed to me to be a blissful favourite of the gods, whether he was a Phrygian or a Carian, one more villainous than Dolon or more unfortunate than Priam. In that situation, constantly activated by these desires, I reaped no joy or pleasure from the other things of life, which I had sufficiently and to spare. I grumbled at my life, finding myself destitute of the most important things and a loser in the lottery of fortune. This is the reason why, as I recall, when I saw you once in Crete tricked out in holiday attire, it was not your intellect or your virtue that I envied, but the softness of the elegantly woven garment and the beautiful wool of your purple cloak that I admired and gaped at (the clasp, I believe, was of gold and had some frivolity worked on it in exquisitely fine intaglio). I followed you about as enchanted as a woman. But now I am rid and purified of all those empty illusions. I have no eyes for gold and silver and can pass them by just like any common stone; and as for your fine robes and tapestries, I swear there's nothing sweeter for me to rest in when I'm full than deep, soft mud. None, then, of such adventitious desires has a place in our souls; our life for the most part is controlled by the essential desires and pleasures.'

For Plutarch, see Q. 247.

190. Can one be too civilised?

Jean-Jacques Rousseau (1712-1778) imagined that without society and within the state of nature, human beings are solitary, peaceful, and often asleep. In this pre-civilised condition our only fears are of pain and hunger. We are simple mute creatures who instinctively feel pity for the suffering of others. Civilisation, alas, corrupts our savage grace.

We are given to two types of self love: *amour de soi* and *amour-propre*. The first is a self-absorbed concern for our own well-being. The second is a restless need to be esteemed, even envied. Within civilisation, among the hordes of fellow citizens, *amour-propre* dominates, and its effects are deleterious. We become aggressive, spiteful and competitive, and this in turn produces material inequalities, which, under the veneer of justice and social order, we then enshrine in law.

Civilisation, in short, is the exchange of noble self-sufficiency for the servile and insatiable longing to be admired.

From *Discourse on the Origin of Inequality* –

'Like the statue of Glaucus, which was so disfigured by time, seas and tempests, that it looked more like a wild beast than a god, the human soul, altered in society by a thousand causes perpetually recurring, by the acquisition of a multitude of truths and errors, by mutations taking place in the constitution of the body, and by the continual jarring of the passions, has, so to speak, changed in appearance, so as to be hardly recognisable. Instead of a being, acting constantly from fixed and invariable principles, instead of that celestial and majestic simplicity, impressed on it by its divine Author, we find in it only the frightful contrast of passion mistaking itself for reason, and of understanding grown delirious...

As the bonds of servitude are formed merely by the mutual dependence of men on one another and the reciprocal needs that unite them, it is impossible to make any man a slave, unless he be first reduced to a situation in which he cannot do without the help of others: and, since such a situation does not exist in a state of nature, everyone is there his own master, and the law of the strongest is of no effect...

Behold man, who was formerly free and independent, in consequence of a multiplicity of new wants, brought into subjection, as it were, to all nature, and particularly to his fellow men; each becomes in some degree a slave, even in becoming the master of others: if rich, they stood in need of the services of others; if poor, of their aid...

The savage man breathes only peace and freedom; he desire only to live and stay idle, even the *ataraxia* of the Stoic falls far short of his profound indifference to every other object. Civilised man, on the other hand, is always moving, sweating, toiling and racking his brains to find still more laborious occupations: he goes on in drudgery to his last moment, and even seeks death to put himself in a position to live, or renounces life to acquire immortality. He pays his court to men in power, whom he hates, and to the wealthy, whom he despises; he stops at nothing to have the honour of serving them; he is not ashamed to value himself on his own meanness and their protection; and, proud of his slavery, he speaks with disdain of those, who have not the honour of sharing it. What a sight would the perplexing and envied labours of a European minister of State present to the eyes of a Caribbean! How many cruel deaths would not this indolent savage prefer to the horrors of such a life, which is seldom even sweetened by the pleasure of doing good! But, for him to see into the motives of all this solicitude, the words *power* and *reputation*, would have to bear some meaning in his mind; he would have to know that there are men who set a value on the opinion of the rest of the world; who can be made happy and satisfied with themselves rather on the testimony of other people than on their own. In reality, the source of all these differences is that the savage lives within himself, while social man lives constantly outside himself, and only knows how to live in the opinion of others, so that he seems to receive the consciousness of his own existence merely from the judgment of others concerning him.'

For Rousseau, see Q. 144.

191. Is it possible to have dignified sex?

St Augustine (354-430) speculated that prior to the Fall Adam possessed total mastery over his erections. He could induce and reduce them at will. (Augustine was assured of this possibility because he knew a man who could sweat on command.) Shortly after eating from the Tree of Knowledge, however, he was met with a rude awakening; self-control had abandoned him. Embarrassed by his sudden powerlessness, he tried to hide it beneath a fig leaf, which only served to make his transgression all the more obvious.

Augustine's conjectures about prelapsarian life are intended to illuminate the sinful nature of lust. The evidence of its sinfulness is the shame it causes us. Why do we not happily consummate our marriages in public (the Cynics – see *Q.* 138 – Crates and Hipparchia did, but that's another story)? Why not give head on the tube? Shame, is Augustine's answer. We are ashamed of lust because it is beyond our control. Since we disobeyed God by eating the forbidden fruit, by way of punishment he has impressed disobedience into the very operation of our bodies.

From *The City of God* –

'Lust seeks for its consummation darkness and secrecy; and this not only when unlawful intercourse is desired, but even such fornication as the earthly city has legalised. Where there is no fear of punishment, these permitted pleasures still shrink from the public eye. Even in brothels where provision is made for this lust, secrecy also is provided; and while lust found it easy to remove the prohibitions of law, shamelessness found it impossible to lay aside the veil of privacy. For even shameless men call this shameful; and though they love the pleasure, dare not display it.

What! does not even conjugal intercourse, sanctioned as it is by law for the propagation of children, legitimate and honourable though it be, does it not seek retirement from every eye? Before the bridegroom fondles his bride, does he not exclude the attendants, and even the groomsmen, and such friends as the closest ties have admitted to the bridal chamber?

The greatest master of Roman eloquence [Cicero] says, that all right actions wish to be set in the light, i.e. desire to be known. This right action, however, has such a desire to be known, that yet it blushes to be seen.

Who does not know what passes between husband and wife that children may be born? Is it not for this purpose that wives are married with such ceremony? And yet, when this well-understood act is gone about for the procreation of children, not even the children themselves, who may already have been born to them, are suffered to be witnesses. This right action seeks the light, in so far as it seeks to be known, but yet dreads being seen. And why so, if not because that which is by nature fitting and decent is so done as to be accompanied, by way of punishment, the feeling of shame?

Hence it is that even the philosophers who have approximated to the truth have avowed that anger and lust are vicious mental emotions, because, even when exercised towards objects which wisdom does not prohibit, they are moved in an ungoverned and inordinate manner, and consequently need the regulation of mind and reason.'

For Augustine, see *Qs.* 18 and 80.

201. Is saying what you mean the same as meaning what you say?

Lewis Carroll's (1832-1898) original title for *Alice's Adventures in Wonderland* was *Alice's Adventures Under Ground*, which raises the question, why did he recast the story's world of nonsense in this way? Why lose the subterranean emphasis? By making this change was Carroll implying that there is no hierarchical relationship between sense and nonsense? Perhaps he came to think of nonsense not as the lack of sense, not hypo-sense, but sense of a different order.

To unravel this a little, it could be argued that since

> nonsense precludes understanding, it thereby precludes deficiency: where there is no understanding there can be no misunderstanding. And so, untrammelled by the demand to 'get it', nonsense conversations are not conducted *with* words but *within* them. That is to say, in a world of nonsense, though we may mean to speak, we do not speak to mean.

'Your hair wants cutting,' said the Hatter. He had been looking at Alice for some time with great curiosity, and this was his first speech.

'You should learn not to make personal remarks,' Alice said with some severity; 'it's very rude.'

The Hatter opened his eyes very wide on hearing this; but all he *said* was, 'Why is a raven like a writing-desk?'

'Come, we shall have some fun now!' thought Alice. 'I'm glad they've begun asking riddles.—I believe I can guess that,' she added aloud.

'Do you mean that you think you can find out the answer to it?' said the March Hare.

'Exactly so,' said Alice.

'Then you should say what you mean,' the March Hare went on.

'I do,' Alice hastily replied; 'at least—at least I mean what I say—that's the same thing, you know.'

'Not the same thing a bit!' said the Hatter. 'You might just as well say that "I see what I eat" is the same thing as "I eat what I see"!'

'You might just as well say,' added the March Hare, 'that "I like what I get" is the same thing as "I get what I like"!'

'You might just as well say,' added the Dormouse, who seemed to be talking in his sleep, 'that "I breathe when I sleep" is the same thing as "I sleep when I breathe"!'

'It *is* the same thing with you,' said the Hatter, and here the conversation dropped, and the party sat silent for a minute, while Alice thought over all she could remember about ravens and writing-desks, which wasn't much.'

212. Is complete fluency in one's native tongue possible?

Imagine your tongue were a person. What would it be like? As an organ expert in conversation and taste, the lingual individual would presumably tend towards the debonair and sybarite. He would make for a fine dinner companion, certainly preferable to a glaring pair of eyes. But imagine affording it responsibilities where rigour and accuracy were required. Would you, for instance, want this person as your surgeon? Would you trust your tongue with your liver?

The writer **G. K. Chesterton** (1874-1936) believed that the tongue was an instrument of the arts and not the sciences. The 'grunts and squeals' it produces are capable of tremendous charm but little accuracy. This is why Plato's general hostility towards poetry is misguided. Plato condemned poetry for failing to articulate truth. He regarded philosophy as a superior pursuit because it utilises reason in order to disclose the nature and essence of reality. But for Chesterton, any activity which relies on language is thereby disqualified from the pursuit of veracity and precision. Trying to ally the tongue with reason is as hopeless as seeking to imbue an inferno with respect.

From *G. F. Watts* –

'Every time one man says to another, "Tell us plainly what you mean?" he is assuming the infallibility of language: that is to say, he is assuming that there is a perfect scheme of verbal expression for all the internal moods and meanings of men. Whenever a man says to another, "Prove your case; defend your faith," he is assuming the infallibility of language: that is to say, he is assuming that a man has a word for every reality in earth, or heaven, or hell. He knows that there are in the soul tints more bewildering, more numberless, and more nameless than the colours of an autumn forest; he knows that there are abroad in the world and doing strange and terrible service in it crimes that have never been condemned and virtues that have never been christened. Yet he seriously believes that these things can every one of them, in all their tones and semi-tones, in all their blends and unions, be accurately represented by an arbitrary system of grunts and squeals. He believes that an ordinary civilised stockbroker can really produce out of his own inside noises which denote all the mysteries of memory and all the agonies of desire. Whenever, on the other hand, a man rebels faintly or vaguely against this way of speaking, whenever a man says that he cannot explain what he means, and that he hates argument, that his enemy is misrepresenting him, but he cannot explain how; that man is a true sage, and has seen into the heart of the real nature of language. Whenever a man refuses to be caught by some dilemma about reason and passion, or about reason and faith, or about fate and free-will, he has seen the truth. Whenever a man declines to be cornered as an egotist, or an altruist, or any such modern monster, he has seen the truth. For the truth is that language is not a scientific thing at all, but wholly an artistic thing, a thing invented by hunters, and killers, and such artists long before science was dreamed of. The truth is simply that – that the tongue is not a reliable instrument, like a theodolite or a camera. The tongue is most truly an unruly member, as the wise saint has called it, a thing poetic and dangerous, like music or fire.'

For Chesterton, see *Q.* 381.

213. Can the description of an object be more realistic than your experience of it?

Sweet is the lore which Nature brings;
Our meddling intellect
Mis-shapes the beauteous forms of things;
– We murder to dissect.

Henri Bergson (1859-1941) shared the sentiment expressed here by William Wordsworth in 'The Tables Turned'. Focusing on language, an agent of the intellect, he claims that we are only able to analyse and describe our sensations by betraying their lived reality. Our sensations and feelings do not consist of stable and discrete parts which can be packaged into words. Conscious states flow, shift and interpenetrate. The orderliness of language cannot convey this flux.

Bergson's imagery of the shadow in the text below is reminiscent of Plato's cave (see Q. 145). Imagine the shadow cast by a posy of flowers. As a shadow alone, we'd fail to see the variety of colours, shapes, textures, the blooming buds, the eventual decay of the petals. If we were to name what we saw, we'd only need one simple word, for the shadow presents itself as one simple thing.

This illustration encapsulates the deficiencies of language. For the sake of social convenience, it transforms the rich bounty of conscious experience into a communicable network of easy words.

From *Time and Free Will* –

'When e.g. I take my first walk in a town in which I am going to live, my environment produces on me two impressions at the same time, one of which is destined to last while the other will constantly change. Every day I perceive the same houses, and as I know that they are the same objects, I always call them by the same name and I also fancy that they always look the same to me. But if I recur, at the end of a sufficiently long period, to the impression which I experienced during the first few years, I am surprised at the remarkable, inexplicable, and indeed inexpressible change which has taken place. It seems that these objects, continually perceived by me and constantly impressing themselves on my mind, have ended by borrowing from me something of my own conscious existence; like myself they have lived, and like myself they have grown old. This is not a mere illusion; for if today's impression were absolutely identical with that of yesterday, what difference would there be between perceiving and recognizing, between learning and remembering? Yet this difference escapes the attention of most of us; we shall hardly perceive it, unless we are warned of it and then carefully look into ourselves. The reason is that our outer and, so to speak, social life is more practically important to us than our inner and individual existence. We instinctively tend to solidify our impressions in order to express them in language. Hence we confuse the feeling itself, which is in a perpetual state of becoming, with its permanent external object, and especially with the word which expresses this object...

Our simple sensations, taken in their natural state, are still more fleeting. Such and such a flavour, such and such a scent, pleased me when I was a child though I dislike them today. Yet I still give the same name to the sensation experienced, and I speak as if only my taste had changed, whilst the scent and the flavour have remained the same. Thus I again solidify the sensation; and when its changeableness becomes so obvious that I cannot help recognizing it, I abstract this changeableness to give it a name of its own and solidify it in the shape of a taste. But in reality there are neither identical sensations nor multiple tastes: for sensations and tastes seem to me to be objects as soon as I isolate and name them, and in the human soul there are only processes. What I ought to say is that every sensation is altered by repetition, and that if it does not seem to me to change from day to day, it is because I perceive it through the object which is its cause, through the word which translates it. This influence of language on sensation is deeper than is usually thought. Not only does language make us believe in the unchangeableness of our sensations, but it will sometimes deceive us as to the nature of the sensation felt. Thus, when I partake of a dish that is supposed to be exquisite, the name which it bears, suggestive of the approval given to it, comes between my sensation and my consciousness; I may believe that the flavour pleases me when a slight effort of attention would prove the contrary. In short, the word with well-defined outlines, the rough and ready word, which stores up the stable, common, and consequently impersonal element in the impressions of mankind, overwhelms or at least covers over the delicate and fugitive impressions of our individual consciousness. To maintain the struggle on equal terms, the latter ought to express themselves in precise words; but these words, as soon as they were formed, would turn against the sensation which gave birth to them, and, invented to show that the sensation is unstable, they would impose on it their own stability.

This overwhelming of the immediate consciousness is nowhere so striking as in the case of our feelings. A violent love or a deep melancholy takes possession of our soul: here we feel a thousand different elements which dissolve into and permeate one another without any precise outlines, without the least tendency to externalize themselves in relation to one another; hence their originality. We distort them as soon as we distinguish a numerical multiplicity in their confused mass: what will it be, then, when we set them out, isolated from one another, in this homogeneous medium which may be called either time or space, whichever you prefer? A moment ago each of them was borrowing an indefinable colour from its surroundings: now we have it colourless, and ready to accept a name. The feeling itself is a being which lives and develops and is therefore constantly changing; otherwise how could it gradually lead us to form a resolution? Our resolution would be immediately taken. But it lives because the duration in which it develops is a duration whose moments, permeate one another. By separating these moments from each other, by spreading out time in space, we have caused this feeling to lose its life and its colour. Hence, we are now standing before our own shadow: we believe that we have analysed our feeling, while we have really replaced it by a juxtaposition of lifeless states which can be translated into words, and each of which constitutes the common element, the impersonal residue, of the impressions felt in a given case by the whole of society. And this is why we reason about these states and apply our simple logic to them: having set them up as genera by the mere fact of having isolated them from one another, we have prepared them for use in some future deduction. Now, if some bold novelist, tearing aside the cleverly woven curtain of our conventional ego, shows us under this appearance of logic a fundamental absurdity, under this juxtaposition of simple states an infinite permeation of a thousand different impressions which have already ceased to exist the instant they are named, we commend him for having known us better than we knew ourselves. This is not the case, however, and the very fact that he spreads out our feeling in a homogeneous time, and expresses its elements by words, shows that he in his turn is only offering us its shadow: but he has arranged this shadow in such a way as to make us suspect the extraordinary and illogical nature of the object which projects it; he has made us reflect by giving outward expression to something of that contradiction, that interpenetration, which is the very essence of the elements expressed. Encouraged by him, we have put aside for an instant the veil which we interposed between our consciousness and ourselves. He has brought us back into our own presence.'

For Bergson, see *Qs*. 19, 126, 265 and 389.

214. Can the painting of a landscape be more realistic than your experience of it?

Friedrich Nietzsche (see *Qs*. 44, 146 and 295) believed that scholars and scientific thinkers were afflicted by a sickness he diagnosed as the Will to Truth. These passive observers of the world suppress their own perspectives in order to achieve an immaculate perception. Using facts as anaesthetics, hooked on truth's torpor, they are a 'race of eunuchs' who would rather defer to the world than create it. Their faith in objectivity and slavish devotion to truth is tantamount to a Will to Death.

At approximately the same time that Nietzsche was articulating these thoughts, **Oscar Wilde** (1854-1900) was in a Soho café having dinner with his lover and expressing very similar sentiments. The ideas kindled over this dinner became his essay 'The Decay of Lying', in which he bemoaned the 'monstrous worship of facts' and the striving for realism in art.

As with Nietzsche's conception of the Will to Truth, Wilde saw the tedious pursuit of faithful representation as the enemy of invention and imagination: 'No great artist ever sees things as they really are. If he did he would cease to be an artist.'

'Life imitates art far more than Art imitates life... A great artist invents a type, and Life tries to copy it, to reproduce it in a popular form, like an enterprising publisher...

Where, if not from the Impressionists, do we get those wonderful brown fogs that come creeping down our streets, blurring the gas-lamps and changing the houses into monstrous shadows? To whom, if not to them and their master, do we owe the lovely silver mists that brood over our river, and turn to faint forms of fading grace curved bridge and swaying barge? The extraordinary change that has taken place in the climate of London during the last ten years is entirely due to this particular school of Art. You smile. Consider the matter from a scientific or a metaphysical point of view, and you will find that I am right. For what is Nature? Nature is no great mother who has borne us. She is our creation. It is in our brain that she quickens to life. Things are because we see them, and what we see, and how we see it, depends on the Arts that have influenced us. To look at a thing is very different from seeing a thing. One does not see anything until one sees its beauty. Then, and then only, does it come into existence. At present, people see fogs, not because there are fogs, but because poets and painters have taught them the mysterious loveliness of such effects. There may have been fogs for centuries in London. I dare say there were. But no one saw them, and so we do not know anything about them. They did not exist till Art had invented them. Now, it must be admitted, fogs are carried to excess. They have become the mere mannerism of a clique, and the exaggerated realism of their method gives dull people bronchitis. Where the cultured catch an effect, the uncultured catch cold. And so, let us be humane, and invite Art to turn her wonderful eyes elsewhere. She has done so already, indeed. That white quivering sunlight that one sees now in France, with its strange blotches of mauve, and its restless violet shadows, is her latest fancy, and, on the whole, Nature reproduces it quite admirably. Where she used to give us Corots and Daubignys, she gives us now exquisite Monets and entrancing Pissarros. Indeed there are moments, rare, it is true, but still to be observed from time to time, when Nature becomes absolutely modern. Of course she is not always to be relied upon. The fact is that she is in this unfortunate position. Art creates an incomparable and unique effect, and, having done so, passes on to other things. Nature, upon the other hand, forgetting that imitation can be made the sincerest form of insult, keeps on repeating this effect until we all become absolutely wearied of it. Nobody of any real culture, for instance, ever talks nowadays about the beauty of a sunset. Sunsets are quite old fashioned. They belong to the time when Turner was the last note in art. To admire them is a distinct sign of provincialism of temperament. Upon the other hand they go on. Yesterday evening Mrs. Arundel insisted on my coming to the window, and looking at the glorious sky, as she called it. Of course I had to look at it. She is one of those absurdly pretty Philistines, to whom one can deny nothing. And what was it? It was simply a very second rate Turner, a Turner of a bad period, with all the painter's worst faults exaggerated and over-emphasized.'

For one of Wilde's key influences, see *Q*. 321.

220. According to Catholicism there are seven deadly sins: wrath, sloth, gluttony, avarice, lust, envy and pride. Which of these is the worst?

When **Lucius Annaeus Seneca** (*c*. 4 BCE-65 CE) received word that Emperor Nero – his former student – had ordered him to commit suicide, he showed no sign of fear. Calmly and without sadness he proceeded to open the veins in his arms. In something of an anti-climax, however, they issued only a trickle rather than a spurt.

To expedite his departure he then sliced at the veins in his ankles and behind his knees, all to no avail. He resorted to hemlock, which was likewise ineffectual. The aging man was almost too deathly to die. Finally, mercifully, he entered a warm bath and was suffocated by the steam.

At no point during this protracted and painful death did he wail or weep. At no point did he lose his temper or grow frustrated. Only the sight of his dying wife, who had chosen to commit suicide with him, threatened to disrupt his composure – a circumstance he averted by having her moved to another room.

Seneca died as he thought we should live: equably, dispassionately, phlegmatically. He regarded emotions as saboteurs of reason which ought to be met with zero tolerance. Every emotion is an excess. The idea of a moderate level of emotion is as nonsensical as a moderate level of insanity. Irrationality does not possess degrees of acceptability. Quite simply, the ideal life is a life without emotion.

The most destructive of all the emotions is anger (or wrath), as he explains in the following essay, 'On Anger', which he addressed to his older brother.

'You have demanded of me, Novatus, that I should write how anger may be soothed, and it appears to me that you are right in feeling especial fear of this passion, which is above all others hideous and wild: for the others have some alloy of peace and quiet, but this consists wholly in action and the impulse of grief, raging with an utterly inhuman lust for arms, blood and tortures, careless of itself provided it hurts another, rushing upon the very point of the sword, and greedy for revenge even when it drags the avenger to ruin with itself. Some of the wisest of men have in consequence of this called anger a short madness: for it is equally devoid of self control, regardless of decorum, forgetful of kinship, obstinately engrossed in whatever it begins to do, deaf to reason and advice, excited by trifling causes, awkward at perceiving what is true and just, and very like a falling rock which breaks itself to pieces upon the very thing which it crushes. That you may know that they whom anger possesses are not sane, look at their appearance; for as there are distinct symptoms which mark madmen, such as a bold and menacing air, a gloomy brow, a stern face, a hurried walk, restless hands, changed colour, quick and strongly-drawn breathing; the signs of angry men, too, are the same: their eyes blaze and sparkle, their whole face is a deep red with the blood which boils up from the bottom of their heart, their lips quiver, their teeth are set, their hair bristles and stands on end, their breath is laboured and hissing, their joints crack as they twist them about, they groan, bellow, and burst into scarcely intelligible talk, they often clap their hands together and stamp on the ground with their feet, and their whole body is highly-strung and plays those tricks which mark a distraught mind, so as to furnish an ugly and shocking picture of self-perversion and excitement...

Next, if you choose to view its results and the mischief that it does, no plague has cost the human race more dear: you will see slaughterings and poisonings, accusations and counter-accusations, sacking of cities, ruin of whole peoples, the persons of princes sold into slavery by auction, torches applied to roofs, and fires not merely confined within city-walls but making whole tracts of country glow with hostile flame. See the foundations of the most celebrated cities hardly now to be discerned; they were ruined by anger. See deserts extending for many miles without an inhabitant: they have been desolated by anger. See all the chiefs whom tradition mentions as instances of ill fate; anger stabbed one of them in his bed, struck down another, though he was protected by the sacred rights of hospitality, tore another to pieces in the very home of the laws and in sight of the crowded forum, bade one shed his own blood by the parricide hand of his son, another to have his royal throat cut by the hand of a slave, another to stretch out his limbs on the cross...

"What, then," asks our adversary, "is a good man not to be angry if he sees his father murdered or his mother outraged?" No, he will not be angry, but will avenge them, or protect them... My father will be murdered: then I will defend him: he has been slain, then I will avenge him, not because I am grieved, but because it is my duty. "Good men are made angry by injuries done to their friends." When you say this, Theophrastus, you seek to throw discredit upon more manly maxims; you leave the judge and appeal to the mob: because everyone is angry when such things befall his own friends, you suppose that men will decide that it is their duty to do what they do: for as a rule every man considers a passion which he recognises to be a righteous one. But he does the same thing if the hot water is not ready for his drink, if a glass be broken, or his shoe splashed with mud. It is not filial piety, but weakness of mind that produces this anger, as children weep when they lose their parents, just as they do when they lose their toys. To feel anger on behalf of one's friends does not show a loving, but a weak mind: it is admirable and worthy conduct to stand forth as the defender of one's parents, children, friends, and countrymen, at the call of duty itself, acting of one's own free will, forming a deliberate judgment, and looking forward to the future, not in an impulsive, frenzied fashion. No passion is more eager for revenge than anger, and for that very reason it is unapt to obtain it: being over hasty and frantic, like almost all desires, it hinders itself in the attainment of its own object, and therefore has never been useful either in peace or war.'

For Seneca, see *Q.* 355.

231. We can see with light but can we see light itself?

Light is all we see. It is not the medium but the object of perception. While you watch a hummingbird sipping from a foxglove, you do not actually see the hummingbird. We can only perceive that which comes into contact with our senses, and it is not a hummingbird dashing towards your retina but reflected waves of light.

Such was the reasoning of the Scottish philosopher **William Hamilton** (1788-1856) in *Lectures on Metaphysics and Logic*.

'[I]t is only a confusion of ideas, or of words, or of both together, to talk of the perception of a distant object, that is, of an object not in relation to our senses. An external object is only perceived inasmuch as it is in relation to our sense, and it is only in relation to our sense, inasmuch as it is present to it. To say, for example, that we perceive by sight the sun or moon, is a false, or an elliptical, expression. We perceive nothing but certain modifications of light in immediate relation to our organ of vision; and so far from Dr [Thomas] Reid being philosophically correct, when he says that "when ten men look at the sun or moon, they all see the same individual object," the truth is that each of these persons sees a different object, because each person sees a different complement of rays, in relation to his individual organ. In fact, if we look alternately with each, we have a different object in our right, and a different object in our left, eye. It is not by perception, but by a process of reasoning, that we connect the objects of sense with existences beyond the sphere of immediate knowledge.'

243. The uterus has a use. Does it have a purpose?

In 1802 William Paley argued that the structural similarities between telescopes and the human eye indicate that if the former was designed, the latter must have been too: 'There is precisely the same proof that the eye was made for vision, as there is that the telescope was made for assisting it. They are made upon the same principles; both being adjusted to the laws by which the transmission and refraction of rays of light are regulated… What could a mathematical-instrument-maker have done more, to show his knowledge of his principle, his application of that knowledge, his suiting of his means to his end… to testify counsel, choice, consideration, purpose?'

Centuries before, however, **Lucretius** (*fl.* 1st c BCE) had already dismissed such an argument. He claimed there the analogy between artefacts and the body is erroneous. Artefacts are invented for the benefit of activities that already exist. Telescopes were designed to enhance the power of sight we already possessed. But this is decidedly unlike the eye itself, for prior to its existence there was no such power as sight.

From a prose translation of *De rerum natura* –

'Do not think that the bright light of the eyes was created in order that we may be able to look before us, or that, in order that we may have power to plant long paces, therefore the tops of shanks and thighs, based upon the feet, are able to bend; or again, that the forearms are jointed to the strong upper arms and hands given us to serve us on either side, in order that we might be able to do what was needful for life. All other ideas of this sort, which men proclaim, by distorted reasoning set effect for cause, since nothing at all was born in the body that we might be able to use it, but what is born creates its own use. Nor did sight exist before the light of the eyes was born, nor pleading in words before the tongue was created, but rather the birth of the tongue came long before discourse, and the ears were created much before sound was heard, and in short all the limbs, I believe, existed before their use came about: they cannot then have grown for the purpose of using them. But, on the other side, to join hands in the strife of battle, to mangle limbs and befoul the body with gore; these things were known long before gleaming darts flew abroad, and nature constrained men to avoid a wounding blow, before the left arm, trained by art, held up the defence of a shield. And of a surety to trust the tired body to rest was a habit far older than the soft-spread bed, and the slaking of the thirst was born before cups. These things, then, which are invented to suit the needs of life, might well be thought to have been discovered for the purpose of using them. But all those other things lie apart, which were first born themselves, and thereafter revealed the concept of their usefulness. In this class first of all we see the senses and the limbs; wherefore, again and again, it cannot be that you should believe that they could have been created for the purpose of useful service.'

For Lucretius, see *Q*. 91.

246. Are meat eaters murderers?

> **Immanuel Kant** (1724-1804) believed that free will elevates humans above animals.
>
> We are autonomous. We act on the basis of motives, reasons for action which we may choose to ignore. Animals, on the contrary, are reactive. Their behaviour is a function of their corporeal nature and the immediate stimuli: 'a dog must eat if he is hungry and has something in front of him; but we, in the same situation, can restrain ourselves'.
>
> Because animals lack freedom, they possess no intrinsic moral worth. There is nothing intrinsically wrong with torturing an animal. Yet, despite Kant's fundamental callousness, his views actually place very high standards on our treatment of animals. This is because he believes that our treatment of animals is liable to affect our treatment of humans, so our treatment of both should be analogous. He is, for instance, against shooting decrepit dogs since he is first and foremost against shooting decrepit butlers. Arguably, then, he should also be opposed to eating (say) kindly cows, lest he wish to condone the consumption of kindly maids.

'Animals are not self-conscious and exist only as means, not for their own sake. Humanity, on the contrary, is not a means. We cannot ask "Why does humanity exist?" Yet we can ask "Why do animals exist?" Nevertheless, our duties towards animals are indirect duties towards humanity. Animals are an analogue of humanity, and by treating them analogously, we thereby promote our duties towards humanity. If a dog has faithfully served his master for many years, treated as an analogue for human service, it deserves reward and should be kept till it dies, even beyond the point at which it can no longer serve. By treating it this way the dog's master is promoting duties towards humanity. Because the actions of animals are analogous to the actions of humans, by performing duties towards one we thereby promote duties towards the other. If a man shoots his dog because the animal can no longer earn his keep, he does not act against the dog, because the dog cannot judge, but his act is inhuman and violates the humanity within himself which it is his duty to show towards mankind. We must show kindness towards animals, if not we shall lose our humanity, for a person who is cruel to animals becomes hardened to other people.'

For Kant, see *Q.* 32.

247. Is eating the body of a dead animal as intimate as having sex with it?

There are many legends surrounding the life of the ancient Greek philosopher Pythagoras. It is said that he dressed all in white, had a thigh of gold, was able to recall his former life as King Midas, communicated with animals (he converted a bear to vegetarianism and persuaded an ox to stop eating beans), calmed the sea and once crossed a river, which, upon his greeting, replied 'Hail Pythagoras!'

It is his alleged vegetarianism (like the pliant ox, he also abstained from beans, which he thought it wrong even to touch) which prompted **Plutarch** (*c.* 46-120 CE) to reference him in 'On the Eating of Flesh'. Given Plutarch's description, our question becomes more specific: Is holding an animal

> carcass to your lips and sucking at its juices a kind of intimacy?

'Can you really ask what reason Pythagoras had for abstaining from flesh? For my part I rather wonder both by what accident and in what state of soul or mind the first man who did so, touched his mouth to gore and brought his lips to the flesh of a dead creature, he who set forth tables of dead, stale bodies and ventured to call food and nourishment the parts that had a little before bellowed and cried, moved and lived. How could his eyes endure the slaughter when throats were slit and hides flayed and limbs torn from limb? How could his nose endure the stench? How was it that the pollution did not turn away his taste, which made contact with the sores of others and sucked juices and serums from mortal wounds?

> The skins shivered; and upon the spits the flesh bellowed, Both cooked and raw; the voice of kine was heard. [From Homer's *Odyssey*, XII]

Though this is an invention and a myth, yet that sort of dinner is really portentous – when a man craves the meat that is still bellowing, giving instructions which tell us on what animals we are to feed while they are still alive uttering their cries, and organizing various methods of seasoning and roasting and serving. It is the man who first began these practices that one should seek out, not him who all too late desisted.'

For Plutarch, see *Q*. 189.

248. Is the life of a human worth more than the life of a goat?

At the age of 37 **Michel de Montaigne** (1533-1592) effectively retired from public life. He had his personal library transported to a tower attached to his family's chateau and there he spent much of the next two decades writing essays on a miscellany of topics, including thumbs, smells and cowardice.

In the following extract from 'Apology for Raymond Sebond' he offers a riposte to the idea that among earth's creatures humans are uniquely special for having been made in the image of God (as Genesis 1:26 states). This idea says more about our vanity than it does our divinity.

'We are to observe that to every thing nothing is more dear and estimable than its being (the lion, the eagle, the dolphin, prize nothing above their own kind); and that every thing assimilates the qualities of all other things to its own proper qualities, which we may indeed extend or contract, but that's all; for beyond that relation and principle our imagination cannot go, can guess at nothing else, nor possibly go out thence, nor stretch beyond it; whence spring these ancient conclusions: of all forms the most beautiful is that of man; therefore God must be of that form. No one can be happy without virtue, nor virtue be without reason, and reason cannot inhabit anywhere but in a human shape; God is therefore clothed in a human figure. *Ita est informatum et anticipatum mentibus nostris, ut homini, quum de Deo cogitet, forma occurrat humana.* "It is so imprinted in our minds, and the fancy is so prepossessed with it, that when a man thinks of God, a human figure ever presents itself to the imagination." Therefore it was that Xenophanes pleasantly said, "That if beasts frame any gods to themselves, as 'tis likely they do, they make them certainly such as themselves are, and glorify themselves in it, as we do. For why may not a goose say thus: 'All the parts of the universe I have an interest in; the earth serves me to walk upon; the sun to light me; the stars have their influence upon me; I have such an advantage by the winds and such by the waters; there is nothing that yon heavenly roof looks upon so favourably as me; I am the darling of nature! Is it not man that keeps, lodges, and serves me? 'Tis for me that he both sows and grinds; if he eats me he does the same by his fellow-men, and so do I the worms that kill and devour him.'" As much might be said by a crane, and with greater confidence, upon the account of the liberty of his flight, and the possession of that high and beautiful region. *Tam blanda conciliatrix, et tam sui est lena ipsa natura.* "So flattering and wheedling a bawd is nature to herself."'

249. Do you have more in common with Michelangelo's David *or an earthworm?*

Charles Darwin (1809-1882) was besotted with worms. He spent decades studying their behaviour, trying to understand their experience of the world. He observed their reactions to the sounds of the piano, the bassoon and of being shouted at. He blew on them, breathed on them, fed them cheese and placed hot pokers near them. And in his book on them, *The Formation of Vegetable Mould Through the Action of Worms, with Observations on Their Habits,* he concluded, 'The plough is one of the most ancient and most valuable of man's inventions; but long before he existed the land was in fact regularly ploughed, and still continues to be thus ploughed by earthworms. It may be doubted whether there are many other animals which have played so important a part in the history of the world, as have these lowly organized creatures'.

This conception of worms as little worker ploughs may explain his fascination – perhaps in them he saw himself. Like a diligent worm, Darwin, through years of slow piecemeal work, managed to transform and enrich the landscape of our scientific understanding.

'We have seen that worms are timid. It may be doubted whether they suffer as much pain when injured, as they seem to express by their contortions. Judging by their eagerness for certain kinds of food, they must enjoy the pleasure of eating. Their sexual passion is strong enough to overcome for a time their dread of light. They perhaps have a trace of social feeling, for they are not disturbed by crawling over each other's bodies, and they sometimes lie in contact. According to Hoffmeister they pass the winter either singly or rolled up with others into a ball at the bottom of their burrows. Although worms are so remarkably deficient in the several sense-organs, this does not necessarily preclude intelligence... and we have seen that when their attention is engaged, they neglect impressions to which they would otherwise have attended; and attention indicates the presence of a mind of some kind. They are also much more easily excited at certain times than at others. They perform a few actions instinctively, that is, all the individuals, including the young, perform such actions in nearly the same fashion. This is shown by the manner in which the species of Perichæta eject their castings, so as to construct towers; also by the manner in which the burrows of the common earth-worm are smoothly lined with fine earth and often with little stones, and the mouths of their burrows with leaves. One of their strongest instincts is the plugging up the mouths of their burrows with various objects; and very young worms act in this manner. But some degree of intelligence appears...

Worms are poorly provided with sense-organs, for they cannot be said to see, although they can just distinguish between light and darkness; they are completely deaf, and have only a feeble power of smell; the sense of touch alone is well developed. They can therefore learn but little about the outside world, and it is surprising that they should exhibit some skill in lining their burrows with their castings and with leaves, and in the case of some species in piling up their castings into tower-like constructions. But it is far more surprising that they should apparently exhibit some degrees of intelligence instead of a mere blind instinctive impulse, in their manner of plugging up the mouths of their burrows. They act in nearly the same manner as would a man, who had to close a cylindrical tube with different kinds of leaves, petioles, triangles of paper, &c., for they commonly seize such objects by their pointed ends. But with thin objects a certain number are drawn in by their broader ends. They do not act in the same unvarying manner in all cases, as do most of the lower animals...'

For Darwin, see Q. 45.

250. If every particle within a statue is in motion, is the statue itself in motion?

For many years **Friedrich Engels** (1820-1895) lived a double life. Diurnally, he was a proficient businessman who actively participated in the marketplace of Victorian capitalism. Nocturnally, however, he worked to develop and advance the cause of communism. In the order of things, it was the diurnal grind which served the nocturnal passion. Indeed, a significant portion of his income was regularly donated to his indigent collaborator Karl Marx, with whom he co-authored *The Communist Manifesto*.

In *Anti-Dühring* he outlined his belief in the 'transitory character of everything'. His sense of the possibility of revolutionary change belonged to a broader metaphysical worldview. The nature of history, society and thought can be seen in the flux and flow of matter: 'nothing is final, absolute, sacred'.

'*Motion is the mode of existence of matter*. Never anywhere has there been matter without motion, nor can there be. Motion in cosmic space, mechanical motion of smaller masses on the various celestial bodies, the motion of molecules as heat or as electrical or magnetic currents, chemical combination or disintegration, organic life – at each given moment each individual atom of matter in the world is in one or other of these forms of motion, or in several forms at once. All rest, all equilibrium, is only relative, and only has meaning in relation to one or other definite form of motion. A body, for example, may be on the ground in mechanical equilibrium, may be mechanically at rest; but this in no way prevents it from participating in the motion of the earth and in that of the whole solar system, just as little as it prevents its most minute physical particles from carrying out the oscillations determined by its temperature, or its atoms from passing through a chemical process. Matter without motion is just as unthinkable as motion without matter. Motion is therefore as uncreatable and indestructible as matter itself… A motionless state of matter is therefore one of the most empty and nonsensical of ideas – a "delirious fantasy" of the purest water.'

254. Is the space between us a something or a nothing?

As well as quarrelling over who first invented calculus, **Gottfried Wilhelm Leibniz** (1646-1716) – whose symbol ∫ for integration we still use – and **Isaac Newton** (1643-1727) also wrangled over the nature of space. Newton believed that in addition to the material objects in the universe, space exists as a separate entity. If all the matter in the universe were to vanish, space would remain, like a sort of empty container. Invisible and immaterial, it is a *thing*, and it exists everywhere, or rather it *is* everywhere. This is a view known as substantivalism.

In contrast to this view is relationism, Leibniz's view. According to relationism, space is not an entity, not a *thing*, it does not exist independently of material things. Rather, it is constituted by the relations between material things. If all the matter in the universe were to vanish, space would vanish too. And if a flitting butterfly were the only thing in existence, it would have no motion since, existing alone, without relation to anything else, it could have no change of place. We are not separated *by* space, our separation *is* space.

The first extract is by Leibniz from his correspondence with Samuel Clarke (Newton's proxy). The second is from an essay Newton appended to his work *Mathematical Principles of Natural Philosophy*.

'I will here show, how men come to form to themselves the notion of space. They consider that many things exist at once, and they observe in them a certain order of co-existence, according to which the relation of one thing to another is more or less simple. This order, is their situation or distance. When it happens that one of those co-existent things changes its relation to a multitude of others, which do not change their relation among themselves; and that another thing, newly come, acquires the same relation to the others, as the former had; we then say, it is come into the place of the former; and this Change, we call a motion in that body, wherein is the immediate cause of the change. And though many, or even all the co-existent things, should change according to certain known rules of direction and swiftness; yet one may always determine the relation of situation, which every co-existent acquires with respect to every other co-existent; and even that relation, which any other co-existent would have to this, or which this would have to any other, if it had not changed, or if it had changed any otherwise. And supposing, or feigning, that among those co-existents, there is a sufficient number of them, which have undergone no change; then we may say, that those which have such a relation to those fixed existents, as others had to them before, have now the *same place* which those others had. And that which comprehends all those places, is called *space*. Which shows, that in order to have an idea of place, and consequently of space, it is sufficient to consider these relations, and the rules of their changes, without needing to fancy any absolute reality out of the things whose situation we consider.'

* * *

'As the order of the parts of time is immutable, so also is the order of the parts of space. Suppose those parts to be moved out of their places, and they will be moved (if the expression may be allowed) out of themselves. For times and spaces are, as it were, the places as well of themselves as of all other things. All things are placed in time as to order of succession; and in space as to order of situation. It is from their essence or nature that they are places; and that the primary places of things should be movable, is absurd. These are therefore the absolute places; and translations out of those places, are the only absolute motions.

But because the parts of space cannot be seen, or distinguished from one another by our senses, therefore in their stead we use sensible measures of them. For from the positions and distances of things from any body considered as immovable, we define all places; and then with respect to such places, we estimate all motions, considering bodies as transferred from some of those places into others. And so, instead of absolute places and motions, we use relative ones; and that without any inconvenience in common affairs; but in philosophical disquisitions, we ought to abstract from our senses, and consider things themselves, distinct from what are only sensible measures of them.'

261. ●, ■, ▲ and ▬ are the only objects in existence. They are positioned as follows -

● ▲

■ ▬

Imagine they are rearranged like so -

▬ ■

▼ ●

Has anything changed?

In *Science and Method* the French philosopher and mathematician **Henri Poincaré** (1854-1912) defended a relationist (see Q. 254) understanding of space.

'It is impossible to picture empty space. All our efforts to imagine pure space from which the changing images of material objects are excluded can only result in a representation in which highly-coloured surfaces, for instance, are replaced by lines of slight colouration, and if we continued in this direction to the end, everything would disappear and end in nothing. Hence arises the irreducible relativity of space.

Whoever speaks of absolute space uses a word devoid of meaning. This is a truth that has been long proclaimed by all who have reflected on the question, but one which we are too often inclined to forget.

If I am at a definite point in Paris, at the Place du Panthéon, for instance, and I say, "I will come back *here* tomorrow;" if I am asked, "Do you mean that you will come back to the same point in space?" I should be tempted to answer yes. Yet I should be wrong, since between now and tomorrow the earth will have moved, carrying with it the Place du Panthéon, which will have travelled more than a million miles. And if I wished to speak more accurately, I should gain nothing, since this million of miles has been covered by our globe in its motion in relation to the sun, and the sun in its turn moves in relation to the Milky Way, and the Milky Way itself is no doubt in motion without our being able to recognise its velocity. So that we are, and shall always be, completely ignorant how far the Place du Panthéon moves in a day. In fact, what I meant to say was, "Tomorrow I shall see once more the dome and pediment of the Panthéon," and if there was no Pantheon my sentence would have no meaning and space would disappear.'

265. Is time composed of parts?

The ancient Greek philosopher Zeno of Elea advanced a number of paradoxes to prove that motion and change are illusions. One of these involved an apparently flying arrow. Consider: motion involves occupying successive positions, but at every instant during the arrow's flight it is only occupying one position – within that single instant it has no time to move between different positions – and so must be at rest, and given that its entire flight consists of such instants, it follows that it is at rest the whole time.

As alluded to in *Q. 19,* **Henri Bergson** (1859-1941) believed that these paradoxes arise when we fall into 'cinematographical' habits of thought which reduce time to a series of states, instants or moments. To understand change we must conceive of time as continuous, as the qualitative transition of potamic becoming, not a leap from one point to the next. This shift in understanding, however, is not without its difficulties: 'becoming shocks the habits of thought and fits ill with the mould of language'.

From *Creative Evolution* –

'That the child can become a youth, ripen to maturity and decline to old age, we understand when we consider that vital evolution is here the reality itself. Infancy, adolescence, maturity, old age, are mere views of the mind, *possible stops* imagined by us, from without, along the continuity of a progress. On the contrary, let childhood, adolescence, maturity and old age be given as integral parts of the evolution, they become *real stops*, and we can no longer conceive how evolution is possible, for rests placed beside rests will never be equivalent to a movement. How, with what is made, can we reconstitute what is being made? How, for instance, from childhood once posited as a *thing*, shall we pass to adolescence, when, by the hypothesis, childhood only is given?

If we look at it closely, we shall see that our habitual manner of speaking, which is fashioned after our habitual manner of thinking, leads us to actual logical deadlocks – deadlocks to which we allow ourselves to be led without anxiety, because we feel confusedly that we can always get out of them if we like: all that we have to do, in fact, is to give up the cinematographical habits of our intellect. When we say "The child becomes a man," let us take care not to fathom too deeply the literal meaning of the expression, or we shall find that, when we posit the subject "child," the attribute "man" does not yet apply to it, and that, when we express the attribute "man," it applies no more to the subject "child." The reality, which is the *transition* from childhood to manhood, has slipped between our fingers. We have only the imaginary stops "child" and "man", and we are very near to saying that one of these stops *is* the other, just as the arrow of Zeno *is*, according to that philosopher, at all the points of the course. The truth is that if language here were moulded on reality, we should not say "The child becomes the man," but "There is becoming from the child to the man." In the first proposition, "becomes" is a verb of indeterminate meaning, intended to mask the absurdity into which we fall when we attribute the state "man" to the subject "child." It behaves in much the same way as the movement, always the same, of the cinematographical film, a movement hidden in the apparatus and whose function it is to superpose the successive pictures on one another in order to imitate the movement of the real object. In the second proposition, "becoming" is a subject. It comes to the front. It is the reality itself; childhood and manhood are then only possible stops, mere views of the mind; we now have to do with the objective movement itself, and no longer with its cinematographical imitation. But the first manner of expression is alone conformable to our habits of language. We must, in order to adopt the second, escape from the cinematographical mechanism of thought.'

For Bergson, see *Qs*. 19, 126, 213 and 389.

267. Does the present have duration?

The Scottish philosopher **Thomas Reid** (1710-1796) believed that there are rifts between our ordinary ways of talking about the world and the philosophical facts of the matter. We might, for instance, say 'I love to watch the falling rain', yet in truth, Reid argues, we have never seen falling rain. He reasons like so:

1. I can only see the present moment. I cannot see what is past.
2. The present moment is instantaneous. It has no duration.
3. Therefore, I can only see what is instantaneous and without duration.
4. Falling rain is a phenomenon with duration. It occurs across instants, not within them.
5. Therefore, I cannot see falling rain.

Reid believes that memory creates the illusion that we *see* falling rain. What we actually see are instantaneous moments threaded together by memory. Without memory we'd have no understanding of change or motion. Our experience of the world would be an unintelligible nightmare of perpetual birth.

(It is worth noting that the meaning of 'vulgar' has narrowed since Reid's time when it was still used to refer to what is ordinary or customary.)

From *Essays on the Intellectual Powers of the Human Mind* –

'It may be here observed, that if we speak strictly and philosophically, no kind of succession can be an object either of the senses, or of consciousness; because the operations of both are confined to the present point of time, and there can be no succession in a point of time; and on that account the motion of a body, which is a successive change of place, could not be observed by the senses alone without the aid of memory.

As this observation seems to contradict the common sense and common language of mankind, when they affirm that they see a body move, and hold motion to be an object of the senses, it is proper to take notice, that this contradiction between the philosopher and the vulgar is apparent only, and not real. It arises from this, that philosophers and the vulgar differ in the meaning they put upon what is called the *present* time and are thereby led to make a different limit between sense and memory.

Philosophers give the name of the *present* to that indivisible point of time, which divides the future from the past: but the vulgar find it more convenient in the affairs of life, to give the name of *present* to a portion of time, which extends more or less, according to circumstances, into the past or future. Hence we say, the present hour, the present year, the present century, though one point only of these periods can be present in the philosophical sense.

It has been observed by grammarians, that the present tense in verbs is not confined to an indivisible point in time, but is so far extended as to have a beginning, middle, and an end; and that in the most copious and accurate languages, these different parts of the present are distinguished by different forms of the verb.

As the purposes of conversation make it convenient to extend what is called the present, the same reason leads men to extend the province of sense, and to carry its limits as far back as they carry the present. Thus a man may say, I saw such a person just now; it would be ridiculous to find fault with this way of speaking, because it is authorised by custom, and has a distinct meaning: but if we speak philosophically, the senses do not testify what we saw, but only what we see; what I saw last moment I consider as the testimony of sense, though it is now only the testimony of memory.

There is no necessity in common life of dividing accurately the provinces of sense and memory; and therefore we assign to sense, not an indivisible point of time, but that small portion of time which we call the present, which has a beginning, middle, and an end.

Hence it is easy to see, that, though in common language we speak with perfect propriety and truth when we say that we *see* a body move, and that motion is an object of sense, yet when as philosophers we distinguish accurately the province of sense from that of memory, we can no more see what is past, though but a moment ago, than we can remember what is present; so that philosophically speaking, it is only by the aid of memory that we discern motion or any succession whatsoever. We see the present place of the body; we remember the successive advance it made to that place: the first can then only give us a conception of motion, when joined to the last.'

For Reid, see *Q*. 124.

268. Does time exist in a vacuum?

Isaac Newton shared similar views on the nature of space and time to those of his teacher **Isaac Barrow** (1630-1677). In his *Geometrical Lectures* Barrow claimed that time, which existed prior to the universe, is not constituted by change or motion. Though we use motion to measure time, we should not confuse the means of measurement with the object of measurement. If everything in the universe suddenly froze, time would not stop. It would continue to flow as it always has, uniformly and unchangingly.

'Just as there was space before the world was founded, and even now there is an infinite space beyond the world (with which God co-exists) ... so before the world and together with the world (perhaps beyond the world) time was, and is... But does time not imply motion? Not at all, I reply, as far as its absolute, intrinsic nature is concerned; no more than rest; the quantity of time depends on neither essentially; whether things run or stand still, whether we sleep or wake, time flows in its even tenor. Imagine all the stars to have remained fixed from their birth; nothing would have been lost to time; as long would that stillness have endured as has continued the flow of this motion. Before, after, at the same time (as far as concerns the rise and disappearance of things), even in that tranquil state would have had their proper existence, and might by a more perfect mind have been perceived. But although those magnitudes are quantities absolutely, independent of all reference to measure, yet we cannot perceive their quantities except by the application of measures; thus time is in itself a quantity, although, that the quantity of time may be distinguished by us, the aid of motion must be called in as a measure by which we judge temporal quantities and compare them with each other; and so time as something measurable implies motion, since if all things had remained unmoved, in no way would we be able to distinguish how much time had flowed past; the age of things would have been indistinguishable to us and its growth would have been undiscoverable.'

274. Does the past contain the future?

Lucretius (see *Qs.* 91 and 243) believed that creation is initiated by the spontaneous swerve of atoms. Without this swerve, there would be no collisions or coalescence among atoms and nothing new would ever emerge. The perpetual newness of the universe is the result of atomic motion breaking the 'bonds of fate' and foiling the 'infinite chain of cause and effect'. If every event was necessitated by a prior cause, as determinism claims, nature would always just be more of the same.

Cicero (see *Q.* 171) lambasted this theory as a 'childish fancy'. He could not abide the notion of atomic spontaneity: every event must be preordained. The scientist and mathematician **Pierre-Simon Laplace** (1749-1827) held a similarly deterministic understanding of the universe. He thought that the laws of nature run the show, and such is their hold that were you equipped with a perfect knowledge of their intricacies, as well as a complete understanding of the universe's current state, you could thereby deduce and foreknow every future event, from tomorrow's lottery numbers to the date of your death.

From *On Probability* –

'All events, even those which on account of their insignificance do not seem to follow the great laws of nature, are a result of it just as necessarily as the revolutions of the sun...

We ought then to regard the present state of the universe as the effect of its anterior state and as the cause of the one which is to follow. Given for one instant an intelligence which could comprehend all the forces by which nature is animated and the respective situation of the beings who compose it – an intelligence sufficiently vast to submit these data to analysis – it would embrace in the same formula the movements of the greatest bodies of the universe and those of the lightest atom; for it, nothing would be uncertain and the future, as the past, would be present to its eyes. The human mind offers, in the perfection which it has been able to give to astronomy, a feeble idea of this intelligence. Its discoveries in mechanics and geometry, added to that of universal gravity, have enabled it to comprehend in the same analytical expressions the past and future states of the system of the world. Applying the same method to some other objects of its knowledge, it has succeeded in referring to general laws observed phenomena and in foreseeing those which given circumstances ought to produce. All these efforts in the search for truth tend to lead it back continually to the vast intelligence which we have just mentioned, but from which it will always remain infinitely removed. This tendency, peculiar to the human race, is that which renders it superior to animals; and their progress in this respect distinguishes nations and ages and constitutes their true glory.'

277. 'Since the future does not yet exist, and you cannot have what does not exist, it follows that you have no future.' Is this correct?

> Like Ludwig Wittgenstein's *Tractatus Logico-Philosophicus*, **Marcus Aurelius's** (121-180) *Meditations* was written on the battlefield. Unlike Wittgenstein, however, the Roman emperor was fighting against invading Germans, not for them.

'Even if you were to live three thousand, or, if you please, thirty thousand years, remember that no man can lose any other life than that which he now lives, neither is he possessed of any other than that which he loses. The longest life, as we commonly speak, and the shortest, come all to the same reckoning. For the present is of the same duration everywhere. Everybody's loss, therefore, is equal, and reaches no further than to a point of time, for no man is capable of losing either the past or the future; for how can one be deprived of what he has not? So that under this consideration there are two notions worth remembering. One is, that Nature treads in a circle, and has much the same face through the whole course of eternity. And therefore it signifies not at all whether a man stands gazing here an hundred, or two hundred, or an infinity of years; for all that he gets by it is only to see the same sights so much the oftener. The other hint is, that when the longest and shortest-lived persons come to die, their loss is equal; they can but lose the present as being the only thing they have; for that which he has not, no man can be truly said to lose.'

For Aurelius's key inspiration, see *Q.* 109.

287. Can pleasure ever be excessive?

The ancient Greek **Cyrenaics** (*c.* 399-275 BCE) adhered to a school of philosophy which crowned pleasure as the ultimate good in life. In contrast to the Epicureans (see *Q.* 103) and Sceptics (see *Q.* 188) who sought ataraxy, a refuge from disquiet, for the Cyrenaics this was not enough. They did not want peace, relief or happiness. They wanted immediate bodily pleasure, and by any means. Nothing in itself is base or dishonourable, only custom and convention make it so. So if theft and adultery do it for you, then steal and cheat. Present pleasure is all that matters.

Why regard pleasure so highly? Because, they claim, it is clearly the thing we most want. Consider the behaviour of infants. Do they ever refuse pleasure? No. Do they continually seek it? Yes. Is their nature fundamentally our nature? Indeed.

No writings of the Cyrenaics survive, so we must rely on their 3rd century biographer Diogenes Laertius in *Lives of the Eminent Philosophers*.

'Those then who adhered to the teaching of Aristippus and were known as Cyrenaics held the following opinions. They laid down that there are two states, pleasure and pain, the former a smooth, the latter a rough motion, and that pleasure does not differ from pleasure nor is one pleasure more pleasant than another. The one state is agreeable and the other repellent to all living things. However, the bodily pleasure which is the end is, according to Panaetius in his work On the Sects, not the settled pleasure following the removal of pains, or the sort of freedom from discomfort which Epicurus accepts and maintains to be the end. They also hold that there is a difference between "end" and "happiness." Our end is particular pleasure, whereas happiness is the sum total of all particular pleasures, in which are included both past and future pleasures.

Particular pleasure is desirable for its own sake, whereas happiness is desirable not for its own sake but for the sake of particular pleasures. That pleasure is the end is proved by the fact that from our youth up we are instinctively attracted to it, and, when we obtain it, seek for nothing more, and shun nothing so much as its opposite, pain. Pleasure is good even if it proceed from the most unseemly conduct, as Hippobotus says in his work On the Sects. For even if the action be irregular, still, at any rate, the resultant pleasure is desirable for its own sake and is good. The removal of pain, however, which is put forward in Epicurus, seems to them not to be pleasure at all, any more than the absence of pleasure is pain. For both pleasure and pain they hold to consist in motion, whereas absence of pleasure like absence of pain is not motion, since painlessness is the condition of one who is, as it were, asleep. They assert that some people may fail to choose pleasure because their minds are perverted; not all mental pleasures and pains, however, are derived from bodily counterparts. For instance, we take disinterested delight in the prosperity of our country which is as real as our delight in our own prosperity. Nor again do they admit that pleasure is derived from the memory or expectation of good, which was a doctrine of Epicurus. For they assert that the movement affecting the mind is exhausted in course of time. Again they hold that pleasure is not derived from sight or from hearing alone. At all events, we listen with pleasure to imitation of mourning, while the reality causes pain. They gave the names of absence of pleasure and absence of pain to the intermediate conditions. However, they insist that bodily pleasures are far better than mental pleasures, and bodily pains far worse than mental pains, and that this is the reason why offenders are punished with the former. For they assumed pain to be more repellent, pleasure more congenial. For these reasons they paid more attention to the body than to the mind. Hence, although pleasure is in itself desirable, yet they hold that the things which are productive of certain pleasures are often of a painful nature, the very opposite of pleasure; so that to accumulate the pleasures which are productive of happiness appears to them a most irksome business.'

For a Victorian Cyrenaic, see *Q.* 321.

293. Is humility a character flaw?

Baruch Spinoza (1632-1677) was a Dutch philosopher whose radical theology led to his excommunication from the local Jewish community. His thoughts on ethics were similarly unorthodox.

He believed that the essence of human nature was the drive to persevere, to increase one's powers of action, and to reject anything that causes a decrease in one's powers of action. The increase in one's power engenders joy, while its decrease induces sadness. To act in accordance with our nature, with our drive to persevere, is in itself virtuous, and so to pursue virtue is to pursue power and joy. Such pursuits, which arise from a rational understanding and fulfilment of our nature, make us active rather than passive beings. With his focus on power and joy, Spinoza sees no value in sombre passions such as humility and repentance. These passions limit and impede us and are thus contrary to our nature. Indeed, since it is in our nature to avoid such states, humility is actually very rare. More often than not humility is feigned, a mask worn by envy and ambition.

From *Ethics* –
'We are wont to call proud the man who boasts too much, who talks of nothing but his own virtues and other people's faults, who wishes to be first; and lastly who goes through life with a style and pomp suitable to those far above him in station. On the other hand, we call humble the man who too often blushes, who confesses his faults, who sets forth other men's virtues, and who, lastly, walks with bent head and is negligent of his attire. However, these emotions, humility and self-abasement, are extremely rare. For human nature, considered in itself, strives against them as much as it can; hence those, who are believed to be most self-abased and humble, are generally in reality the most ambitious and envious...

Humility is not a virtue; that is, it does not arise from reason. Humility is the sadness arising from a man's contemplation of his own weakness. Now in so far as a man knows himself by true reason, to that extent he is assumed to understand his own essence, that is, his own power. Therefore if a man, in contemplating himself, perceives some weakness in himself, it is not by virtue of his understanding himself, but by virtue of his power of activity being checked. But, if we assume that a man perceives his own weakness by virtue of understanding something stronger than himself, by the knowledge of which he determines his own power of activity, this is the same as saying that we conceive that a man understands himself distinctly because his power of activity is aided. Therefore humility, or the sadness which arises from a man's contemplation of his own weakness, does not arise from true contemplation or reason, and is not a virtue but a passive emotion.'

295. She is incapable of feeling guilt. Is this a sickness or a blessing?

According to the *Catechism of the Catholic Church*, 'Freedom makes man *responsible* for his acts' – a claim which, on one level, appears contradictory. Are responsibilities not a hindrance to freedom? Is freedom not the absolution from accountability and judgment?

Friedrich Nietzsche (1844-1900) believed that the connection between free will and responsibility was forged in order to subjugate. By labelling a person responsible, we are thereby justified in our oppression – called 'punishment' – of that person. The concept of free will was invented so that we might find others guilty, so that we might dominate them, so that we might poison them with passivity, dependence and cowardice: justice is institutionalised sadism.

To overcome the fetters of morality and end the enervation of guilt, we must, as Nietzsche wrote in *Twilight of the Idols*, free ourselves from the belief in free will.

'At present we no longer have any mercy upon the concept "free-will": we know only too well what it is—the most egregious theological trick that has ever existed for the purpose of making mankind "responsible" in a theological manner,—that is to say, to make mankind dependent upon theologians. I will now explain to you only the psychology of the whole process of inculcating the sense of responsibility. Wherever men try to trace responsibility home to anyone, it is the instinct of punishment and of the desire to judge which is active. Becoming is robbed of its innocence when any particular condition of things is traced to a will, to intentions and to responsible actions. The doctrine of the will was invented principally for the purpose of punishment,—that is to say, with the intention of tracing guilt. The whole of ancient psychology, or the psychology of the will, is the outcome of the fact that its originators, who were the priests at the head of ancient communities, wanted to create for themselves a right to administer punishments—or the right for God to do so. Men were thought of as "free" in order that they might be judged and punished—in order that they might be held guilty: consequently every action had to be regarded as voluntary, and the origin of every action had to be imagined as lying in consciousness (—in this way the most fundamentally fraudulent character of psychology was established as the very principle of psychology itself). Now that we have entered upon the opposite movement, now that we immoralists are trying with all our power to eliminate the concepts of guilt and punishment from the world once more, and to cleanse psychology, history, nature and all social institutions and customs of all signs of those two concepts, we recognise no more radical opponents than the theologians, who with their notion of "a moral order of things," still continue to pollute the innocence of Becoming with punishment and guilt. Christianity is the metaphysics of the hangman.

What then, alone, can our teaching be?—That no one gives man his qualities, neither God, society, his parents, his ancestors, nor himself (—this non-sensical idea which is at last refuted here, was taught as "intelligible freedom" by Kant, and perhaps even as early as Plato himself). No one is responsible for the fact that he exists at all, that he is constituted as he is, and that he happens to be in certain circumstances and in a particular environment. The fatality of his being cannot be divorced from the fatality of all that which has been and will be. This is not the result of an individual intention, of a will, of an aim, there is no attempt at attaining to any "ideal man," or "ideal happiness" or "ideal morality" with him,—it is absurd to wish him to be careering towards some sort of purpose. *We* invented the concept "purpose"; in reality purpose is altogether lacking.

One is necessary, one is a piece of fate, one belongs to the whole, one is in the whole,—there is nothing that could judge, measure, compare, and condemn our existence, for that would mean judging, measuring, comparing and condemning the whole. *But there is nothing outside the whole!* The fact that no one shall any longer be made responsible, that the nature of existence may not be traced to a *causa prima* [first cause], that the world is an entity neither as a sensorium nor as a spirit—*this alone is the great deliverance,*—thus alone is the innocence of Becoming restored…'

For Nietzsche, see *Qs.* 44 and 146.

305. I hold a belief that is of tremendous help to me, but I find evidence to suggest that it is false. Would it be more rational to ignore the evidence or abandon the belief?

William James's (1842-1910) understanding of truth can be summarised in this basic argument:

1. We ought to only believe those ideas that will serve a good life.
2. By definition, the truth is that which we ought to believe.
3. Therefore, the truth refers to those ideas that will serve a good life.

The first premise follows from the conviction that nothing is more valuable than a good life, and given the value of truth, James concludes that there can be no distinction between what is good and what is true.

As a theory which seeks to remain rooted in the practicalities of living, it is fitting that it germinated from a crisis in James's own life. At the age of 28, amid recurring depression and a general aimlessness, he was one day struck by a sudden wave of dread, an awareness of 'the pit of insecurity beneath the surface of life' and 'a horrible fear of my own existence'. For weeks after he suffered from fears of solitude and the dark.

After reading an essay on the nature of free will, however, James resolved to try to change his life by embracing the concept of free will: 'My first act of free will shall be to believe in free will... [I shall] believe in my individual reality and creative power'.

Though his resolve had little effect – he continued without direction for several more years – in his experimental attitude towards beliefs, his willingness to employ and test ideas out, we see a nascent form of his later philosophy.

From *Pragmatism* –

'*The true is the name of whatever proves itself to be good in the way of belief, and good, too, for definite, assignable reasons.* Surely you must admit this, that if there were *no* good for life in true ideas, or if the knowledge of them were positively disadvantageous and false ideas the only useful ones, then the current notion that truth is divine and precious, and its pursuit a duty, could never have grown up or become a dogma. In a world like that, our duty would be to *shun* truth, rather. But in this world, just as certain foods are not only agreeable to our taste, but good for our teeth, our stomach, and our tissues; so certain ideas are not only agreeable to think about, or agreeable as supporting other ideas that we are fond of, but they are also helpful in life's practical struggles. If there be any life that it is really better that we should lead, and if there be any idea which, if believed in, would help us to lead that life, then it would be really *better for us* to believe in that idea, *unless, indeed, belief in it incidentally clashed with other greater vital benefits.*

"What would be better for us to believe"! This sounds very like a definition of truth. It comes very near to saying "what we *ought* to believe": and in *that* definition none of you would find any oddity. Ought we ever not to believe what it is *better for us* to believe? And can we then keep the notion of what is better for us, and what is true for us, permanently apart?'

For James, see *Qs*. 114 and 121.

306. Imagine you saw a file of angels pass through your body and disappear. Would it be possible to prove whether the experience had been real or illusory?

Throughout her life the Spanish mystic **St Teresa of Ávila** (1515-1582) was predisposed towards states of emotional intensity. As a child she attempted to run away from home to Moorish territories in search of martyrdom (she was turned round by her uncle), as a teenager she was an ardent reader of romantic tales of chivalry, and as an adult she developed new forms of prayer which led to experiences of overwhelming ecstasy.

Owing to its depiction by the sculptor Bernini, her most famous religious experience involved the sudden appearance of an angel: 'In his hands I saw a great golden spear, and at the iron tip there appeared to be a point of fire. This he plunged into my heart several times so that it penetrated my entrails. When he pulled it out, I felt that he took them with it, and left me utterly consumed by the great love of God. The pain was so severe that it made me utter several moans.'

Her experiences were various. At times the divine beings were not perceived in the external environment but appeared to her from within. They did not always possess form but manifested as an invisible presence. Occasionally she levitated, though this got on her nerves.

These experiences were greeted by those she told with scepticism. Some suspected she was under the influence of the devil. In the passage below, taken from her autobiography *The Life of Saint Teresa*, she defends the veracity of her experiences. Among her contentions is the idea that the effects of a given experience are testament to its reality, and that the goodness of those effects is testament to the goodness of their cause. Her experiences had the effect of transforming her life for the better, indicating a cause both beneficent and wondrous.

'It is the most impossible of all impossible things that all this may be the work of the imagination. There is no ground whatever for the supposition; for the very beauty and whiteness of one of our Lord's Hands are beyond our imagination altogether. How is it that we see present before us, in a moment, what we do not remember, what we have never thought of, and, moreover, what, in a long space of time, the imagination could not compass, because, as I have just said, it far transcends anything we can comprehend in this life? This, then, is not possible. Whether we have any power in the matter or not will appear by what I am now going to say.

If the vision were the work of a man's own understanding – setting aside that such a vision would not accomplish the great results of the true one, nor, indeed, any at all – it would be as the act of one who tries to go to sleep, and yet continues awake, because sleep has not come. He longs for it, because of some necessity or weakness in his head: and so he lulls himself to sleep, and makes efforts to procure it, and now and then thinks he has succeeded; but, if the sleep be not real, it will not support him, nor supply strength to his head: on the contrary, his head will very often be the worse for it. So will it be here, in a measure; the soul will be dissipated, neither sustained nor strengthened; on the contrary, it will be wearied and disgusted. But, in the true vision, the riches which abide in the soul cannot be described; even the body receives health and comfort.

I urged this argument, among others, when they told me – as they often did – that my visions came from the evil one, and that I imagined them myself. I made use of certain illustrations, as well as I could, and as our Lord suggested to me. But all was to little purpose; for as there were most holy persons in the place – in comparison with whom I was a lost soul – whom God did not lead by this way, they were at once filled with fear; they thought it all came through my sins. And so my state was talked about, and came to the knowledge of many; though I had spoken of it to no one, except my confessor, or to those to whom he commanded me to speak of it.

I said to them once, "If they who thus speak of my state were to tell me that a person with whom I had just conversed, and whom I knew well, was not that person, but that I was deluding myself, and that they knew it, I should certainly trust them rather than my own eyes. But if that person left with me certain jewels, and if, possessing none previously, I held the jewels in my hand as pledges of a great love, and if I were now rich, instead of poor as before, I should not be able to believe this that they said, though I might wish it." These jewels I could now show them, for all who knew me saw clearly that my soul was changed, and so my confessor said; for the difference was very great in every way, and my confessor himself testified to the fact, since it was now different in every respect, and this was no fancy but something that everyone could most distinctly see. As I was formerly so wicked, I said, I could not believe that Satan, if he wished to deceive me and take me down to hell, would have recourse to means so adverse to his purpose as this, of rooting out my faults, implanting virtues and spiritual strength; for I saw clearly that I had become at once another person through the instrumentality of these visions.'

307. Generally speaking, should we trust appearances?

Arthur Eddington (1882-1944) was an English astrophysicist who, in addition to providing the first empirical confirmation of Albert Einstein's contention that light must bend as it passes near massive objects, made significant advances in our understanding of the internal structure of stars. Of more dubious scientific value, however, was his calculation that there are precisely 15, 747, 724, 136, 275, 002, 577, 605, 653, 961, 181, 555, 468, 044, 717, 914, 527, 116, 709, 366, 231, 425, 076, 185, 631, 031, 296 protons in the universe.

In the 1920s Eddington delivered a lecture series, later published as *The Nature of the Physical World*, on the recent advances in physics. He began by informing the audience that the world we experience is largely an illusion.

'I have settled down to the task of writing these lectures and have drawn up my chairs to my two tables. Two tables! Yes; there are duplicates of every object about me—two tables, two chairs, two pens.

This is not a very profound beginning to a course which ought to reach transcendent levels of scientific philosophy. But we cannot touch bedrock immediately; we must scratch a bit at the surface of things first. And whenever I begin to scratch the first thing I strike is—my two tables.

One of them has been familiar to me from earliest years. It is a commonplace object of that environment which I call the world. How shall I describe it? It has extension; it is comparatively permanent; it is coloured; above all it is substantial. By substantial I do not merely mean that it does not collapse when I lean upon it; I mean that it is constituted of "substance" and by that word I am trying to convey to you some conception of its intrinsic nature. It is a thing; not like space, which is a mere negation...

Table No. 2 is my scientific table. It is a more recent acquaintance and I do not feel so familiar with it. It does not belong to the world previously mentioned, that world which spontaneously appears around me when I open my eyes... My scientific table is mostly emptiness. Sparsely scattered in that emptiness are numerous electric charges rushing about with great speed; but their combined bulk amounts to less than a billionth of the bulk of the table itself. Notwithstanding its strange construction it turns out to be an entirely efficient table. It supports my writing paper as satisfactorily as table No. 1; for when I lay the paper on it the little electric particles with their headlong speed keep on hitting the underside, so that the paper is maintained in shuttlecock fashion at a nearly steady level. If I lean upon this table I shall not go through; or, to be strictly accurate, the chance of my scientific elbow going through my scientific table is so excessively small that it can be neglected in practical life. Reviewing their properties one by one, there seems to be nothing to choose between the two tables for ordinary purposes; but when abnormal circumstances befall, then my scientific table shows to advantage. If the house catches fire my scientific table will dissolve quite naturally into scientific smoke, whereas my familiar table undergoes a metamorphosis of its substantial nature which I can only regard as miraculous...

I need not tell you that modern physics has by delicate test and remorseless logic assured me that my second scientific table is the only one which is really there—wherever "there" may be. On the other hand I need not tell you that modern physics will never succeed in exorcising that first table—strange compound of external nature, mental imagery and inherited prejudice—which lies visible to my eyes and tangible to my grasp.'

311. 'We are never free of moods,' wrote the philosopher Martin Heidegger. Do you agree?

The following extract is taken from a letter **Herman Melville** (1819-1891) wrote to the novelist Nathaniel Hawthorne in which he warns against constructing philosophical principles on the foundation of temporary feelings. Yet, if Heidegger is right – if, in the words of Ralph Waldo Emerson, 'Life is a train of moods like a string of beads' – is there any hope for philosophy? Can we rise above the mind's celerity to find lasting truth?

'In reading some of Goethe's sayings, so worshipped by his votaries, I came across this, "*Live in the all.*" That is to say, your separate identity is but a wretched one, – good; but get out of yourself, spread and expand yourself, and bring to yourself the tinglings of life that are felt in the flowers and the woods, that are felt in the planets Saturn and Venus, and the Fixed Stars. What nonsense! Here is a fellow with a raging toothache. "My dear boy," Goethe says to him, "you are sorely afflicted with that tooth; but you must live in the all, and then you will be happy!" As with all great genius, there is an immense deal of flummery in Goethe, and in proportion to my own contact with him, a monstrous deal of it in me… This "all" feeling, though, there is some truth in. You must often have felt it, lying on the grass on a warm summer's day. Your legs seem to send out shoots into the earth. Your hair feels like leaves upon your head. This is the all feeling. But what plays the mischief with the truth is that men will insist upon the universal application of a temporary feeling or opinion.'

For Melville, see *Q.* 88.

315. Could an evil act ever be worthy of admiration?

Thomas De Quincey (1785-1859) regarded murder as performance art. While most of its practitioners are second-rate, geniuses do reside among its ranks. According to De Quincey, John Williams, an alleged murderer from the early 19th century, was one such genius: 'Like Aeschylus or Milton in poetry, like Michael Angelo in painting, he has carried his art to a point of colossal sublimity'.

Williams was accused of murdering the inhabitants of two households in the East End of London. At around midnight on December 7th, 1811, a husband, wife, infant and the husband's apprentice were murdered in the comfort of their home. Twelve days later, not far from the first massacre, at approximately the same time, a husband, wife and their maid were also murdered by an intruder. The bodies in both cases presented an admixture of bludgeoned skulls and slit throats.

De Quincey referred to these acts as 'the sublimest and most entire in their excellence that ever were committed'. At the time, thoughts on the nature of the sublime were very much in the air. Immanuel Kant had expounded his belief that the feeling of the sublime was evoked by the prospect of powerful and overwhelming natural threats, such as thunderstorms and hurricanes. The sense of our physical helplessness causes displeasure, but within the sublime, this displeasure is met with the pleasurable awareness that there are things more valuable to us than mere survival, things that would ennoble us to face our fears and confront the forces of nature. In that sense, nature has no dominion over us.

How might these ideas apply to murder? Perhaps for De Quincey the sublimity of murder consists in the murderer resisting the dominion of nature by, as it were, *becoming* a force of nature, by acting with all the violence, caprice and injustice of nature. The murderer mocks death by donning its robes.

Though De Quincey's enjoyment may seem macabre and unintelligible, it is noteworthy that murder is ubiquitous in art, from Agamemnon's bath to Desdemona's bed. And if we admire the depiction of murder, do we not, in a way, admire the idea of it?

From 'On Murder Considered as One of the Fine Arts' –

'I am for morality, and always shall be, and for virtue and all that; and I do affirm, and always shall, (let what will come of it,) that murder is an improper line of conduct—highly improper; and I do not stick to assert, that any man who deals in murder, must have very incorrect ways of thinking, and truly inaccurate principles; and so far from aiding and abetting him by pointing out his victim's hiding-place, as a great moralist of Germany declared it to be every good man's duty to do, I would subscribe one shilling and sixpence to have him apprehended, which is more by eighteen-pence than the most eminent moralists have subscribed for that purpose. But what then? Everything in this world has two handles. Murder, for instance, may be laid hold of by its moral handle, (as it generally is in the pulpit, and at the Old Bailey;) and *that*, I confess, is its weak side; or it may also be treated *aesthetically*, as the Germans call it, that is, in relation to good taste...

[W]hat says the Stagyrite [Aristotle]? He (in the Fifth Book, I think it is, of his Metaphysics,) describes what he calls χλεπτήν τέλειον, i.e. *a perfect thief*; and, as to Mr Howship, in a work of his on Indigestion, he makes no scruple to talk with admiration of a certain ulcer which he had seen, and which he styles 'a beautiful ulcer' ...

But the truth is, that, however objectionable *per se*, yet, relatively to others of their class, both a thief and an ulcer may have infinite degrees of merit. They are both imperfections, it is true; but to be imperfect being their essence, the very greatness of their imperfection becomes their perfection. *Spartam nactus es, hanc exorna* [Sparta is yours: adorn it]. A thief like Autolycus or Mr Barrington, and a grim phagedaenic ulcer, superbly defined, and running regularly through all its natural stages, may no less justly be regarded as ideals after *their* kind, than the most faultless moss-rose amongst flowers, in its progress from bud to 'bright consummate flower;' or, amongst human flowers, the most magnificent young female, apparelled in the pomp of womanhood. And thus not only the ideal of an inkstand may be imagined, (as Mr Coleridge demonstrated in his celebrated correspondence with Mr Blackwood,) in which, by the way, there is not so much, because an inkstand is a laudable sort of thing, and a valuable member of society; but even imperfection itself may have its ideal or perfect state.

Really, gentlemen, I beg pardon for so much philosophy at one time, and now, let me apply it. When a murder is in the paulo-postfuturum tense [the verb form for an event that is about to happen], and a rumour of it comes to our ears, by all means let us treat it morally. But suppose it over and done... Suppose the poor murdered man to be out of his pain, and the rascal that did it off like a shot, nobody knows whither; suppose, lastly, that we have done our best, by putting out our legs to trip up the fellow in his flight, but all to no purpose—'abiit, evasit,' &c.—why, then, I say, what's the use of any more virtue? Enough has been given to morality; now comes the turn of Taste and the Fine Arts. A sad thing it was, no doubt, very sad; but *we* can't mend it.

Therefore let us make the best of a bad matter; and, as it is impossible to hammer anything out of it for moral purposes, let us treat it aesthetically, and see if it will turn to account in that way. Such is the logic of a sensible man, and what follows? We dry up our tears, and have the satisfaction perhaps to discover, that a transaction, which, morally considered, was shocking, and without a leg to stand upon, when tried by principles of Taste, turns out to be a very meritorious performance. Thus all the world is pleased; the old proverb is justified, that it is an ill wind which blows nobody good; the amateur, from looking bilious and sulky, by too close an attention to virtue, begins to pick up his crumbs, and general hilarity prevails. Virtue has had her day; and henceforward, *Vertu* and Connoisseurship have leave to provide for themselves. Upon this principle, gentlemen, I propose to guide your studies, from Cain to Mr Thurtell. Through this great gallery of murder, therefore, together let us wander hand in hand, in delighted admiration, while I endeavour to point your attention to the objects of profitable criticism.'

For De Quincey, see *Q.* 162.

318. Can beauty be terrifying?

Andy Warhol once wrote, 'I always hear myself saying, "She's a beauty!" or "He's a beauty!" or "What a beauty!" but I never know what I'm talking about. I honestly don't know what beauty is...' Had he read less Truman Capote and more **Edmund Burke** (1729-97), he may well have found out.

From *A Philosophical Enquiry into the Origin of Our Ideas of the Sublime and Beautiful* –

'I am told that, in most languages, the objects of love are spoken of under diminutive epithets. It is so in all the languages of which I have any knowledge. In Greek the *ιον* and other diminutive terms are almost always the terms of affection and tenderness. These diminutives were commonly added by the Greeks to the names of persons with whom they conversed on terms of friendship and familiarity. Though the Romans were a people of less quick and delicate feelings, yet they naturally slid into the lessening termination upon the same occasions. Anciently, in the English language, the diminishing *ling* was added to the names of persons and things that were the objects of love. Some we retain still, as darling (or little dear), and a few others. But to this day, in ordinary conversation, it is usual to add the endearing name of *little* to everything we love; the French and Italians make use of these affectionate diminutives even more than we. In the animal creation, out of our own species, it is the small we are inclined to be fond of; little birds, and some of the smaller kinds of beasts. A great beautiful thing is a manner of expression scarcely ever used; but that of a great ugly thing is very common. There is a wide difference between admiration and love. The sublime, which is the cause of the former, always dwells on great objects, and terrible; the latter on small ones, and pleasing; we submit to what we admire, but we love what submits to us; in one case we are forced, in the other we are flattered, into compliance. In short, the ideas of the sublime and the beautiful stand on foundations so different, that it is hard, I had almost said impossible, to think of reconciling them in the same subject, without considerably lessening the effect of the one or the other upon the passions. So that, attending to their quantity, beautiful objects are comparatively small.

The next property constantly observable in such objects is *Smoothness*. A quality so essential to beauty, that I do not now recollect anything beautiful that is not smooth. In trees and flowers, smooth leaves are beautiful; smooth slopes of earth in gardens; smooth streams in the landscape; smooth coats of birds and beasts in animal beauties; in fine women, smooth skins; and in several sorts of ornamental furniture, smooth and polished surfaces. A very considerable part of the effect of beauty is owing to this quality; indeed the most considerable...

On closing this general view of beauty, it naturally occurs that we should compare it with the sublime; and in this comparison there appears a remarkable contrast. For sublime objects are vast in their dimensions, beautiful ones comparatively small; beauty should be smooth and polished; the great, rugged and negligent: beauty should shun the right line, yet deviate from it insensibly; the great in many cases loves the right line; and when it deviates, it often makes a strong deviation: beauty should not be obscure; the great ought to be dark and gloomy: beauty should be light and delicate; the great ought to be solid, and even massive. They are indeed ideas of a very different nature, one being founded on pain, the other on pleasure; and, however they may vary afterwards from the direct nature of their causes, yet these causes keep up an eternal distinction between them, a distinction never to be forgotten by any whose business it is to affect the passions...

When we have before us such objects as excite love and complacency, the body is affected, so far as I could observe, much in the following manner: the head reclines something on one side; the eyelids are more closed than usual, and the eyes roll gently with an inclination to the object; the mouth is a little opened, and the breath drawn slowly, with now and then a low sigh; the whole body is composed, and the hands fall idly to the sides. All this is accompanied with an inward sense of melting and languor. These appearances are always proportioned to the degree of beauty in the object, and of sensibility in the observer. And this gradation from the highest pitch of beauty and sensibility, even to the lowest of mediocrity and indifference, and their correspondent effects, ought to be kept in view, else this description will seem exaggerated, which it certainly is not. But from this description it is almost impossible not to conclude that beauty acts by relaxing the solids of the whole system.'

For Burke, see *Q*. 370.

320. Can art be immoral?

Bronzino's *An Allegory with Venus and Cupid* emerged from its 1958 restoration at the National Gallery a markedly more salacious painting.

To behold the painting prior to its restoration one would have seen a depiction of Venus embraced by a naked Cupid, who is cradling her head with one hand and fondling her breast with the other. The restoration revealed, however, that Venus's tongue, which is touching her son's lips, and her nipple, which is held between his fingers, had been painted over. Originally, moreover, there had been no sprig of myrtle covering both Cupid's inviting arse and the quiver angled suggestively towards it, nor a loincloth hiding Venus's genitalia. Evidently, over the course of its four-hundred-year life, this work of art had been deemed too good to dispose of yet too indecent to preserve.

For **Clive Bell** (1881-1964) – art critic and member of

the Bloomsbury Group – such censorship is fundamentally misguided. It misses the point of what art is. To look at a painting as a work of art is to focus on form alone; the content of the painting is entirely independent of its artistic value. A visual work of art cannot be immoral since, as art, it represents nothing. It is simply a configuration of colour, shape and space. As Bell declared, the 'first commandment of art' is 'Thou shalt create form'. Seen purely as art, there is, for instance, no arse in Bronzino's painting, only two overlapping parabolas.

In other words, art is not to be read but experienced. And to experience 'aesthetic emotion' we need know nothing of a painting's meaning, origin or history.

From *Art* –

'To appreciate a work of art we need bring with us nothing from life, no knowledge of its ideas and affairs, no familiarity with its emotions. Art transports us from the world of man's activity to a world of aesthetic exaltation. For a moment we are shut off from human interests; our anticipations and memories are arrested; we are lifted above the stream of life. The pure mathematician rapt in his studies knows a state of mind which I take to be similar, if not identical. He feels an emotion for his speculations which arises from no perceived relation between them and the lives of men, but springs, inhuman or super-human, from the heart of an abstract science. I wonder, sometimes, whether the appreciators of art and of mathematical solutions are not even more closely allied…

A painter too feeble to create forms that provoke more than a little aesthetic emotion will try to eke that little out by suggesting the emotions of life. To evoke the emotions of life he must use representation. Thus a man will paint an execution, and, fearing to miss with his first barrel of significant form, will try to hit with his second by raising an emotion of fear or pity.

But if in the artist an inclination to play upon the emotions of life is often the sign of a flickering inspiration, in the spectator a tendency to seek, behind form, the emotions of life is a sign of defective sensibility always. It means that his aesthetic emotions are weak or, at any rate, imperfect. Before a work of art people who feel little or no emotion for pure form find themselves at a loss. They are deaf men at a concert. They know that they are in the presence of something great, but they lack the power of apprehending it. They know that they ought to feel for it a tremendous emotion, but it happens that the particular kind of emotion it can raise is one that they can feel hardly or not at all. And so they read into the forms of the work those facts and ideas for which they are capable of feeling emotion, and feel for them the emotions that they can feel—the ordinary emotions of life. When confronted by a picture, instinctively they refer back its forms to the world from which they came. They treat created form as though it were imitated form, a picture as though it were a photograph. Instead of going out on the stream of art into a new world of aesthetic experience, they turn a sharp corner and come straight home to the world of human interests. For them the significance of a work of art depends on what they bring to it; no new thing is added to their lives, only the old material is stirred. A good work of visual art carries a person who is capable of appreciating it out of life into ecstasy: to use art as a means to the emotions of life is to use a telescope for reading the news. You will notice that people who cannot feel pure aesthetic emotions remember pictures by their subjects; whereas people who can, as often as not, have no idea what the subject of a picture is. They have never noticed the representative element, and so when they discuss pictures they talk about the shapes of forms and the relations and quantities of colours. Often they can tell by the quality of a single line whether or no a man is a good artist. They are concerned only with lines and colours, their relations and quantities and qualities; but from these they win an emotion more profound and far more sublime than any that can be given by the description of facts and ideas.'

321. Does art have a function?

> The ideas of the ancient Greek Cyrenaics (see *Q.* 287) reverberate through the Victorian writings of **Walter Pater** (1839-1894). Pater's *The Renaissance* was a key influence in the development of aestheticism, the movement which held that art should neither edify nor educate, that it is closer to a lover than a teacher, existing for its own sake, for the sake of beauty alone. Like motes of dust sparkling in the light, Pater saw existence as a sequence of vanishing moments. Life requires us to cleave ourselves to the fleeting present and gild it with passion's radiance.

'One of the most beautiful passages of Rousseau is that in the sixth book of the *Confessions*, where he describes the awakening in him of the literary sense. An undefinable taint of death had clung always about him, and now in early manhood he believed himself smitten by mortal disease. He asked himself how he might make as much as possible of the interval that remained; and he was not biassed by anything in his previous life when he decided that it must be by intellectual excitement, which he found just then in the clear, fresh writings of Voltaire. Well! we are all *condamnés*, as Victor Hugo says: we are all under sentence of death but with a sort of indefinite reprieve – *les hommes sont tous condamnés à mort avec des sursis indéfinis*: we have an interval, and then our place knows us no more. Some spend this interval in listlessness, some in high passions, the wisest, at least among "the children of this world," in art and song. For our one chance lies in expanding that interval, in getting as many pulsations as possible into the given time. Great passions may give us this quickened sense of life, ecstasy and sorrow of love, the various forms of enthusiastic activity, disinterested or otherwise, which come naturally to many of us. Only be sure it is passion – that it does yield you this fruit of a quickened, multiplied consciousness. Of such wisdom, the poetic passion, the desire of beauty, the love of art for its own sake, has most. For art comes to you proposing frankly to give nothing but the highest quality to your moments as they pass, and simply for those moments' sake.'

For Pater's great admirer, see *Q*. 214.

324. Is perfume art?

Should you wish to picture **Samuel Taylor Coleridge** (1772-1834) writing these words, imagine a 46-year-old man huddled over his desk, possibly high on opium, with 'large projecting eyebrows' and 'eyes rolling beneath them like a sea with darkened lustre', a mouth 'gross, voluptuous, open, eloquent', a chin 'good-humoured and round', a nose 'small, feeble', and a body 'inclining to the corpulent'. Such were William Hazlitt's (see *Qs*. 134 and 328) observations on first meeting his idol.

In *Essays on the Principles of Genial Criticism* Coleridge explains that art exists to excite the particular pleasure aroused by beauty. Beauty is harmony, the 'unity of the manifold, the coalescence of the diverse'. Seemingly, then, works such as Yves Klein's ultramarine monochrome paintings fail as art since there are no parts, only fields of a single hue. Coleridge thought the same of odours. While they are agreeable, they cannot be beautiful, for, he implied, unlike the eyes and ears, the nose cannot discern parts.

'The Beautiful, contemplated in its essentials, that is, in *kind* and not in *degree*, is that in which the *many*, still seen as many, becomes *one*. Take a familiar instance, one of a thousand. The frost on a window-pane has by accident crystallized into a striking resemblance of a tree or a seaweed. With what pleasure we trace the parts, and their relations to each other, and to the whole! Here is the stalk or trunk, and here the branches or sprays — sometimes even the buds or flowers. Nor will our pleasure be less, should the caprice of the crystallization represent some object disagreeable to us, provided only we can see or fancy the component parts each in relation to each, and all forming a whole. A lady would see an admirably painted tiger with pleasure, and at once pronounce it beautiful, — nay, an owl, a frog, or a toad, who would have shrieked or shuddered at the sight of the things themselves. So far is the Beautiful from depending wholly on association, that it is frequently produced by the mere removal of associations. Many a sincere convert to the beauty of various insects, as of the dragon-fly, the fangless snake, &c., has Natural History made, by exploding the terror or aversion that had been connected with them.

The most general definition of beauty, therefore, is — that I may fulfil my threat of plaguing my readers with hard words — Multeity in Unity. Now it will be always found, that whatever is the definition of the *kind*, independent of degree, becomes likewise the definition of the highest degree of that kind. An old coach-wheel lies in the coachmaker's yard, disfigured with tar and dirt (I purposely take the most trivial instances) — if I turn away my attention from these, and regard the *figure* abstractly, "still," I might say to my companion, "there is beauty in that wheel, and you yourself would not only admit, but would feel it, had you never seen a wheel before. See how the rays proceed from the centre to the circumferences, and how many different images are distinctly comprehended at one glance, as forming one whole, and each part in some harmonious relation to each and to all." But imagine the polished golden wheel of the chariot of the Sun, as the poets have described it: then the figure, and the real thing so figured, exactly coincide. There is nothing heterogeneous, nothing to abstract from: by its perfect smoothness and circularity in width, each part is (if I may borrow a metaphor from a sister sense) as perfect a melody, as the whole is a complete harmony. This, we should say, is beautiful throughout. Of all "the many," which I actually see, each and all are really reconciled into unity; while the effulgence from the whole coincides with, and seems to represent, the effluence of delight from my own mind in the intuition of it.

It seems evident then, first, that beauty is harmony, and subsists only in composition, and secondly, that the first species of the Agreeable can alone be a component part of the beautiful, that namely which is naturally consonant with our senses by the pre-established harmony between nature and the human mind; and thirdly, that even of this species, those objects only can be admitted (according to rule the first) which belong to the eye and ear, because they alone are susceptible of distinction of parts.'

325. Can art make you a better person?

The art critic Matthew Arnold advised that 'we are not to take *Anna Karenina* as a work of art; we are to take it as a piece of life. A piece of life it is. The author has not invented and combined it, he has seen it.' **Leo Tolstoy** (1828-1910), however, would have rejected this distinction between art and life. Tolstoy argued that art is the transmission of feelings between the artist and the beholder. The art work is a solvent of difference. It fuses and unites. So there is no artifice involved: genuine feelings are transmitted, true fellowship is engendered.

A consequence of Tolstoy's view is that a work of art produced in isolation is thereby incapable of artistic value. Indeed, Tolstoy believed that the more people a work of art can unite, the greater it is. Art should express universal emotions. With this in mind, while he praised Charles Dickens' *A Christmas Carol,* he censured Beethoven's Ninth Symphony for being too long and complicated for 'normal people'.

From *What is Art?* –

'To see the aim and purpose of art in the pleasure we get from it, is like assuming (as is done by people of the lowest moral development, e.g. by savages) that the purpose and aim of food is the pleasure derived when consuming it.

Just as people who conceive the aim and purpose of food to be pleasure cannot recognise the real meaning of eating, so people who consider the aim of art to be pleasure cannot realise its true meaning and purpose, because they attribute to an activity the meaning of which lies in its connection with the other phenomena of life, the false and exceptional aim of pleasure. People come to understand that the meaning of eating lies in the nourishment of the body, only when they cease to consider that the object of that activity is pleasure. And it is the same with regard to art. People will come to understand the meaning of art only when they cease to consider that the aim of that activity is beauty, that is to say, pleasure...

In order correctly to define art, it is necessary, first of all, to cease to consider it as a means to pleasure and to consider it as one of the conditions of human life. Viewing it in this way we cannot fail to observe that art is one of the means of intercourse between man and man.

Every work of art causes the receiver to enter into a certain kind of relationship both with him who produced, or is producing, the art, and with all those who, simultaneously, previously, or subsequently, receive the same artistic impression.

Speech, transmitting the thoughts and experiences of men, serves as a means of union among them, and art acts in a similar manner. The peculiarity of this latter means of intercourse, distinguishing it from intercourse by means of words, consists in this, that whereas by words a man transmits his thoughts to another, by means of art he transmits his feelings.

The activity of art is based on the fact that a man, receiving through his sense of hearing or sight another man's expression of feeling, is capable of experiencing the emotion which moved the man who expressed it. To take the simplest example; one man laughs, and another who hears becomes merry; or a man weeps, and another who hears feels sorrow... a man expresses his feeling of admiration, devotion, fear, respect, or love to certain objects, persons, or phenomena, and others are infected by the same feelings of admiration, devotion, fear, respect, or love to the same objects, persons, and phenomena.

And it is upon this capacity of man to receive another man's expression of feeling and experience those feelings himself, that the activity of art is based.

If a man infects another or others, directly, immediately, by his appearance, or by the sounds he gives vent to at the very time he experiences the feeling; if he causes another man to yawn when he himself cannot help yawning, or to laugh or cry when he himself is obliged to laugh or cry, or to suffer when he himself is suffering that does not amount to art.

Art begins when one person, with the object of joining another or others to himself in one and the same feeling, expresses that feeling by certain external indications. To take the simplest example: a boy, having experienced, let us say, fear on encountering a wolf, relates that encounter; and, in order to evoke in others the feeling he has experienced, describes himself, his condition before the encounter, the surroundings, the wood, his own lightheartedness, and then the wolf's appearance, its movements, the distance between himself and the wolf, etc. All this, if only the boy when telling the story, again experiences the feelings he had lived through and infects the hearers and compels them to feel what the narrator had experienced, is art. If even the boy had not seen a wolf but had frequently been afraid of one, and if, wishing to evoke in others the fear he had felt, he invented an encounter with a wolf, and recounted it so as to make his hearers share the feelings he experienced when he feared the wolf, that also would be art. And just in the same way it is art if a man, having experienced either the fear of suffering or the attraction of enjoyment (whether in reality or in imagination), expresses these feelings on canvas or in marble so that others are infected by them. And it is also art if a man feels or imagines to himself feelings of delight, gladness, sorrow, despair, courage, or despondency and the transition from one to another of these feelings, and expresses these feelings by sounds, so that the hearers are infected by them, and experience them as they were experienced by the composer…

Art like speech is a means of communication and therefore of progress, that is, of the movement of humanity forward towards perfection. Speech renders accessible to men of the latest generations all the knowledge discovered by the experience and reflection, both of preceding generations and of the best and foremost men of their own times; art renders accessible to men of the latest generations all the feelings experienced by their predecessors and also those felt by their best and foremost contemporaries. And as the evolution of knowledge proceeds by truer and more necessary knowledge dislodging and replacing what was mistaken and unnecessary, so the evolution of feeling proceeds by means of art – feelings less kind and less necessary for the well-being of mankind being replaced by others kinder and more needful for that end. That is the purpose of art. And, speaking now of its subject-matter, the more art fulfils that purpose the better the art, and the less it fulfils it the worse the art.'

326. Is poetry flammable?

Does Verdi's *Requiem* cease to exist when it is not being performed? Is every performance a kind of resurrection? If not, this leads one to wonder what sort of thing the *Requiem* actually is. If it does not perish beyond the final notes of the 'Libera me', if it continues to exist in silence, then apparently it is not audible in essence.

According to the English philosopher and archaeologist **R. G. Collingwood** (1889-1943) a work of art is an imaginary thing. The sounds heard during a performance of Verdi's *Requiem* are not the music but the music's medium. We find the music *through* the notes, not within them.

The distinction between the work of art and its tangible medium applies to all art forms. Leonardo, for instance, while working on the *Last Supper* would stand for hours staring at the incomplete painting. It was during these pauses that the true composition was taking place. The painting is not the realisation of the imagination. The mural itself is not the *Last Supper*. The mural is its vehicle, the means by which we can access Leonardo's imaginary composition.

From *The Principles of Art* –

'When a man makes up a tune, he may and very often does at the same time hum it or sing it or play it on an instrument. He may do none of these things, but write it on paper. Or he may both hum it or the like, and also write it on paper at the same time or afterwards. Also he may do these things in public, so that the tune at its very birth becomes public property... But all these are accessories of the real work, though some of them are very likely useful accessories. The actual making of the tune is something that goes on in his head, and nowhere else.

I have already said that a thing which "exists in a person's head" and nowhere else is alternatively called an imaginary thing... Hence the making of a tune is an instance of imaginative creation. The same applies to the making of a poem, or a picture, or any other work of art...

When, speaking of a work of art (tune, picture, &c.), we mean by art a specific craft, intended as a stimulus for producing specific emotional effects in an audience, we certainly mean to designate by the term "work of art" something that we should call real. The artist as magician or purveyor of amusement is necessarily a craftsman making real things, and making them out of some material according to some plan. His works are as real as the works of an engineer, and for the same reason.

But it does not at all follow that the same is true of an artist proper. His business is not to produce an emotional effect in an audience, but, for example, to make a tune. This tune is already complete and perfect when it exists merely as a tune in his head, that is, an imaginary tune. Next, he may arrange for the tune to be played before an audience. Now there comes into existence a real tune, a collection of noises. But which of these two things is the work of art? Which of them is the music? The answer is implied in what we have already said: the music, the work of art, is not the collection of noises, it is the tune in the composer's head. The noises made by the performers, and heard by the audience, are not the music at all; they are only means by which the audience, if they listen intelligently (not otherwise), can reconstruct for themselves the imaginary tune that existed in the composer's head.

This is not a paradox. It is not something παρά δόξαν, contrary to what we ordinarily believe and express in our ordinary speech. We all know perfectly well, and remind each other often enough, that a person who hears the noises the instruments make is not thereby possessing himself of the music. Perhaps no one can do that unless he does hear the noises; but there is something else which he must do as well. Our ordinary word for this other thing is listening; and the listening which we have to do when we hear the noises made by musicians is in a way rather like the thinking we have to do when we hear the noises made, for example, by a person lecturing on a scientific subject. We hear the sound of his voice; but what he is doing is not simply to make noises, but to develop a scientific thesis. The noises are meant to assist us in achieving what he assumes to be our purpose in coming to hear him lecture, that is, thinking this same scientific thesis for ourselves. The lecture, therefore, is not a collection of noises made by the lecturer with his organs of speech; it is a collection of scientific thoughts related to those noises in such a way that a person who not only hears but thinks as well becomes able to think these thoughts for himself. We may call this the communication of thought by means of speech, if we like; but if we do, we must think of communication not as an "imparting" of thought by the speaker to the hearer, the speaker somehow planting his thought in the hearer's receptive mind, but as a "reproduction" of the speaker's thought by the hearer, in virtue of his own active thinking.

The parallel with listening to music is not complete. The two cases are similar at one point, dissimilar at another. They are dissimilar in that a concert and a scientific lecture are different things, and what we are trying to "get out of" the concert is a thing of a different kind from the scientific thoughts we are trying to "get out of" the lecture. But they are similar in this: that just as what we get out of the lecture is something other than the noises we hear proceeding from the lecturer's mouth, so what we get out of the concert is something other than the noises made by the performers. In each case, what we get out of it is something which we have to reconstruct in our own minds, and by our own efforts; something which remains for ever inaccessible to a person who cannot or will not make efforts of the right kind, however completely he hears the sounds that fill the room in which he is sitting.'

328. Has Shakespeare outlived his life?

Consider these claims regarding the nature of language:

- We have a shared understanding of words (if we didn't, communication would be impossible).
- Given that words are shared but our mental states are particular to us, it follows that words cannot be mental entities.
- Given, further, that a deaf person can understand words even though she has never heard them spoken, as can a blind person who has never seen them written, it follows that words are neither visible nor audible – they are not physical entities.

Similar thoughts led the German philosopher Gottlob Frege to conclude that language exists in a 'third realm' beyond the realms of the mental and the physical: unlike dreams, it is outside of our minds, unlike sand, it is immaterial. (Take note, the logic of the third bullet point is rather suspect.)

If this is correct, if words have neither the evanescence of the mental nor the senescence of the physical, then perhaps they are, as **William Hazlitt** (1778-1830) wrote, 'things that last for ever'.

From his essay 'On Thought and Action' –

'Actions pass away and are forgotten, or are only discernible in their effects: conquerors, statesmen, and kings live but by their names stamped on the page of history. Hume says rightly that more people think about Virgil and Homer (and that continually) than ever trouble their heads about Caesar or Alexander. In fact, poets are a longer-lived race than heroes: they breathe more of the air of immortality. They survive more entire in their thoughts and acts. We have all that Virgil or Homer did, as much as if we had lived at the same time with them: we can hold their work in our hands, or lay them on our pillows, or put them to our lips. Scarcely a trace of what the others did is left upon the earth, so as to be visible to common eyes. The one, the dead authors, are living men, still breathing and moving in their writings. The others, the conquerors of the world, are but the ashes in an urn. The sympathy (so to speak) between thought and thought is more intimate and vital than that between thought and action. Thought is linked to thought as flame kindles into flame: the tribute of admiration to the manes of departed heroism is like burning incense in a marble monument. Words, ideas, feelings, with the progress of time harden into substances: things, bodies, actions, moulder away, or melt into a sound, into thin air! – Yet though the Schoolmen in the Middles Ages disputed more about the texts of Aristotle than the battle of Arbela, perhaps Alexander's Generals in his lifetime admired his pupil [Alexander] as much and liked him better. For not only a man's actions are effaced and vanish with him; his virtues and generous qualities die with him also: his intellect only is immortal and bequeathed unimpaired to posterity. Words are the only things that last for ever.'

For Hazlitt, see *Q*. 134.

330. Does anything ever happen without a cause?

'Where the individual begins, life begins. The two are inseparable, life and individuality,' wrote **D. H. Lawrence** (1885-1930).

Noting that 'individual' derives from the Latin *individualis*, meaning indivisible, helps to clarify Lawrence's meaning. A given organism, such as yourself, is not a combination of inherited parts. You are not merely a reconfiguration of the old but something new and irreducibly different. You cannot look to your parents to find yourself. Your ancestry is insignificant. The past does not contain you. Your existence is unprecedented. You are inexplicable, unfathomable, a singularity.

From *Psychoanalysis and the Unconscious* –

'[I]n every individual organism, an individual nature, an individual consciousness, is spontaneously created at the moment of conception. We say *created*. And by *created* we mean spontaneously appearing in the universe, out of nothing. *Ex nihilo nihil fit* [From nothing comes nothing]. It is true that an individual is also generated. By the fusion of two nuclei, male and female, we understand the process of generation. And from the process of generation we may justly look for a new unit, according to the law of cause and effect. As a natural or automatic result of the process of generation we may look for a new unit of existence. But the nature of this new unit must derive from the natures of the parents, also by law. And this we deny. We deny that the nature of any new creature derives from the natures of its parents. The nature of the infant is *not* just a new permutation-and-combination of elements contained in the natures of the parents. There is in the nature of the infant that which is utterly unknown in the natures of the parents. Something which could never be derived from the natures of all the existent individuals or previous individuals. There is in the nature of the infant something entirely new, underived, underivable, something which is, and which will for ever remain, *causeless*. And this something is the unanalysable, undefinable reality of individuality. Every time at the moment of conception of every higher organism an individual nature incomprehensibly arises in the universe, out of nowhere. Granted the whole cause-and-effect process of generation and evolution, still the individual is not explained. The individual unit of consciousness and being which arises at the conception of every higher organism arises by pure creation, by a process not susceptible to understanding, a process which takes place outside the field of mental comprehension, where mentality, which is definitely limited, cannot and does not exist.

This causeless created nature of the individual being is the same as the old mystery of the divine nature of the soul. Religion was right and science is wrong. Every individual creature has a soul, a specific individual nature the origin of which cannot be found in any cause-and-effect process whatever. Cause-and-effect will not explain even the individuality of a single dandelion. There is no assignable cause, and no logical reason, for individuality. On the contrary, individuality appears in defiance of all scientific law, in defiance even of reason.'

For Lawrence, see *Q*. 147.

349. He believes that God exists. She believes that He does not. Is one of them wrong?

On a question such as this **Sextus Empiricus** (*fl.* 3rd c) would offer no judgment. He was a Pyrrhonian Sceptic who believed that tranquillity can be only achieved in matters of philosophy or theology by abstaining from belief; a kind of epistemic celibacy. For any philosophical claim, the Sceptic will nullify its power by finding an equally convincing contrary claim. By cancelling out every argument, the Sceptic is happily left with nothing. Unusually, then, for a philosophical school, Scepticism is not a set of beliefs but rather a method or skill.

From *Outlines of Pyrrhonism* –

'The originating cause of Scepticism is, we say, the hope of attaining quietude. Smart and energetic people who were perturbed by the contradictions in things and in doubt as to which of the alternatives they ought to accept, were led on to inquire what is true in things and what false, hoping by the settlement of the question to attain quietude. The main basic principle of the Sceptic system is that of opposing to every proposition an equal proposition; for we believe that as a consequence of this we end by ceasing to dogmatise...

Our next subject will be the End of the Sceptic system. Now an "End" is "that for which all actions or reasonings are undertaken, while it exists for the sake of none"; or, otherwise, "the ultimate object of appetency." We assert still that the Sceptic's End is quietude in respect of matters of opinion and moderate feeling in respect of things unavoidable. For the Sceptic, having set out to philosophise with the object of passing judgment on the sense-impressions and ascertaining which of them are true and which false, so as to attain quietude thereby, found himself involved in contradictions of equal weight, and being unable to decide between them suspended judgment; and as he was thus in suspense there followed, as it happened, the state of quietude in respect of matters of opinion...

The Sceptic, in fact, had the same experience which is said to have befallen the painter Apelles. Once, they say, when he was painting a horse and wished to represent in the painting the horse's foam, he was so unsuccessful that he gave up the attempt and flung at the picture the sponge on which he used to wipe the paints off his brush, and the mark of the sponge produced the effect of a horse's foam. So, too, the Sceptics were in hopes of gaining quietude by means of a decision regarding the disparity of the objects of sense and of thought, and being unable to effect this they suspended judgment; and they found that quietude, as if by chance, followed upon their suspense, even as a shadow follows its substance.'

For Sextus Empiricus's Sceptical forebear, see *Q*. 188.

350. He believes that God exists. She believes that He does not. Is there a significant difference between them?

> **Tertullian** (*c.* 160-220) was an early Latin theologian from Carthage who famously wrote these perplexing lines: 'The Son of God died; it is believable because it is foolish. And having been buried he resurrected; it is certain because it is impossible.'
>
> In his *Apology* Tertullian argued that a profound difference exists between Christians and non-Christians. Christians alone possess a distinctive kind of purity constituted by their conviction that our thoughts ought to be as virtuous as our actions, their fear of eternal punishment and their belief in the ever-present eye of God.
>
> The chasm is arguably at its greatest between Christians and philosophers: 'What have philosopher and Christian in common, — the disciple of Greece and the disciple of heaven, — the business of the one with reputation, of the other with salvation, — the man of words and the man of deeds, — the builder and the destroyer, — the friend and the foe of error, — the man who corrupts the truth, and the man who restores it and proclaims it — the thief of truth and its guardian?'

'We, then, alone are innocent. What is surprising in that, if it must be so? And it must be. Innocence we have been taught by God; in its perfection we know it, as revealed by a perfect teacher; faithfully we keep it as committed to us by one who reads the heart and cannot be despised. It was but man's opinion that gave you your idea of innocence, man's authority that enjoined it. So your rule of life is neither complete nor does it inspire such fear as to lead to true innocence. Man's skill to make clear what is truly good is no more than his authority to enforce it; the one may as easily be mistaken as the other despised. And to come to the point, which is the ampler saying: Thou shalt not kill, or, Do not even be angry? Which is more perfect, to forbid adultery or to prohibit a single lustful look? Which is the deeper law, to restrain from doing evil or from even speaking it? Which is the more thorough, not to permit the doing of an injury or to allow no retaliation? Though at the same time you must recognize that your own laws, which seem to tend to innocence, drew from the divine law, which is the more ancient pattern. We have spoken already of the date of Moses.

But what authority can man's laws have, when a man may have the luck to evade them, again and again undiscovered in his guilt, sometimes to despise them, as he breaks them of choice or of necessity? Think over all this, remembering how short is any punishment that will not continue after death. That is why Epicurus makes light of all torture and pain; if it is slight, he says, you may despise it, if it is great it will not be long. Yes! We who are examined in the sight of God who sees all, we who foresee an eternal punishment from His hand, we well may be the only ones to attain innocence; since, at once from fullness of knowledge, from the difficulty of concealment, from the greatness of the torture (not long, but eternal), we fear Him…'

For early Christian theologians, see *Q*. 65 and *Q*. 356.

351. Could an omnipotent being create a tennis ball that was not a tennis ball?

Here we have two conflicting extracts from two different philosophers. The first is collated from various letters written by **René Descartes** (1596-1650). The second is from *Summa theologiae* by **Thomas Aquinas** (1225-1274).

'In general we can be quite certain that God can do whatever we are able to understand, but not that He cannot do what we are unable to understand. For it would be presumptuous to think that our imagination extends as far as His power… [T]he power of God can have no limit… I would not even dare to say that God cannot arrange that a mountain should exist without a valley, or that one and two should not make three; but I only say that He has given me a mind of such a nature that I cannot conceive of a mountain without a valley or a sum of one and two which would not be three, and so on, and that such things imply contradictions in my conception.'

* * *

'That which implies being and non-being at the same time is repugnant to the idea of an absolutely possible thing, within the scope of the divine omnipotence. For such cannot come under the divine omnipotence, not because of any defect in the power of God, but because it has not the nature of a feasible or possible thing. Therefore, everything that does not imply a contradiction in terms, is numbered amongst those possible things, in respect of which God is called omnipotent: whereas whatever implies contradiction does not come within the scope of divine omnipotence, because it cannot have the aspect of possibility. Hence it is better to say that such things cannot be done, than that God cannot do them. Nor is this contrary to the word of the angel who said, saying: *No word shall be impossible with God.* For whatever implies a contradiction cannot be a word, because no intellect can possibly conceive such a thing.'

For Descartes, see *Q*. 26.

355. Can we give back to our parents more than we have received from them?

It is written in Jewish rabbinic literature, 'Honour the body that bore you, and the breasts that gave you suck, maintain your parents, for your parents took part in your creation.

For man owes his existence to God, to his father, and to his mother. When a human being honours his parents, God says: "I consider it as if I had dwelled among men and they had honoured Me," but if people do not honour their parents, God says: "It is good that I do not dwell among men, or they would have treated Me superciliously, too."'

From a philosophical perspective, these moral prescriptions arguably commit what is known as the genetic fallacy, namely, the attribution of undue significance to the origins of things. **Lucius Annaeus Seneca** (*c.* 4 BCE-65 CE) would concur. He claimed that the cause of our existence is of little importance to our ongoing lives. Beginnings in themselves warrant no special reverence: the tree should not humble itself before the seed.

From 'On Benefits' –

'I could never have obtained anything without having previously received the boon of existence from my parents; yet it does not follow from this that whatever I obtain is less than that without which I could not obtain it. If my nurse had not fed me when I was a child, I should not have been able to conduct any of those enterprises which I now carry on, both with my head and with my hand, nor should I ever have obtained the fame which is due to my labours both in peace and war; would you on that account argue that the services of a nurse were more valuable than the most important undertakings? Yet is not the nurse as important as the father, since without the benefits which I have received from each of them alike, I should have been alike unable to effect anything? If I owe all that I now can do to my original beginning, I cannot regard my father or my grandfather as being this original beginning; there always will be a spring further back, from which the spring next below is derived. Yet no one will argue that I owe more to unknown and forgotten ancestors than to my father; though really I do owe them more, if I owe it to my ancestors that my father begat me...

"Whatever I have bestowed upon my father," says my opponent, "however great it may be, yet is less valuable than what my father has bestowed upon me, because if he had not begotten me, it never could have existed at all." By this mode of reasoning, if a man has healed my father when ill, and at the point of death, I shall not be able to bestow anything upon him equivalent to what I have received from him; for had my father not been healed, he could not have begotten me. Yet think whether it be not nearer the truth to regard all that I can do, and all that I have done, as mine, due to my own powers and my own will? Consider what the fact of my birth is in itself; you will see that it is a small matter, the outcome of which is dubious, and that it may lead equally to good or to evil; no doubt it is the first step to everything, but because it is the first, it is not on that account more important than all the others...

It is not a good thing to live, but to live well. "But," say you, "I do live well." True, but I might have lived ill; so that your part in me is merely this, that I live. If you claim merit to yourself for giving me mere life, bare and helpless, and boast of it as a great boon, reflect that this you claim merit for giving me is a boon which I possess in common with flies and worms. In the next place, if I say no more than that I have applied myself to honourable pursuits, and have guided the course of my life along the path of rectitude, then you have received more from your benefit than you gave; for you gave me to myself ignorant and unlearned, and I have returned to you a son such as you would wish to have begotten...

"But," says our opponent, "whatever you do, whatever you are able to give to your father, is part of his benefit bestowed upon you." So it is the benefit of my teacher that I have become proficient in liberal studies; yet we pass on from those who taught them to us, at any rate from those who taught us the alphabet; and although no one can learn anything without them, yet it does not follow that whatsoever success one subsequently obtains, one is still inferior to those teachers. There is a great difference between the beginning of a thing and its final development; the beginning is not equal to the thing at its greatest, merely upon the ground that, without the beginning, it could never have become so great.'

For Seneca, see *Q*. 220.

356. 'They fuck you up, your mum and dad,' wrote the poet Philip Larkin. Do you agree?

In *The Life and Times of Tristram Shandy, Gentleman* the eponymous hero attributes his shortcomings in life to the clumsy circumstances of his conception. Had his mother not interrupted his father during the act by asking whether he'd forgotten to wind the clock, Tristram's life would have assumed a different complexion: 'I wish either my father or my mother, or indeed both of them, as they were in duty both equally bound to it, had minded what they were about when they begot me; had they duly consider'd how much depended upon what they were then doing;—that not only the production of a rational Being was concerned in it, but that possibly the happy formation and temperature of his body, perhaps his genius and the very cast of his mind;—and, for aught they knew to the contrary, even the fortunes of his whole house might take their turn from the humours and dispositions which were then uppermost…'

In an altogether more solemn text, *Homilies on Leviticus*, the early Christian theologian **Origen** (*c.* 185-254) – a man reputed to have castrated himself – finds agreement with Tristram Shandy. The climate of our conception does matter, however, unlike Shandy, Origen believes that the process is ineluctably damning. Since we were conceived through the concupiscence of our parents, we are born polluted, stained by their sin, and this is why as infants we must be baptised. Put plainly, their fucking fucked us up.

'But if you would hear what other saints also think of that birth [in the flesh], hear David saying, "I was conceived in iniquities, and in sins did my mother bear me," showing that whatsoever soul is born in the flesh is polluted by the defilement of iniquity and sin...

Whosoever cometh into this world is said to be made in a certain contamination. Wherefore also Scripture saith, "No one is clean from defilement, not even if his life be one day." For from the very fact, that he was placed in his mother's womb, and takes the matter of his body from the origin of his father's seed, he may be said to be contaminated in father and in mother. Or know you not, that when the male child is forty days old, it is offered at the altar, to be purified there, as having been polluted in the conception itself, either of the paternal seed or the maternal womb. Every man, then, was polluted in father and in mother, but Jesus, my Lord, alone entered pure into this generation; He was not defiled in his mother [being a virgin]. For He entered a body undefiled... He was not defiled then in his mother, but neither was he in his father. For Joseph yielded no part in his generation, except ministry and love.'

For early Christian theologians, see *Qs*. 65 and 350.

359. There is a list that details every fact about you. There is another list that details every fact about the full-stop at the end of this sentence. Is your list longer?

From *Centuries of Meditations* by the poet and Anglican clergyman **Thomas Traherne** (*c.* 1637-1674) –

'Suppose a river, or a drop of water, an apple or a sand, an ear of corn, or an herb: God knoweth infinite excellencies in it more than we: He seeth how it relateth to angels and men; how it proceedeth from the perfect Lover to the most perfectly Beloved; how it representeth all His attributes; how it conduceth in its place, by the best of means to the best of ends: and for this cause it cannot be beloved too much. God the Author and God the End is to be beloved in it; Angels and men are to be beloved in it; and it is highly to be esteemed for all their sakes. O what a treasure is every sand when truly understood!'

361. Do babies know that they exist?

In the passage below from 'An Introduction to the Philosophy of Consciousness', the St Andrews philosopher **James Frederick Ferrier** (1808-1864) argues that maturation cannot be wholly mimetic. The notion that independence can be taught is an absurdity: if everything we said or did was derived from a lesson we'd received, we'd be a mere copy of what went before. To become a separate being we must acquire abilities we cannot learn.

For Ferrier, the formative act in one's life as an independent being is the first use of the word 'I'. We cannot be taught how to use this word; it requires deviation from the environment. This primal deviation is the start of consciousness and thus constitutes a kind of second birth. Prior to the ability to use the first-person pronoun, an infant cannot be considered conscious and therefore cannot know that it exists as a distinct being. Indeed, prior to this point the infant does not exist as a distinct being. Only through the assertion of self-awareness do we become a self.

'It is a well-known fact that children, for some time after they acquire the use of language, speak of themselves *in the third person*, calling themselves John, Tom, or whatever else their names may be. Some speak thus for a longer, others for a shorter period; but all of them invariably speak for a certain time after this fashion. What does this prove, and how is it to be accounted for?

In the first place, it proves that they have not yet acquired the notion of their own personality. Whatever their intellectual or rational state may in other respects be, they have not combined with it the conception of *self*. In other words, it proves that as yet they are unconscious. They as yet exist merely *for others*, not *for themselves*...

So long, then, as this state of things continues, the human being is to be regarded as leading altogether mere animal life, as living completely under the dominion and within the domain of nature. The law of its whole being is the law of causality. Its sensations, feelings of every kind, and all its exercises of reason are mere effects, which again in their turn are capable of becoming causes. It cannot be said to be without "mind," if by the attribution of "mind" to it we mean that it is subject to various sensations, passions, desires, &c.; but it certainly is without consciousness, or that notion of self, that realisation of its own personality, which, in the subsequent stages of its existence, accompanies these modifications of its being...

For let it be particularly noted that the notion of self is a great deal more than a mere notion, — that is to say, it possesses far more than a mere logical value and contents — it is absolutely genetic or creative. *Thinking* oneself "I" *makes* oneself "I"; and it is only *by thinking* himself "I" that a man *can* make himself "I"; or, in other words, change an unconscious thing into that which is now a conscious self. Nothing else will or can do it. So long as a Being does *not* think itself "I", it does not and cannot become "I". No other being, no being except itself, can make it "I" ...

But now mark the moment when the child pronounces the word "I", and knows what this expression means. Here is a new and most important step taken. Let no one regard this step as insignificant, or treat our mention of it lightly and superciliously; for, to say the least of it, it is a step the like of which in magnitude and wonder the human being never yet took, and never shall take again, throughout the whole course of his rational and immortal career. We have read in fable of Circaean charms, which changed men into brutes; but here in this little monosyllable is contained a truer and more potent charm, the spell of an inverted and unfabulous enchantment, which converts the *feral* into the *human* being. The origination of this little monosyllable lifts man out of the natural into the moral universe. It places him, indeed, upon a perilous pre-eminence, being the assertion of nothing less than his own absolute independence...

We have already stated that the child's employment of language previous to his use of the word "I" may be accounted for upon the principle of imitation, or that at any rate it falls to be considered as a mere illustration of the general law of cause and effect. He hears other people applying certain sounds to designate certain objects; and when these objects or similar ones are presented, or in any way recalled, to him, the consequence is, that he utters the same sounds in connection with their presence. All this takes place, very naturally, under the common law of association. But neither association, nor the principle of imitation, nor any conceivable modification of the law of cause and effect, will account for the child's use of the word "I". In originating and using this term, he reverses, or runs counter to all these laws, and more particularly performs a process diametrically opposed to any act of imitation. Take an illustration of this: A child hears another person call a certain object a "table": well, the power of imitation naturally leads him to call the same thing, and any similar thing, a "table". Suppose, next, that the child hears this person apply to himself the word "I": In this case, too, the power of imitation would naturally (that is to say, letting it operate here in the same way as it did in the case of the table) lead the child to call that man "I". But is this what the child does? No. As soon as he becomes conscious, he ceases, so far at least as the word "I" is concerned, to be an imitator. He still applies the word "table" to the objects to which other people apply that term; and in this he imitates them. But with regard to the word "I" he applies this expression to a thing totally different from that which he hears all other people applying it to. They apply it to themselves, but he does not apply it *to them,* but *to himself*; and in this he is not an imitator, but the absolute originator of a new notion, upon which he now, and henceforth, takes up his stand, and which leads him on in the career of a destiny most momentous, and altogether anomalous and new...

In the use and understanding of this word every man must be altogether *original*. No person can *teach* to another its true meaning and right application; for this reason, that no two human beings ever use it, or ever can use it, in the same sense or apply it to the same being: a true but astounding paradox, which may be thus forcibly expressed. Every one rightly calls himself by a name which no other person can call him by without being convicted of the most outrageous and almost inconceivable insanity. The word "I" in *my* mouth as applied to *you* would prove me to be a madman. The word "I" in *your* mouth as applied to *me* would prove you to be the same. Therefore, I cannot by any conceivability teach you what it means, nor can you teach me. We must both of us originate it first of all independently for ourselves, and then we can understand one another.'

367. In the absence of the law, would we still have rights?

In the passage below from *A Discourse of Natural Religion,* the English philosopher **Samuel Clarke** (1675-1729) rails against the view that morality is a social convention. He believes that the differences between right and wrong are facts of nature. The law no more invented morality than Newton invented gravity. Indeed, if there were no morality prior to the law, there would be no standard by which to judge it. If we possessed no rights prior to the Universal Declaration of Human Rights, then the rights declared would be entirely arbitrary. We would have no basis for either praising or criticising the document.

Moreover, without a natural understanding that we ought to honour agreements, such a document would be worthless. Of course, we could stipulate within the document that our consent to it is binding, but this would then require a further stipulation that stipulations are binding, and so on *ad infinitum*. The obligation to honour our agreements and remain loyal to our promises is a precondition, not a consequence, of such compacts.

'Now if the destruction of mankind by each other's hands be such an evil, that, to prevent it, it was fit and reasonable that men should enter into compacts to preserve each other, then, before any such compacts, it was manifestly a thing unfit and unreasonable in itself that mankind should all destroy one another. And if so, then for the same reason it was also unfit and unreasonable, antecedent to all compacts, that any one man should destroy another arbitrarily and without any provocation, or at any time when it was not absolutely and immediately necessary for the preservation of himself; which is directly contradictory to Mr. Hobbes's first supposition, of there being no natural and absolute difference between good and evil, just and unjust, antecedent to positive compact. And in like manner, all others, who, upon any pretence whatsoever, teach that good and evil depend originally on the constitution of positive laws, whether divine or human, must unavoidably run into the same absurdity: For, if there be no such thing as good and evil in the nature of things, antecedent to all laws, then neither can any one law be better than another, nor any one thing whatever be more justly established and enforced by laws, than the contrary; nor can any reason be given why any laws should ever be made at all: But all laws equally will be either arbitrary and tyrannical, or frivolous and needless, because the contrary might with equal reason have been established, if, before the making of the laws, all things had been alike indifferent in their own nature. There is no possible way to avoid this absurdity, but by saying, that, out of things in their own nature absolutely indifferent, those are chosen by wise governors to be made obligatory by law, the practice of which they judge will tend to the public benefit of the community. But this is an express contradiction in the very terms. For, if the practice of certain things tends to the public benefit of the world, and the contrary would tend to the public disadvantage, then those things are not in their own nature indifferent, but were good and reasonable to be practised before any law was made, and can only for that very reason be wisely enforced by the authority of laws. Only here it is to be observed, that, by the public benefit, must not be understood the interest of any one particular nation, to the plain injury or prejudice of the rest of mankind, any more than the interest of one city or family, in opposition to their neighbours of the same country. But those things only are truly good in their own nature which either tend to the universal benefit and welfare of all men, or at least are not destructive of it. The true state, therefore, of this case, is plainly this: Some things are in their own nature good and reasonable, and fit to be done; such as keeping faith, and performing equitable compacts, and the like; and these receive not their obligatory power from any law or authority, but are only declared, confirmed, and enforced by penalties upon such as would not perhaps be governed by right reason only. Other things are in their own nature absolutely evil; such as breaking faith, refusing to perform equitable compacts, cruelly destroying those who have neither directly nor indirectly given any occasion for any such treatment, and the like: And these cannot, by any law or authority whatsoever, be made fit and reasonable, or excusable to be practised.'

368. In the absence of the law, would we still have property?

The 17th century philosopher Samuel Freiherr von Pufendorf argued that within the state of nature, prior to the existence of any form of government, if a person were to pluck an acorn from a wild oak tree and swallow it, despite it being nestled in her belly, the acorn would not be her property. Pufendorf believed that property was a convention that required agreement from other people.

John Locke (1632-1704) disagreed with this. He regarded property as metaphysical rather than conventional in nature. Starting from the claim that our body is our property, he then argued that whatever becomes 'mixed' with our body via our actions thereby becomes our property. As we interact with an object, we sort of spill over the bounds of our bodies and subsume it. The fly you swat away thereby becomes an extension of your body. The air you exhale is rightfully yours. The particles of lunar dust in Neil Armstrong's footprints are as much his property as the feet with which he used to make them.

From *Two Treatises of Government* –

'Though the earth, and all inferior creatures, be common to all men, yet every man has a property in his own person: this no body has any right to but himself. The *labour* of his body, and the *work* of his hands, we may say, are properly his. Whatsoever then he removes out of the state that nature hath provided, and left it in, he hath mixed his *labour* with, and joined to it something that is his own, and thereby makes it his *property*. It being by him removed from the common state nature hath placed it in, it hath by this *labour* something annexed to it, that excludes the common right of other men: for this *labour* being the unquestionable property of the labourer, no man but he can have a right to what that is once joined to, at least where there is enough, and as good, left in common for others.

He that is nourished by the acorns he picked up under an oak, or the apples he gathered from the trees in the wood, has certainly appropriated them to himself. No body can deny but the nourishment is his. I ask then, when did they begin to be his? when he digested? or when he eat? or when he boiled? or when he brought them home? or when he picked them up? and it is plain, if the first gathering made them not his, nothing else could. That labour put a distinction between them and common: that added something to them more than nature, the common mother of all, had done; and so they became his private right.'

For Locke, see *Qs*. 60 and 71.

370. Should MPs in the House of Commons be permitted to call each other cunts?

As it is, merely referring to a fellow MP as a 'little squirt' will see you suspended from the House of Commons for 'disorderly conduct', as Dennis Skinner can attest (a serial offender, he was also suspended for 'pompous sod' and 'dodgy Dave', in reference to the former prime minister David Cameron).

Edmund Burke (1729-1797) would have welcomed such protocol. He believed that manners are not simply a decorative addition to society but its underlying support. The foundation and not the frieze. Indeed, Burke implies that rudeness and morality are incompatible. A society not blessed with the grace of good manners, not suffused with the 'spirit of the gentleman', is a society no citizen could love: vulgarity precludes virtue.

The 'barbarous philosophy' Burke references below is the egalitarianism of the French Revolution. By eliminating the majesty of rank – God and king – the French were only able to establish order through tyranny. But order should not be imposed on society via the threat of punishment. We should not rely on fear as an instrument of obedience. Obedience should arise from our reverence for the law, respect for each other and love of our country. (When Burke speaks of love, he is speaking of languor – see *Q.* 318 – so for him manners are essentially an opiate.)

From *Reflections on the Revolution in France* and *Letters on a Regicide Peace* –

'On the scheme of this barbarous philosophy, which is the offspring of cold hearts and muddy understandings, and which is as void of solid wisdom, as it is destitute of all taste and elegance, laws are to be supported only by their own terrors, and by the concern which each individual may find in them from his own private speculations, or can spare to them from his own private interests. In the groves of *their* academy, at the end of every vista, you see nothing but the gallows. Nothing is left which engages the affections on the part of the commonwealth. On the principles of this mechanic philosophy, our institutions can never be embodied, if I may use the expression, in persons; so as to create in us love, veneration, admiration, or attachment. But that sort of reason which banishes the affections is incapable of filling their place. These public affections, combined with manners, are required sometimes as supplements, sometimes as correctives, always as aids to law. The precept given by a wise man [Horace], as well as a great critic, for the construction of poems, is equally true as to states. *Non satis est pulchra esse poemata, dulcia sunto* [It is not enough for poems to be fine, they must charm]. There ought to be a system of manners in every nation which a well-formed mind would be disposed to relish.

To make us love our country, our country ought to be lovely.'

* * *

'Manners are of more importance than laws. Upon them, in a great measure the laws depend. The law touches us here and there, and now and then. Manners are what vex or soothe, corrupt or purify, exalt or debase, barbarise or refine us, by a constant, steady, uniform, insensible operation, like that of the air we breathe in. They give their whole form and colour to our lives. According to their quality, they aid morals, they supply them, or they totally destroy them.'

For Burke, see *Q*. 318.

371. Could you trust a politician who had an awful taste in music?

We can take from **John Ruskin** (1819-1900) a test for determining the merit of a given artwork. If you find yourself standing before a painting unsure of its quality, ask yourself this: would it be admitted into a show curated by angels?

Ruskin believed that there is no distinction between art and morality. Beauty is an object of 'moral perception', that is to say, goodness and beauty are one and the same. Taste, therefore, is a moral sense. Given the stakes, it is appropriate to respond to bad art with contempt. It is right and fitting for art to inspire enmity and argument. To admire bad art is to delight in the praise of hateful things and offend the sensibility of angels.

From the essay 'Traffic' –

'I want you to think a little of the deep significance of this word "taste"; for no statement of mine has been more earnestly or oftener controverted than that good taste is essentially a moral quality. "No," say many of my antagonists, "taste is one thing, morality is another. Tell us what is pretty: we shall be glad to know that; but we need no sermons – even were you able to preach them, which may be doubted."

Permit me, therefore, to fortify this old dogma of mine somewhat. Taste is not only a part and an index of morality; – it is the ONLY morality. The first, and last, and closest trial question to any living creature is, "What do you like?" Tell me what you like, and I'll tell you what you are. Go out into the street, and ask the first man or woman you meet, what their "taste" is; and if they answer candidly, you know them, body and soul...

But you may answer, "Is the liking for outside ornaments, – for pictures, or statues, or furniture, or architecture, a moral quality?" Yes, most surely, if a rightly set liking. Taste for *any* pictures or statues is not a moral quality, but taste for good ones is. Only here again we have to define the word "good." I don't mean by "good," clever – or learned – or difficult in the doing. Take a picture by Teniers, of sots quarrelling over their dice; it is an entirely clever picture; so clever that nothing in its kind has ever been done equal to it; but it is also an entirely base and evil picture. It is an expression of delight in the prolonged contemplation of a vile thing, and delight in that is an "unmannered," or "immoral" quality. It is "bad taste" in the profoundest sense – it is the taste of the devils. On the other hand, a picture of Titian's, or a Greek statue, or a Greek coin, or a Turner landscape, expresses delight in the perpetual contemplation of a good and perfect thing. That is an entirely moral quality – it is the taste of the angels. And all delight in fine art, and all love of it, resolves themselves into simply love of that which deserves love. That deserving is the quality which we call "loveliness" – (we ought to have an opposite word, hateliness, to be said of the things which deserve to be hated); and it is not an indifferent nor optional thing whether we love this or that; but it is just the vital function of all our being. What we *like* determines what we *are*, and is the sign of what we are; and to teach taste is inevitably to form character.'

For Ruskin, see Q. 149.

374. Is a high-school massacre the act of a crazed individual or a crazed society?

The notion that *society* can act at all raises a host of related questions. Can society think? Is it conscious? Does it have a body? To answer in the affirmative would seem to indicate that society is a sort of being or organism. The English sociologist and philosopher **Herbert Spencer** (1820-1903) thought exactly this. He claimed that societies are naturally occurring organisms which, like the rest of the organic world, are subject to the laws of evolution. Sociology is therefore a branch of biology.

From his essay 'The Social Organism' –

'Societies agree with individual organisms in four conspicuous peculiarities:

1. That commencing as small aggregations, they insensibly augment in mass: some of them eventually reaching ten thousand times what they originally were.

2. That while at first so simple in structure as to be considered structureless, they assume, in the course of their growth, a continually-increasing complexity of structure.

3. That though in their early, undeveloped states, there exists in them scarcely any mutual dependence of parts, their parts gradually acquire a mutual dependence; which becomes at last so great, that the activity and life of each part is made possible only by the activity and life of the rest.

4. That the life of a society is independent of, and far more prolonged than, the lives of any of its component units; who

are severally born, grow, work, reproduce, and die, while the body-politic composed of them survives generation after generation, increasing in mass, in completeness of structure, and in functional activity...

On the other hand, the leading differences between societies and individual organisms are these...

That though the living tissue whereof an individual organism consists, forms a continuous mass, the living elements of a society do not form a continuous mass; but are more or less widely dispersed over some portion of the Earth's surface. This, which at first sight appears to be an absolute distinction, is one which yet to a great extent fades when we contemplate all the facts. For, in the lower divisions of the animal and vegetal kingdoms, there are types of organization much more nearly allied, in this respect, to the organization of a society, than might be supposed—types in which the living units essentially composing the mass, are dispersed through an inert substance, that can scarcely be called living in the full sense of the word. It is thus with some of the *Protococci* and with the Nostoceae, which exist as cells imbedded in a viscid matter. It is so, too, with the *Thalassicollæ*—bodies made up of differentiated parts, dispersed through an undifferentiated jelly. And throughout considerable portions of their bodies, some of the *Acalephæ* exhibit more or less this type of structure. Now this is very much the case with a society. For we must remember that though the men who make up a society are physically separate, and even scattered, yet the surface over which they are scattered is not one devoid of life, but is covered by life of a lower order which ministers to their life. The vegetation which clothes a country makes possible the animal life in that country; and only through its animal and vegetal products can such a country support a society. Hence the members of the body-politic are not to be regarded as separated by intervals of dead space, but as diffused through a space occupied by life of a lower order. In our conception of a social organism, we must include all that lower organic existence on which human existence, and therefore social existence, depend. And when we do this, we see that the citizens who make up a community may be considered as highly vitalized units surrounded by substances of lower vitality, from which they draw their nutriment: much as in the cases above instanced...

[Another] difference is that while the ultimate living elements of an individual organism are mostly fixed in their relative positions, those of the social organism are capable of moving from place to place. But here, too, the disagreement is much less than would be supposed. For while citizens are locomotive in their private capacities, they are fixed in their public capacities. As farmers, manufacturers, or traders, men carry on their businesses at the same spots, often throughout their whole lives; and if they go away occasionally, they leave behind others to discharge their functions in their absence. Each great centre of production, each manufacturing town or district, continues always in the same place; and many of the firms in such town or district, are for generations carried on either by the descendants or successors of those who founded them. Just as in a living body, the cells that make up some important organ severally perform their functions for a time and then disappear, leaving others to supply their places; so, in each part of a society the organ remains, though the persons who compose it change. Thus, in social life, as in the life of an animal, the units as well as the larger agencies formed of them, are in the main stationary as respects the places where they discharge their duties and obtain their sustenance. And hence the power of individual locomotion does not practically affect the analogy...

Thus we find but little to conflict with the all-important analogies. Societies slowly augment in mass; they progress in complexity of structure; at the same time their parts become more mutually dependent; their living units are removed and replaced without destroying their integrity; and the extents to which they display these peculiarities are proportionate to their vital activities. These are traits that societies have in common with organic bodies.'

376. What is the greater misfortune, to be a woman or a man?

The French philosopher Jean-Paul Sartre characterised the difference between penetrating and being penetrated as that between filling and being filled. The latter he thought was particularly desirable for us because we are troubled by the void at the heart of existence. We long to be stuffed whole. To become complete beings.

Perhaps such an idea was the reason why **Ovid** (43 BCE-17 CE) thought it right to have Tiresias – who had been both a man and a woman – confirm the Jovian hypothesis that sex between men and women is more pleasurable for women.

From Arthur Golding's 1567 translation of *Metamorphoses* –

'Now while these things were done on earth and that by
fatal doom
The twice-born Bacchus had a time to man's estate to come,
They say that Jove, disposed to mirth, as he and Juno sat
A-drinking nectar after meat, in sport and pleasant rate
Did fall a-jesting with his wife and said, "A greater pleasure
In Venus' games ye women have than men beyond all
measure."
She answered, "No." To try the truth they both of them
agree
The wise Tiresias in this case indifferent judge to be,
Who both the man and woman's joys by trial understood.
For finding once two mighty snakes engendering in a wood,
He strake them overthwart the backs; by means whereof,
behold,

(As strange a thing to be of truth as ever yet was told)
He, being made a woman straight, seven winters lived so.
The eighth he, finding them again, did say unto them tho,
"And if to strike ye have such power as for to turn their
shape
That are the givers of the stripe, before you hence escape
One stripe now will I lend you more." He strake them as
beforn,
And straight returned his former shape in which he first was
born.
Tiresias, therefore being ta'en to judge this jesting strife,
Gave sentence on the side of Jove. The which the queen, his
wife,
Did take a great deal more to heart than needed and in spite,
To wreak her teen upon her judge, bereft him of his sight.'

381. 'Life, friends, is boring,' wrote the poet John Berryman. Is this an adequate justification for suicide?

G. K. Chesterton's (1874-1936) antipathy towards suicide is predicated on the view that it involves the annihilation of the world. He does not countenance the thought that suicide may be an act of hatred not towards the world but one's self; an act not of world murder but self murder. For Chesterton, no act can equal the squalor of suicide, no sin can sink lower, for it is the 'refusal to take an interest in existence'.

The force of his acrimony is perhaps indicative of a kind of phobia; aphanisis is a possible candidate. The psychoanalyst Ernest Jones coined this term to refer to what he saw as one of our most profound fears: the death of our capacity for pleasure. To be afflicted by aphanisis is to be impervious to the world's delights. It is the inability to enjoy anything or anyone. A hopeless inanition. This is what Chesterton sees in the suicidal person and he cannot bear it. By construing suicidal acedia as a 'refusal', an act of will, he gives it the guise of a choice and so himself refuses to consider it as something we may be powerless against.

From *Orthodoxy* –

'Under the lengthening shadow of Ibsen, an argument arose whether it was not a very nice thing to murder one's self. Grave moderns told us that we must not even say "poor fellow," of a man who had blown his brains out, since he was an enviable person, and had only blown them out because of their exceptional excellence. Mr. William Archer even suggested that in the golden age there would be penny-in-the-slot machines, by which a man could kill himself for a penny. In all this I found myself utterly hostile to many who called themselves liberal and humane. Not only is suicide a sin, it is the sin. It is the ultimate and absolute evil, the refusal to take an interest in existence; the refusal to take the oath of loyalty to life. The man who kills a man, kills a man. The man who kills himself, kills all men; as far as he is concerned he wipes out the world. His act is worse (symbolically considered) than any rape or dynamite outrage. For it destroys all buildings: it insults all women. The thief is satisfied with diamonds; but the suicide is not: that is his crime. He cannot be bribed, even by the blazing stones of the Celestial City. The thief compliments the things he steals, if not the owner of them. But the suicide insults everything on earth by not stealing it. He defiles every flower by refusing to live for its sake. There is not a tiny creature in the cosmos at whom his death is not a sneer. When a man hangs himself on a tree, the leaves might fall off in anger and the birds fly away in fury: for each has received a personal affront. Of course there may be pathetic emotional excuses for the act. There often are for rape, and there almost always are for dynamite. But if it comes to clear ideas and the intelligent meaning of things, then there is much more rational and philosophic truth in the burial at the cross-roads and the stake driven through the body, than in Mr. Archer's suicidal automatic machines. There is a meaning in burying the suicide apart. The man's crime is different from other crimes – for it makes even crimes impossible.

About the same time I read a solemn flippancy by some free thinker: he said that a suicide was only the same as a martyr. The open fallacy of this helped to clear the question. Obviously a suicide is the opposite of a martyr. A martyr is a man who cares so much for something outside him, that he forgets his own personal life. A suicide is a man who cares so little for anything outside him, that he wants to see the last of everything. One wants something to begin: the other wants everything to end. In other words, the martyr is noble, exactly because (however he renounces the world or execrates all humanity) he confesses this ultimate link with life; he sets his heart outside himself: he dies that something may live. The suicide is ignoble because he has not this link with being: he is a mere destroyer; spiritually, he destroys the universe.'

For Chesterton, see *Q.* 212.

389. Is it possible to invent new emotions?

The relative inertia of language may lead one to conclude that new emotions seldom arise. Certainly there are innovations – 'nostalgia' (with reference to time), 'angst' and 'wanderlust' are all 20th century additions – but the rate of linguistic innovation seemingly lags behind the creative evolution of fashion, the arts and technology. And for our purposes, we need to consider whether these new names constitute the invention of new emotions or whether they are just new words for old emotions, or, perhaps, new words for new but naturally emerging emotions.

Henri Bergson (1859-1941) claimed that new emotions are

certainly invented, but he thought that we should not use language as a measure of emotional abundance. Language only works in generalities. In fact, new emotions are constantly being invented through the arts. The invention of new music, for instance, is the invention of new emotions.

In a way, this is perhaps rather obvious. Consider a song you are particularly fond of. Though the song may generally relate to, say, the sorrows or ecstasy of love, can the feeling you experience while listening to it be caused by anything else, or is it particular to that song? Did that feeling exist within you prior to the first time you heard it? And if the feeling is not particular to that song, why return to it?

From *Two Sources of Morality and Religion* –

'Are you going to say that we are here in the realm of art and not among real things, that therefore we are playing at emotion, that our feeling is purely imaginative, and that, anyway, the musician could not produce this emotion in us, suggest it without causing it, if we had not already experienced it in real life, where it was caused by an object from which art had merely to detach it? That would be to forget that joy and sorrow, pity and love are words expressing generalities, words which we must call upon to express what music makes us feel, whereas each new musical work brings with it new feelings, which are created by that music, and within that music, are defined and delimited by the lines, unique of their kind, of the melody or symphony. They have therefore not been extracted from life by art; it is we who, in order to express them in words, are driven to compare the feeling created by the artist with the feeling most resembling it in life. But let us then take states of emotion caused in effect by certain things and, as it were, prefigured in them. Those ordained by nature are finite, that is to say limited in number. They are recognizable because they are destined to spur us on to acts answering to needs. The others, on the contrary, are real inventions, comparable to those of the musician, at the origin of which there has always been a man. Thus mountains may, since the beginning of time, have had the faculty of rousing in those who looked upon them certain feelings comparable with sensations, and which were indeed inseparable from mountains. But Rousseau created in connection with them a new and original emotion. This emotion has become current coin, Rousseau having put it into circulation. And even to-day it is Rousseau who makes us feel it, as much and more than the mountains. True, there are reasons why this emotion, sprung from the heart of Jean-Jacques, should fasten on to mountains rather than any other object; the elementary feelings, akin to sensations, which were directly aroused by mountains must have been able to harmonize with the new emotion. But Rousseau gathered them together, gave them their places, henceforth as mere harmonics in a sound for which he provided, by a true creation, the principal tone. It is the same with love of nature in general. Nature has ever aroused feelings which are almost sensations; people have always enjoyed the pleasant shade, the cool waters, etc., in fine all those things suggested in the word "amoenus" by which the Romans described the charm of the country. But a fresh emotion, surely the creation of some person or persons, has arisen and used these pre-existing notes as harmonics, and produced in this way something to be compared with the fresh tones of a new instrument, what we call in our respective countries the sentiment of nature. The fundamental tone thus introduced might have been different, as is the case in the East, in Japan especially, the timbre would then have been different. Feelings akin to sensation, closely bound up with the objects which give rise to them, are indeed just as likely to attract a previously created emotion as they are to connect with an entirely new one. This is what happened with love. From time immemorial woman must have inspired man with an inclination distinct from desire, but in immediate contact, as though welded to it, and pertaining both to feeling and to sensation. But romantic love has a definite date: it sprang up during the Middle Ages on the day when some person or persons conceived the idea of absorbing love into a kind of supernatural feeling, into religious emotion as created by Christianity and launched by the new religion into the world. When critics reproach mysticism with expressing itself in the same terms as passionate love, they forget that it was love which began by plagiarizing mysticism, borrowing from it its fervour, its raptures, its ecstasies: in using the language of a passion it had transfigured, mysticism has only resumed possession of its own.'

For Bergson, see *Qs*. 19, 126, 213, and 265.

397. Herodotus wrote of an Indian tribe that ate its dead. Is this practice any stranger than cremation or burial?

> **Herodotus** (*c*. 484-420 BCE) is considered history's first historian. He wrote only one book, *The Histories*, which documented the failed attempt of the Persian empire to conquer Greece.

'[I]f one should propose to all men a choice, bidding them select the best customs from all the customs that there are, each race of men, after examining them all, would select those of his own people; thus all think that their own customs are by far the best... Now of the fact that all men are thus wont to think about their customs, we may judge by many other proofs and more specially by this which follows: Darius [king of Persia] in the course of his reign summoned those of the Greeks who were present in his land and asked them for what price they would consent to eat their fathers when they died; and they answered that for no price would they do so. After this Darius summoned those Indians who are called Callatiae, who eat their parents, and asked them in presence of the Greeks, who understood what they said by help of an interpreter, for what payment they would consent to consume with fire the bodies of their fathers when they died; and they cried out aloud and bade him not to speak of so horrid an act. So firmly rooted are these beliefs – I think that Pindar spoke rightly in his verse when he said that custom is lord of all.'

IFF
BOOKS

ACADEMIC AND SPECIALIST

Iff Books publishes non-fiction. It aims to work with authors and titles that augment our understanding of the human condition, society and civilisation, and the world or universe in which we live.

If you have enjoyed this book, why not tell other readers by posting a review on your preferred book site.

Is There an Afterlife?

David Fontana

Is there an Afterlife? If so what is it like? How do Western ideas of the afterlife compare with Eastern? David Fontana presents the historical and contemporary evidence for survival of physical death.

Paperback: 978-1-90381-690-5

Nothing Matters

a book about nothing

Ronald Green

Thinking about Nothing opens the world to everything by illuminating new angles to old problems and stimulating new ways of thinking.

Paperback: 978-1-84694-707-0 ebook: 978-1-78099-016-3

Panpsychism

The Philosophy of the Sensuous Cosmos

Peter Ells

Are free will and mind chimeras? This book, anti-materialistic but respecting science, answers: No! Mind is foundational to all existence.

Paperback: 978-1-84694-505-2 ebook: 978-1-78099-018-7

Punk Science

Inside the Mind of God

Manjir Samanta-Laughton

Many have experienced unexplainable phenomena; God, psychic abilities, extraordinary healing and angelic encounters. Can cutting-edge science actually explain phenomena previously thought of as 'paranormal'?

Paperback: 978-1-90504-793-2

The Vagabond Spirit of Poetry

Edward Clarke

Spend time with the wisest poets of the modern age and of the past, and let Edward Clarke remind you of the importance of poetry in our industrialized world.

Paperback: 978-1-78279-370-0 ebook: 978-1-78279-369-4